Sex and Gender

Recent Titles in the

CONTEMPORARY WORLD ISSUES
Series

Books in the **Contemporary World Issues** series address vital issues in today's society such as genetic engineering, pollution, and biodiversity. Written by professional writers, scholars, and nonacademic experts, these books are authoritative, clearly written, up-to-date, and objective. They provide a good starting point for research by high school and college students, scholars, and general readers as well as by legislators, businesspeople, activists, and others.

Each book, carefully organized and easy to use, contains an overview of the subject, a detailed chronology, biographical sketches, facts and data and/or documents and other primary source material, a forum of authoritative perspective essays, annotated lists of print and nonprint resources, and an index.

Readers of books in the Contemporary World Issues series will find the information they need in order to have a better understanding of the social, political, environmental, and economic issues facing the world today.

Sex and Gender

A REFERENCE HANDBOOK

David E. Newton

ABC-CLIO™

An Imprint of ABC-CLIO, LLC
Santa Barbara, California • Denver, Colorado

Library of Congress Cataloging-in-Publication Data

Names: Newton, David E., author.
Title: Sex and gender : a reference handbook / David E. Newton.
Description: Santa Barbara, California : ABC-CLIO, [2017] | Series: Contemporary world issues | Includes bibliographical references and index.
Identifiers: LCCN 2017002214 (print) | LCCN 2017015770 (ebook) | ISBN 9781440854804 (ebook) | ISBN 9781440854798 (alk. paper)
Subjects: LCSH: Sex role. | Gender identity.
Classification: LCC HQ1075 (ebook) | LCC HQ1075 .N49 2017 (print) | DDC 305.3—dc23
LC record available at https://lccn.loc.gov/2017002214

ISBN: 978-1-4408-5479-8
EISBN: 978-1-4408-5480-4

21 20 19 18 17   1 2 3 4 5

This book is also available as an eBook.

ABC-CLIO
An Imprint of ABC-CLIO, LLC

ABC-CLIO, LLC
130 Cremona Drive, P.O. Box 1911
Santa Barbara, California 93116-1911
www.abc-clio.com

This book is printed on acid-free paper ∞

Manufactured in the United States of America

Everything begins and ends with sex.
Except when it doesn't.

Preface

Few topics in human society are of such basic importance as sex and gender. Indeed, throughout human history, cultures have been organized to a considerable extent on the basis of what it is that defines "maleness" and "femaleness," what the characteristic features of those traits are, and how they can best be utilized in human organizations. This process has always involved, however, a complex mix of the biological traits with which individuals are born (a person's sex) and the social, cultural, economic, political, and other factors by which a society makes use of those traits (his or her gender).

That pattern holds true today. Modern cultures attempt to understand the strengths that males and females can each bring to a society and how their natural traits and abilities can best be put to use in building a strong association that can solve problems of every type in everyday life.

But this process often does not run smoothly, especially when fundamental questions begin to arise because of changing views as to what it means to be a "man" or a "woman" in modern culture. These questions sometimes appear in stark form, as when some number of individuals decide and began to act on the realization that their biological sex and social gender are incongruent, and they begin to deal with a host of problems created by transgenderism.

In other cases, issues that have percolated around the edges of society for hundreds of years move to the center stage, where cultures are forced to think about and deal with questions that have never been fully resolved. So the battle against gender inequality that has surged to the front of public attention in the 21st century raises the most basic questions as to what the proper roles of men and women are in society, a question that has simmered largely in the background since the earliest days of civilization.

This book is not able to deal with all of the difficult problems associated with sex and gender in society. The focus here on topics, such as the biology of sexual development, the development of gender roles, transvestism, transgenderism, gender roles, and affectional orientation, reflects our efforts to shine a light on some of the most challenging issues that individuals at all ages must face. But we acknowledge that other issues should, but do not, appear in the book, issues such as asexuality, maternity leave, sexual harassment, and contraception. Space is simply not available for the full range of topics that might be included in a book on sex and gender.

This book is intended as an introduction to the topic of sex and gender and a guide to further research on the topic. The first two chapters deal with a review of the history and background of the two topics (Chapter 1) and a discussion of some of the most important issues relating to these topics (Chapter 2). Chapter 3 provides a group of contributors with an opportunity to present their own perspectives on some specific aspect of the topic, with essays on subjects such as gender identity on the web, diet culture and gender expectations, personal experiences in coming out as a gay man and as a transgender person, and gender dysphoria in films.

Chapter 4 consists of brief sketches of important individuals and organization in the field of sex and gender, while Chapter 5 provides data and statistics on some important aspects of the topic, along with selections from laws, court cases, and other documents relevant to the topic. A critical resource is the annotated bibliography in Chapter 6 that provides the reader with a large number of print and electronic resources for further study. Chapter 7 then offers a chronology of important events in history relating to sex and gender, while a glossary provides essential terms found in the book and likely to be encountered in future research.

Sex and Gender

Introduction

On May 13, 2016, the U.S. Department of Justice and the U.S. Department of Education jointly issued a letter to schools and colleges across the nation regarding the use of bathroom facilities by transgender students. Its main point was that

> As a condition of receiving Federal funds, a school agrees that it will not exclude, separate, deny benefits to, or otherwise treat differently on the basis of sex any person in its educational programs or activities unless expressly authorized to do so under Title IX or its implementing regulations. The Departments treat a student's gender identity as the student's sex for purposes of Title IX and its implementing regulations. This means that a school must not treat a transgender student differently from the way it treats other students of the same gender identity. ("Dear Colleague Letter on Transgender Students" 2016)

Two weeks later, 11 states filed suit in federal court against provisions of the letter. In July, 10 more states filed a similar

Transgender sign with a woman, male, and transgender symbol. Some lawmakers across the United States believe that transgender students should be required to use only those facilities that correspond with their birth sex. Others say they should be allowed to use the facilities of their choice. (Karenr/Dreamstime.com) suit against the requirements outlined in the "Dear Colleagues" letter. The argument posed by the states was that the provisions of Title IX (which prohibits sex discrimination in schools and colleges) refer only to *sex*, and not to *gender identity*. The states argued that

> The State of Nebraska and nine additional States seek a declaration that the Department of Education ("ED") has violated the Administrative Procedure Act and numerous other federal laws by rewriting the unambiguous term "sex" under Title VII and Title IX to include "gender identity," thereby seeking to control even local school determinations regarding how best to designate locker room and bathroom assignments. . . .
>
> The letter confirmed that the federal executive branch has formalized its new definition of the term "sex" and threatened enforcement action against any of the more than 100,000 elementary and secondary schools that receive federal funding if those schools choose to provide students with showers, locker rooms, and restrooms designated by biological sex, consistent with one's genes and anatomy. ("United States District Court for the District of Nebraska" 2016)

Male and *female*? *Man* or *woman*? *Boy* and *girl*? Most people probably think they are pretty sure what these terms mean. They are used in everyday conversation, apparently with the understanding that their meanings are clear. But *sex* versus *gender identity*? Here the difference (if there is one) may not seem quite so clear. If someone says that "he" is a "man," isn't that clear that the person's sex and gender identity are both "male"?

Actually, the answer to that question is "no." A person's *sex* and *gender identity* are not necessarily congruent. And the precise meanings of these two terms and the differences between them lie at some of the most fundamental issues in all of human history. They may also form the basis of some of the most contentious social issues facing Americans and other people around the world today. The goal of this book is to provide an introduction to the concepts of sex and gender identity, how those concepts are based in human anatomy and physiology, how they have developed over the centuries, and how they have inspired arguments like those involving school bathrooms and locker rooms.

Basic Definitions

At the outset, then, are the two most important definitions needed for this discussion: What do the terms *sex* and *gender identity* mean?

Sex

According to one respected resource, the *Merriam-Webster* dictionary, the term *sex* refers to "either of the two major forms of individuals that occur in many species and that are distinguished respectively as female or male especially on the basis of their reproductive organs and structures," or, as a secondary definition, "the sum of the structural, functional, and behavioral characteristics of organisms that are involved in reproduction marked by the union of gametes and that distinguish males and females" (*Merriam-Webster* 2016). Thus, a person's sex can usually (but not always) be determined simply by observing his or her reproductive organs. The presence of a penis suggests that a person is a male; the presence of a vagina indicates a female.

A person's sex can also be determined by one's genetic makeup. Humans normally have 23 pairs of chromosomes, the structures on which genes occur. Twenty-two of those pairs are the same in both males and females; they are said to be *autosomes*. The 23rd pair is different in males and females. In females, the two members of the pair are identical and are called *X chromosomes*. In males, the 23rd chromosome pair contains one X chromosome and one Y chromosome. This chromosome pair is called the *sex chromosome*, or *allosome*. The presence of the Y chromosome is generally taken as an indication that a person is a male. The absence of the Y chromosome is an indication that the person is a female. (For a brief review of this topic, see "Human Heredity" 2016.)

Sex, thus, is a biological phenomenon. It is determined by a person's genetic makeup and by well-defined anatomical features of a human or other organism. Sex is not a learned characteristic. No one has to teach a female how to be a member of the female sex; that "label" comes as naturally as does the ability to speak or to learn.

Gender

By contrast, gender identity is a social and/or psychological concept. A person who carries a Y chromosome and male anatomical structures may think of himself as a female. That is, he may choose to use words, gestures, clothing, and other characteristics that are more commonly associated with females than they are with males. Conversely, an individual with a vagina, ovaries, and other female genitalia may think and want to act as a male. Individuals whose sexual self-image is different from their biological sex are said to be *transgender*. (In order to balance definitions, many transgender individuals refer to men and women whose sex and gender identity are congruent as *cisgender* individuals.)

The cause of transgenderism is not known, although a number of possible causes have been suggested. Some experts believe that changes may occur to a fetus that result in an imbalance between one's genetic makeup (XX or XY chromosome) and one's genital structures. Another possibility is that chemical changes occur from internal or external causes that lead to a disjunction between the sexual characteristics one is born with and those that seem natural to the brain. Any number of cultural and psychological factors may also be involved in the development of a transgender identity. For example, some cultures recognize as normal and natural not just two genders, but three, four, or even more genders. Some people who grow up in those cultures select a third, fourth, or other gender as readily as others who select "male" or "female," no matter their biological sex ("Understanding Transgender" 2009).

The term *transsexual* is sometimes used as a synonym for *transgender*. Both terms should be used with some caution since an individual may simply want to live one's life as a person of the opposite gender (a man wearing dresses rather than a suit, for example), and thus be considered to be *transgender*. Or he or she may also wish to have surgery that actually results in exchanging one set of genitalia for the opposite set, in which case one is also *transsexual*.

One other term that is sometimes a source of confusion is *transvestite*, which refers to a person who prefers to dress in the clothing of and, often, appear in public as a member of the opposite sex. For example, there are many biological males who are happily married with families who enjoy dressing up in women's clothing and socializing with other men with similar interests, or even going shopping with their (approving) wives. Female transvestites are less common in today's world, almost certainly because of differing social expectations of the sexes. That is, a man's dressing as a woman represents a risky social act because it means (whether one approves or not) taking a lower social class role, while a woman's dressing as a man represents an act of upward social mobility, which may actually gain approval. The act of dressing in the clothing of someone of the opposite sex is called *cross-dressing*. Transvestites who choose to appear, and often perform, in public may also be called *drag queens*.

Relatively little research has been conducted on transvestism, and there is little understanding or agreement as to the factors that cause the condition. Most transvestites insist that their desire to cross-dress has nothing to do with their wanting to be a member of the opposite sex. That is, male transvestites are not in the least interested in becoming a woman; they are not transgender or transsexual. They do, however, offer a variety of reasons for wanting to wear women's clothes and makeup, such as

- feeling a sense of "relief," similar to that a drug addict might experience after having a "hit" of a drug;
- experiencing a sense of "naturalness," that is, recognizing that wearing women's clothing is as "correct" as wearing men's clothing;
- having sexual feelings about the appearance and feel of women's clothing;
- experiencing a sense that the person is more attractive as a woman than he is as a man;
- acknowledging a "feminine" aspect of one's own personality that is otherwise entirely absent from one's life, without ever wanting to *become* a woman (Coleman 1996; Griffiths 2012; "Why Be a TV?" 2008).

Transvestism is poorly understood at least partly because the practice appears to be rather uncommon in modern industrialized society and most people involved in cross-dressing prefer to keep their preferences private. Scattered studies provide modest amounts of demographic data, but hardly enough to allow researchers to provide some dependable model of the "average" transvestite (Docter and Prince 1997). Even psychiatrists, psychologists, and other mental health workers appear to be uncertain as to how to classify transvestism, if at all, and when and how, again, to provide counseling and guidance for people who engage in such behavior (Lopes 2016; "Transvestic Fetishism" 2016).

One of the most fascinating points to note about transvestism is its persistent occurrence in human history. Compared to the limited literature on transvestism in the modern world, a large body of research has been produced on the practice in earlier societies, ranging from at least as early as biblical times to early 20th-century America. The phenomenon has been recorded among biblical cultures, in ancient Greece, in imperial Rome, among medieval saints, and within virtually every human culture that has been studied, from remote Pacific Islands throughout Native American tribal societies to the busy neighborhoods of Elizabethan London. (Among the extensive literature on transvestism, see, for example, Miller 1999; Schmidt-Hori 2009; "20 Most Historically Famous Crossdressers" 2012; and Vedeler 2008.)

In some ways, the most interesting of all scholarly articles on transvestism is a chapter devoted to "passing women" in the United States between 1782 and 1920 in Jonathan Katz's monumental work, *Gay American History*. Katz provides a number of very detailed stories about women who chose to "pass" as men by dressing as men, taking on male occupations, and even, in some cases, marrying a woman and forming a stable long-term relationship with her. Katz quotes extensively from source documents describing what the lives of these individuals were like, in almost all case chosen "not as imitation of men, but as real women, women who refused to accept the traditional, socially assigned fate of their sex, women whose particular revolt took the form of passing as men" (Katz 1976, 209). It perhaps can be taken as some small measure of social progress that women today are seldom forced to the act of trying to "pass" as men in order to work for an equal place in society.

Sexual Differentiation in Humans

As noted previously, a person's biological sex is determined ultimately by the composition of chromosome 23. If a person has two X chromosomes present, that person will ultimately become a female; if a Y chromosome is present, the person will become a male. But the process by which one's sexual status is actually expressed is more complicated than would seem to be the case from this brief definition.

When a sperm cell enters an ovum (egg), the process of embryogenesis (the formation of the embryo) begins. The fertilized cell divides a number of times, forming in sequence a two-cell, four-cell, eight-cell, sixteen-cell—and so on—body known as an *embryo*. At this stage of development, all embryos look essentially the same, whether the 23rd chromosome they contain is an XX or an XY. Images of the early embryo give no evidence whatsoever as to whether that embryo will evolve into a female or into a male. (For images of the embryo at this state, see "What to Expect" 2016.)

The early embryo does contain, however, two structures involved in the eventual development of one's sexual status, the Wolffian duct and the Müllerian duct, also known as the mesonephric and paramesonephric ducts, respectively. The Wolffian duct has the capacity to develop into male sex organs, and the Müllerian duct into female sex organs. (For an illustration, see "Sexual Differentiation" 2016.)

The ultimate fate of the two duct systems is determined by a gene on the short arm of the Y chromosome known as the SRY gene (for *s*ex-determining *r*egion on the *Y* chromosome). If the Y chromosome is present, the SRY gene eventually becomes active, releasing a protein, testosterone, that initiates the conversion of the Wolffian duct into the male sex organs, the penis, testes, scrotum, and prostate gland. During this process, the Müllerian duct degenerates and eventually disappears, making it impossible for female sex organs to develop.

If no Y chromosome is present (that is, if the person is a female with an XX 23rd chromosome), it is the Müllerian system that begins to develop, eventually becoming the fallopian tubes, uterus, and upper part of the vagina that make up part of the female reproductive system. In this case, it is the Wolffian system that begins to degenerate and disappear so that no male sexual features can develop.

This sequence of events often explains the somewhat remarkable comment that "all humans start out as females." Of course, not all embryos actually begin as females because many of them contain a Y chromosome, which predisposes their becoming males. But for a short period early in their existence—before the SRY gene has become active—all embryos do *seem* to be female. And, in fact, males carry some modest reminders of the female component from which they arose, reminders such as nipples that have no adult function, a penis that is essentially an enlarged clitoris, and the raphe line on the scrotum that, without testosterone, would become the labia and vagina (Adewale 2016; Schultz 2014; Sokol and Sokol 2007).

In any case, the structures that begin to develop at this stage of embryogenesis are those organs involved in the process of human reproduction, including the penis, scrotum, testes, epididymis, vas deferens, prostate gland, seminal vesicles, and urethra in the male; and the vagina, clitoris, ovaries, fallopian tubes, uterus, cervix, and vaginal canal in the female. These sexual organs continue to grow until a baby is born and continue to grow with the rest of the body thereafter. Once a child reaches puberty, however, an important change takes place: those organs begin to function in such a way as to make reproduction possible.

Disorders of Sexual Development

The preceding description of sexual development in humans requires an important caveat, one that applies to most discussions of human sexuality. Events and conditions related to human sexuality often are not quite what they seem, not as simple and straightforward as an explanation like the one above may suggest. That is, some type of error may occur in a process that leads to a result not typically observed. Chromosomes and the genes they contain, for example, are not fixed structures in the body; they are, instead, often in motion, especially during the process of meiosis. During this movement, a variety of changes can occur in genes and chromosomes: bits of one or the other may break off, portions that come into contact with each other may exchange segments, or duplication may go awry and additional copies may be formed. Consider a simple example in the process of sexual differentiation.

Under most circumstances, the union of a sperm and an ovum results in four possible chromosomal arrangements, as shown in Figure 1.1. The offspring produced in the mating process shown here are, of course, typical males (XY chromosome) and females (XX chromosomes). But errors may occur during the union of sperm and ovum, which result in the formation of atypical chromosomal arrangements. A person who inherits one such arrangement will not develop the typical, straightforward male or female sexual characteristics produced by the 23rd XY and XX chromosome structures.

One of the most common chromosomal abnormalities occurs when an offspring inherits only one X chromosome, rather than an XX or XY combination. The condition is known as Turner syndrome. The child is a female because she lacks a Y chromosome, but she experiences a number of physical variations, such as a short stature, diminished sexual features, and

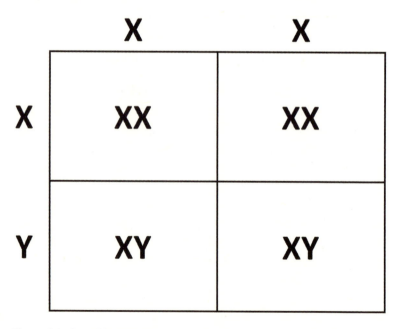

Figure 1.1   Possible chromosomal arrangements from sperm and ovum

a number of other atypical features, such as a webbed neck and poorly developed eyes and ears. Turner children may survive to adulthood, but they experience atypical sexual development and other physical problems. The condition appears in about one of 2,000 live births (Daniel 2016).

Another common chromosomal abnormality occurs when an embryo receives an extra X chromosome, resulting in a XXY genotype. The presence of the Y chromosome means that the child will be a male, but one with atypical features such as enlarged breasts, reduced male sexual features, reduced motor skills, and some compromised mental functions. The condition is also known as Klinefelter syndrome and may appear in a number of chromosomal variations, such as XXY, XXXY, XXXXY, and XXYY (Chen 2016). The disorder occurs in about 1 out of every 500 to 1,000 live births, while variations are less common (1 in 18,000 to 50,000 live births for XXXY and XXYY, and 1 in 85,000 to 100,000 live births for XXXXY; Linden, Bender, and Robinson 1995). (For a discussion of other chromosomal abnormalities, see "Genetic Components of Sex and Gender" 2016; Hutcheson 2016; O'Neil 2013. The frequencies of various types of chromosomal disorders are listed in "How Common Is Intersex?" 2016.)

Interruptions in the typical process of sexual differentiation in humans can lead to the development of a condition known as *hermaphroditism*, in which both male and female sexual organs are present. The term comes from the name of a Greek god, Hermaphroditus, or Hermaphroditos, the offspring of Hermes and Aphrodite. When the water nymph Salmacis fell in love with Hermaphroditus (a very handsome male at the time), she prayed to be united with him forever. The gods took her at her word, and literally merged their two bodies, producing a new individual with a complete set of male and female sexual organs.

Most plants and a large number of plant genera are hermaphroditic, the latter including tunicates, snails, slugs, some fish, and

a few invertebrate. Individual animals in these categories generally have both male and female organs and reproduce asexually.
By some estimates, there may be as many as 65,000 hermaphroditic species (Jarne and Auld 2006).

Hermaphroditism exists among humans also, although so-
called true hermaphroditism is very rare. It is characterized by
the presence of both ovarian (female) and testicular (male) tissue, which may be present in a single organ (called the *ovotestis*)
or in two separate organs. More common is so-called pseudohermaphroditism, in which case a person has a single genetic
sex, but is born with ambiguous genitalia such that it is difficult to determine whether the individual is a male or a female
simply by visual inspection (Utiger 2016).

The term *hermaphroditism* is now largely obsolete. For some
time, individuals interested in the topic of sexual differentiation have believed that *hermaphroditism* and related terms are
misleading and stigmatizing and should be replaced by one (or
more) neutral term. For some time, then, the preferred term
to describe such conditions as those described above had become *intersex*, defined as "a general term used for a variety of
conditions in which a person is born with a reproductive or
sexual anatomy that doesn't seem to fit the typical definitions
of female or male" (Dreger et al. 2005). Some of the specific
conditions included within the term were clitoromegaly (large
clitoris), Klinefelter's syndrome, micropenis (small penis),
ovotestes, Swyer syndrome (a condition in which a person
has no gonads of any type), and Turner's syndrome ("Intersex
Conditions" 2016).

Over time, specialists began to argue that the term *intersex*
was also too ambiguous for an adequate discussion of problems related to atypical sexual differentiation. Finally, the
Lawson Wilkins Pediatric Endocrine Society and the European Society for Paediatric Endocrinology sponsored an international conference in Chicago, Illinois, on October 27–31,
2005, to resolve issues surrounding the terminology and
treatment of intersex and related conditions. The so-called

Chicago Consensus came up with a new type of terminology and ways of thinking about conditions such as those discussed here, which were subsumed with the general name of *disorders of sex development*, or DSD (Hughes et al. 2006). The Chicago Consensus provides the basis from which experts in the field now talk about atypical development of sex characteristics prior to birth. (For one of the best discussions of DSD, see Consortium on the Management of Disorders of Sex Development 2006.)

Some forms of DSD are life-threatening conditions that must be treated as soon as possible after birth (see, for example, Bowen 2003). Most forms of DSD do not pose such serious threats, but are problematic issues for the newborn child and its parents. Perhaps the most difficult of those issues is how the sex of a newborn is to be determined when sexual characteristics are ambiguous, as may be the case with clitoromegaly or micropenis. One option is to have surgery performed to clarify the appearance of external genitalia so that the child can be raised unambiguously as male or female. Another option is to hold off on such surgery until later in life, or to have an individual live with the genitalia with which he or she was born. The last of these options, once somewhat vigorously opposed by some experts in the field, is now widely seen as a reasonable and successful way of dealing with issues related to DSD.

The prognosis for individuals born with DSD is highly variable, depending on the specific type of problem involved, the effectiveness of treatment, and other factors. While some people certainly face a number of daily challenges that non-DSD individuals do not encounter, many live happy, successful lives that are not noticeably different from their non-DSD family, neighbors, friends, and the general community. Chapter 2 of this book includes a discussion of some of the personal, social, ethical, and other issues involved in decisions early in an individual's life with regard to possible sex assignment surgery. (The literature of intersex individuals in human history is large. See, for example, Brisson 2002; Cleminson and García 2013; Hillman 2013; Long 2006; and Reis 2009.)

Intersex in History

Most discussions of human sexuality implicitly assume the concept of binary sexuality, that is, the existence of two, and only two, types of sex: male and female. In fact, the average person might be expected to think of human sexuality exclusively in those terms. But throughout human history, most cultures have at least considered the possibility of some third (or fourth or more) type of sexuality, some "third sex," "intersex," or other sexual designation. (Note that, in 2014, Facebook acknowledged the possibility of 71 different genders [Williams 2016].)

For example, clay tablets dating to about 2000 BCE inform the Sumerian tale of the creation of humans. Included in that description is an explanation that other types of humans, in addition to male and female, were created during the formation of the human species. According to that story, the Mother Goddess Ninmah, in a somewhat inebriated state, took clay left over from the making of males and females to construct four other human forms, for two of which no description remains. But the tablets do contain descriptions of the other two "alternative" human forms:

> she (Ninmah) made into a woman who cannot give birth. Enki [Ninmah's companion] upon seeing the woman who cannot give birth, Decreed her fate, destined her to be stationed in the "woman house."
>
> The . . . she (Ninmah) made into one who has no male organ, who has no female organ. Enki, upon seeing him who has no male organ, who has no female organ, To stand before the king, decreed as his fate. ("Chapter 2: Myths of Origins" 2011)

A somewhat later text (about 1700 BCE) provides a similar description of the creation of a not-male, not-female type of human:

> In addition, let there be a third category among the peoples,
>
> Among the peoples women who bear and women who do not bear.
>
> Let there be among the peoples the Pasittu-demon to snatch the baby from the lap of her who bore it.
>
> Establish Ugbabtu-women, Entu-women and Igistu-women
>
> And let them be taboo and so stop childbirth. ("Atrahasis Epic: The Flood Story, 18th Century BCE" 2016)

Reference to a "third category" of humans appears in manuscripts from many other early cultures. For example, one of the fundamental documents of the Hindu religion, the Laws of Manu, explains that

> A male child is produced by a greater quantity of male seed, a female child by the prevalence of the female; if (both are) equal, a hermaphrodite or a boy and a girl; if (both are) weak or deficient in quantity, a failure of conception (results). ("Indian History Sourcebook" 1998, chapter III, section 49)

By the second half of the 19th century, some scholars were beginning to think about the possibility of a "third sex" in other than mythological terms. Two of the pioneers in this developing field of sexology, Magnus Hirschfeld and Karl Heinrich Ulrichs, suggested the possibility of a third sex somewhere between pure male and pure female. Their thinking arose out of efforts to understand the phenomenon of same-sex attraction ("homosexuality") which also, for the first time in history, had become a legitimate (at least in some circles) topic of scientific research. Hirschfeld introduced the term *third sex* in 1899 to describe a number of sexual forms—such as homosexuality, bisexuality, transvestism, transsexualism, and hermaphroditism—that could not be subsumed under a strictly binary system of sexuality. He actually believed that there were no such things as "pure males" and "pure females," but that all humans possessed the biological requisites and emotional attributes to express both male and female features to at least some extent. In the majority of cases, he acknowledged, people present themselves, at the very least, as "very much male" or "very much female." But, in fact, the existence of nontraditional sexualities was evidence of the great variability and flexibility present in the human race as a whole (Bauer 2015).

Ulrichs went somewhat further than Hirschfeld in the sense that he clearly labeled the group of "intersexed" people that Hirschfeld had defined; he called them *urnings* or *Uranians*, after the Greek goddess Aphrodite Uranus, who was said to have been created out of the testicles of the god Uranus (Norton 2008; "Urning: Etymology" 2016).

The issue of how to deal with problems of intersexuality grew in importance in the 1950s with the question as to how newborn children with ambiguous genitalia should be treated: what happens, that is, when a baby or a young child has external genitalia that make it difficult to unhesitatingly assign that individual as a "male" or a "female" or a "boy" or a "girl." One answer to that question was provided by John Money, then a professor of pediatrics and medical psychology at Johns Hopkins University, a post he held from 1951 until his death in 2006. Money made his position clear on that issue in a 1955 article, "An Examination of Some Basic Sexual Concepts: The Evidence of Human Hermaphroditism." He and his coauthors wrote that "[s]exual behavior and orientation as male or female does not have an innate, instinctive basis." Those characteristics, he argued, develop only as an individual grows and is exposed to a host of social and environmental factors (Money, Hampson, and Hampson 1955, 301).

The case for which Money and his colleagues became best known involved an individual by the name of David Reimer, whose case arose not because of intersex issues (he was not an intersex child), but because his penis had been mutilated at the age of eight months as the result of a botched circumcision procedure. Money recommended as the simplest possible solution to this problem: using surgery to provide David with female genitalia and have him raised as a girl. He later pointed to this event as one of his most successful ways of dealing with problems involving ambiguous genitalia.

The problem, as it turned out, is that the surgery ultimately did not "take," as Money hoped and thought that it might. That is, Reimer never really identified as a female, but thought of himself and behaved as a male. One person who had doubts about Money's theory of sexual development was Milton Diamond, professor of anatomy and reproductive biology at the University of Hawaii at Manoa. It was Diamond's view that events that occur prior to a child's birth predispose that child toward a male or female sexuality, and surgical adjustments to external genitalia do not alter the ultimate direction of those factors. Diamond was intrigued by Money's research and asked for additional information about the David Reimer case, but was denied that request. Diamond eventually found Reimer, however, and discovered that he was not only living as a man, but had married and was the father of three adopted children. Diamond and Money eventually engaged in a vigorous public debate over the basis of one's sexuality and the treatment of intersex issues, a dispute that has eventually resolved largely in Diamond's view of the question (Colapinto 2004; "David Reimer: The Boy Who Was Raised as a Girl" 2004; "What's the History behind the Intersex Rights Movement?" 2008).

Puberty

From birth to the age of about ten, children continue to grow mentally and physically, adopting more of the physical characteristics of adults. At that age, however, a fairly dramatic bodily change begins to take place: puberty. *Puberty* is defined as the period in an individual's life when his or her body develops the capability of reproduction. The age at which puberty occurs differs over a somewhat broad scale, depending on any number of factors, including sex, a person's genetic makeup, nutritional patterns, environmental factors, ethnicity, social and economic factors, one's general health, and cultural factors (Hockenbury and Hockenbury 2016, 395–396).

The physical changes that take place during puberty are often (almost always) accompanied by a number of emotional changes, most of which can be traced directly to the physical changes. Of major importance is the fact that a young person quite suddenly is faced with a "new body" with which he or she is unfamiliar. It takes a person a while to recognize, acknowledge, and learn how to deal with that new body. It is hardly surprising, then, that boys and girls on the way to becoming men and women have to change the way they think, feel, and act. Psychologists have long recognized this difficult period of life that is sometimes called a time of *Sturm und Drang* ("storm and stress"), a concept first mentioned by American psychologist William H. Burnham and later developed by his colleague, G. Stanley Hall (Burnham 1889; Hall 1904). (Modern psychologists tend to believe that Burnham and Hall may somewhat have overstressed the "storm" aspect of this image, but agree that puberty is almost certainly a period of considerable "stress." See, for example, Vitelli 2013.)

Whatever the theoretical speculation, there seems to be little doubt that puberty is often accompanied by some difficult mental and emotional adjustments, such as the following:

- There is a new and different understanding of one's own sexuality. Since a person's sexual system has been largely dormant in the years preceding puberty, having powerful new feelings about one's own sexual capabilities can be disturbing with questions as to what one can and should do with one's new potentials.

- These feelings may prompt a person to think about gender roles, try out "being a man" or "being a woman," in terms of clothing, language, behavior, and other actions to see how that gender role fits one's feelings about it.

- One's new sexual capabilities may also prompt new thoughts as to how one relates with other individuals. Old friends may no longer seem "right" for the "new me," while others may be added to the list of friends.

- Changes in one's sexuality may also prompt a host of new feelings about oneself. The challenge of figuring out ways of handling the "new body" may at times seem overwhelming, perhaps prompting a variety of responses, such as unusual sensitivity to the world around oneself, an inability to cope with problems, and a loss of knowing where to go and whom to ask about questions.

Changes such as these may cause a person to behave in ways that seem entirely different from what one was like as a child: wanting to withdraw from parents, siblings, and friends; just "giving up" from time to time and fighting back against the people one knows and loves best; becoming angry over things that aren't actually very important; insisting on doing exactly what one wants to do, even though that may change five minutes from now; and believing that "no one understands me" and I'm the only person who is having this problems, even though I don't have the least idea as to how to solve any of them (Gongala 2016).

Gender Development

The concept of *gender* involves two essential components: gender identity and gender role. *Gender identity* refers to one's self-image as being male or female. An individual who sees and thinks of himself as a male is said to have a male gender identity, and one who sees and thinks of herself as a female, to have a female gender identity. *Gender role*, on the other hand, is the presentation that one makes of himself or herself as either a male or a female. That presentation involves the clothes one wears, the way one speaks, the interests one might have, and so on—all behaviors that are established by societal rules and customs as being those that make up "a man" or "a woman." Thus, one might be able to guess a person's gender role simply by noticing how that individual sits in a chair: a woman with her knees together and a man with his legs spread apart.

In most cases, a person's biological sex and gender identity and gender role are congruent. That is, an individual with a vagina is likely to think of herself as a female and to act as one, while an individual with a penis is likely to think of himself as a male and to act as one. But these straightforward examples are by no means *always* the case. In fact, incongruities among biological sex, gender identity, and gender role are not at all uncommon, and are the subject of further consideration later in this book.

How does a person's gender identity develop? That question is one that has been of considerable interest to researchers over the past few decades. In spite of a number of studies of humans and experimental animals (mostly rats), researchers are still unclear about the exact process by which gender identity develops within the uterus, although some trends are beginning to appear. One fact that is now well known is that the human brain, like the fetus itself, is essentially the same at the earliest stages of life. But sometime between the 12th and 18th weeks of pregnancy, male fetuses experience a surge of testosterone flow that begins to produce significant changes in the fetal brain. (Note that this change occurs about a month after the first release of testosterone that results in the formation of male sexual organs.) Some parts of the male brain—the corpus callosum, amygdala, cerebellum, and portions of the preoptic area of the hypothalamus—grow and develop to a greater extent than they do in the female brain, which receives a much lower supply of testosterone. These changes in the brain are permanent and provide an important part of the explanation as to why male and female brains are truly different from each other in a number of important ways ("Gender Identity and Gender Development" 2016).

The important point with regard to gender identity is that the brain changes produced by these prenatal hormonal changes often (but not always) can be traced to specific types of gender identity in a young child's life. Evidence for this conclusion comes in some cases from studies of individuals who have *not* experienced typical prenatal hormonal changes. The case study of David Reimer, provided above, is often cited as an especially significant example of the persistence of prenatal gender identity formation in spite of fairly dramatic efforts to shape that identity (genital surgery and social indoctrination; Brannon 2016, 138–139; Dingfelder 2004; Swaab and Garcia-Falguereas 2009).

"Learning" one's gender identity goes, of course, far beyond a series of biological changes that take place in the brain prior to birth. That process is also strongly influenced by a host of environmental clues from parents, siblings, other family members, neighbors, friends, the media, and society at large. Those environmental clues may begin while a child is still in the womb, when an ultrasound reveals to its parents (who have chosen to learn) what its biological sex will be. Parents who actually see that their baby is going to be a girl, for example, can certainly be excused for beginning to think and plan in terms of having a baby girl in their homes in the next few months. They are likely to start talking to each other and to everyone else they meet how eager they are to have "her" and all the wonderful things they are going to give "her" and the wonderful times they will have with "her." The parents have already begun to construct a series of expectations designed for the baby's "herness" before she ever appears in the outside world.

And then, from the moment of birth, that process continues. Think of all the ways in which parents and others deal with a child that reinforces that child's gender identity:

- blue clothing, bedding, and other supplies for a boy; pink for a girl;
- dolls for girls; toy guns for boys;
- understanding and acceptance of weakness and dependency for girls; expectations and demands for strength and leadership for boys;
- gentle and supportive language for girls and more "tough it up" language for boys;
- books on science and nature for boys; books on homemaking for girls (Brown 2014).

The list goes on, as does the practice, generally into elementary and high school, into college, and beyond. Even in today's "better informed" and "more sensitive" world, people are constantly reminded by those around them as to what their gender identity ought to be. (Yes, there are still golf clubs that do not admit female members, and women's book clubs that are reluctant to accept male members.)

Two points should be made about this very entrenched system of confirming an individual's gender identity. First, the process clearly has some social benefits in that it contributes to the maintenance of a formal structure for society. That structure makes clear what it is that the society expects of males and what it expects of females, allowing people to "settle in" to a societal role with which (almost) everyone can be comfortable.

At the same time, the deficiencies of this model have become increasingly obvious and troublesome over the past century, with more and more people asking whether certain societal roles should be restricted to one gender and other roles to the other gender. A great many parents today work very hard to ensure that, insofar as possible, their children, of whatever gender, have equal opportunities in choice of clothing, toys to play with, books to read, courses to pursue in school, sports to play, and other activities. That mind-set is certainly one to be admired and respected, although it may also be associated with a number of personal and social issues, about which more will be said later in this book.

Transgenderism

The discussion of gender identity thus far describes the process that most commonly occurs in humans, one that is "normal" and "natural." And this is a good time to stop for a moment and talk about these two terms.

Normal and Natural

Normal and *natural* are two perfectly good terms with clear definitions. *Normal*, for example, in the field of mathematics means "the most common result in a series of measurements." In ethics and related fields, it refers to a standard that has been established by a reputable authority, to which everyone is expected to adhere. One might say that being right-handed is *normal* simply because most people are right-handed. Being left-handed is *abnormal* because it is not the most common handedness trait among humans.

The word *natural*, as should be obvious, refers to something that occurs in the natural world. Being able to walk and talk is *natural* for humans because, for the most part, those are skills that nearly all people have. Being able to fly is *unnatural* because humans, without the aid of an airplane or some other device, are not able to fly.

The problem with these two terms is that they are often used not as descriptions of a trait, but as value judgments. The literature is full of comments to the effect, for example, that same-sex attraction is "abnormal" and "unnatural" with the implication that there is something wrong with same-sex attraction. Well, same-sex attraction is certainly "abnormal" in that it is not the majority characteristic among human beings. But neither is being a mental genius, which must be regarded as being "abnormal" for the same reason. And same-sex attraction is certainly not "unnatural." Biologists have known for a very long time that many species in the animal world display same-sex attraction, as do some humans. So, whatever else it may be, same-sex attraction is not "unnatural." It is just one more type of attraction between individuals that exist in the animal world.

The message of this digression, then, is that one must always read, speak, and write of "normal" and "natural" events only as terms of description and not as value judgments. Value judgments can certainly be made about behaviors and actions, but they should not be phrased in the terms of *normality* and *naturalness*.

This brings us back to the discussion of gender identity: how it develops and, now, how it can sometimes deviate from the typical ("normal"?) pattern, a phenomenon known as *transgenderism*.

Transgenderism is a subject that received relatively little attention by the general public in the United States until the early 21st century. Then, quite suddenly, it blossomed into a subject of articles in the popular press, on television, and across the Internet, as well as the topic of social, political, and even athletic concern, both in the United States and worldwide. Discussions began to appear on a fairly regular basis as to what it meant to be "transgender" and of what concern this subject could be to the general non-transgender public. In some ways, the most striking event that occurred during this period was the announcement by (the former) Bruce Jenner, one of the nation's premier Olympic athletes that he was, in fact, transgender and would be transitioning to the female gender after having lived for 65 years as a man (Bernstein 2015).

Transgenderism in History

In fact, individuals who "feel uncomfortable in their own bodies," who "know" that "their physical body does not reflect their true sexuality," who "are living a lie" as to the most important traits of their own lives, or who otherwise live as one gender while possessing the physical body of someone of the opposite biological sex have been a part of human societies for untold centuries. And further, these individuals often play readily acknowledged and often important and highly respected roles in the communities in which they live.

A review of the appearance of transgenderism in human history does involve, however, some special cautions. In the first place, the further back one goes in history, the less complete and the less reliable are the data on the subject. That is, we can feel fairly safe in talking about transgenderism in the mid-20th century, but very cautious in referring to examples from the 10th century BCE. One of the major features of this problem is the uncertainty as to what people of the time and—perhaps more importantly—scholars who study the subject mean by "transgenderism" at any particular point in history. Some researchers who have written about the topic in ancient Middle East cultures (such as Mesopotamia and Sumeria), for example, may conflate transgenderism with cross-dressing or with homosexuality, when these three topics, as understood today, are entirely different from each other. (That this practice has survived almost to the present day is reflected in a definition of the term *transgender* in the San Francisco Municipal Code text adopted in 1998.)

"Transgender" is used as an umbrella term that includes female and male cross dressers, transvestites, drag queens or kings, female and male impersonators, intersexed individuals, pro-operative, post-operative, and non-operative transsexuals, masculine females, feminine males, all persons whose perceived gender or anatomic sex may be incongruent with their gender expression and all persons exhibiting gender characteristics and identities which are perceived to be androgynous. ("California's Trans Rights Collective" 2016)

The city has since changed this definition to one that more closely fits that generally accepted by the transgender community.

Given those cautions, however, a fair amount of data exists about what appears to be "sex changes" as early as about 3500 BCE. For example, Ishtar (also known as Inanna), the goddess of love, sex, fertility, and war in ancient Sumeria, is thought to have had the ability "to change men into women and women into men" in order to serve her more effectively. (She apparently achieved the first of these procedures by crushing a man's testicles between two rocks.) Ishtar herself is sometimes depicted as a woman with a beard, reinforcing the cross-gender feature of her character (Platine 2003; "Posts from the 'Transgender' Category" 2016; Whitaker 2016; for the original text on this topic, see Dalley 2008, 305).

A more complete understanding of the role of transgenderism in human history can be gleaned from the story of *hijras*, a term used to describe male-to-female transsexuals dating to the earliest periods of Indian history. Hijras trace their history to a number of classic myths involving the goddess Bahucara Mata, the deity Ramachandra (Rama), the Lord Shiva, and/ or the Sanskrit epic tale, *Mahabharata*. Each of these sources contains one or more descriptions of males undergoing some type of transformation in which they reappear as females. For example, one of the manifestations in which the Lord Shiva appears is the half-man, half-woman form known as Ardhanarishvara, who appeared fully formed from the head of the Brahma. Many hijras worship the Lord Shiva, therefore, as the progenitor of their gender ("Ardhanarishvara—The Symbolic Unity of Nature and Knowledge" 2016; DelliSwararao 2016).

Hijras survive today in modern India as a distinct group of individuals who carry on a tradition that is now more than 2,000 years old. Over the centuries, however, their position in society has diminished, falling from favored temple workers to rejected members of a low caste of the Indian population. Most still undergo sex change procedures and depend on alms from the public and support from their local communities for the necessities of life. They retain a few of their special privileges from their ancient past. For example, they are often held in high regard as a favorable presence at weddings and the birth of children, an appearance for which a hijra will earn a modest "good luck" fee. Hijras can also be found on busy city streets, asking for alms from passersby, many of whom respond with a small gift for fear of offending someone (hijra) thought to have special spiritual powers. For a short period of each year, the hijras even come in for special recognition because of their unique status in Indian society. During the Mayana Kollai festival, they dress in special costumes, sing and dance on public streets, and are invited into private homes, where they give residents prized special blessings for the rest of the year (Feit 2016; McCarthy 2014; "Why Are Hijras Worshiped in India?" 2015). (In April 2014, the Indian Supreme Court took the unprecedented action of declaring hijras an officially recognized "third sex" groups, with privileges similar to those afforded biological men and women in the country.)

One of the best known examples of transgender cultures can be found much closer to home: the berdaches, individuals found among certain Native American tribes who were biological males, but who generally lived as females and assumed many roles traditionally assigned to that sex. The earliest reports of berdaches can be found in the writings of European explorers who were generally shocked and puzzled when they encountered the practice during their travels. One of the earliest of these records can be found in the writings of the Spanish explorer Alvar Núñez Cabeza de Vaca, who wrote in about 1530:

> During the time that I was thus among these people I saw a devilish thing, and it is that I saw one man married to another, and that these are impotent, effeminate men and they go about dressed as women, and do women's tasks and shoot with a bow and carry great burdens . . . and they are huskier than the other men, and taller. (Katz 1976, 285; similar examples are cited in chapter 4 of Katz's book.)

Perhaps the most difficult problem for early explorers was not just the moral outrage they felt against such non-Christian practices as same-sex relationships, but the difficulty in placing such relationships within the traditional binary (male/female) model of sexuality they brought with them to North America. Among most Native American tribes, sexuality was a good deal more fluid than that model, allowing for at least a "third sex" (and perhaps more) for individuals like the berdaches who were "part men and part women." Europeans invented the term *berdache* for the individuals they described, from the French term for the passive partner in the act of sodomy or a boy prostitute. In reaction to the continued use of this term, a group of Native American LGBTQ individuals and their allies decided in 1990 to suggest a new term to describe this traditional form of behavior, *two spirit*, to reflect the ability of such individuals to transcend a single sex or gender role ("spirit") and express the characteristics of both sexes and genders ("Two Spirit 101" 2016).

The Native American population in pre-European conquest days was hardly a unified system, with various tribes having some quite distinctive characteristics. Thus, two spirit people were not found in every tribe, although they were common in tribes such as the Arapahos, Arikaras, Assiniboines, Blackfoot, Cheyennes, Comanches, Plains Crees, Crows, Gros Ventres, Hidatsas, Kansas, Kiowas, Mandans, Plains Ojibwas, Omahas, Osages, Otoes, Pawnees, Poncas, Potawatomis, Quapaws, and Winnebagos, each with their own name for the individuals and practices involved ("Berdache" 2011).

Berdaches typically "discovered" their role in life as children, sometimes (as with modern-day transgender individuals) simply by recognizing and acknowledging a feeling that they belonged to the gender opposite that of their biological sex. Often, however, children claim to have received a "call" in their dreams to take on the role of a two spirit person. In adult life, such individuals might play a variety of roles, usually subsuming those otherwise classified as "female," such as cooking, gathering, caring for children, and performing a variety of crafts, such as beading, weaving, and quilting. They often played some important basic political, religious, military, ceremonial, and other roles in the society, such as leading the singing and praying at important tribal ceremonies (Roscoe 2015; Williams 1986).

Most discussions of berdaches focus on male-to-female individuals, but female-to-male transgender individuals also existed. These were biological females who, as they grew older, took on the appearance and social responsibilities of males, such as hunting and engaging in armed battles. Various tribes had their own names for the two categories of berdaches, such as *he'emen* for male-to-female and *hetaneman* for female-to-male among the Cheyenne and *agokwa* and *okitcitakwe*, respectively, among the Ojibawa ("The Two-Spirit Tradition" 2013; for an especially well-known case of a female-to-male two spirit person, see Katz 1976, 304–308). Two spirit people today often (but not always) identify themselves as members of the LGBTQAI (lesbian, gay, bisexual, transgender, queer/questioning, asexual/ally, intersex) community and participate in its activities (Navoti 2016).

A person can live as someone of the opposite gender successfully, as untold numbers of specific individuals have done over the centuries; no surgical or other procedures are needed, as long as one's dress, outward appearance, manner of speaking, and other characteristic traits are observed (see, for example, Katz 1976, chapter 3). That such is the case would have been important for long periods in human history before effective and humane methods of sex reassignment surgery were available. (The term *sex reassignment surgery* (SRS) refers to surgical and other procedures by which a person's genitalia are changed from those of one sex to those of the opposite sex.)

Before such procedures were available—and even today in places where they are not available or not provided—other methods are available for achieving the same results. The possibly apocryphal tale of story of Ishtar's crushing a man's testicles is an example of such a procedure; although undoubtedly profoundly painful, the procedure is effective in disrupting the normal biological functions that make a man "male." According to some observers, Native American tribes achieved the same result by having young males ride horses for long periods of time, similarly damaging beyond repair their testicles and neutering them biologically (Conway 2006; "OtherWise Elders and Saints" 2016).

Today, surgical procedures used in SRS are based essentially on the same principles as those used throughout history, but they are immeasurably more sophisticated and more successful. The first such procedures involved the surgical removal of the penis and testicles in male-to-female surgeries and, perhaps, the construction of an artificial vagina and related structures. Female-to-male procedures involved the removal of the breasts, uterus, and ovaries, and, in some cases, construction of an artificial penis.

The early history of sex reassignment surgery is somewhat obscure, partly because of the opprobrium attached to such procedures as well as, in many cases, legal restrictions against them. Interest in SRS began to appear in the second decade of the 20th century as studies of human sexuality in general became more popular and more widely accepted as a legitimate topic of medical investigation. It is difficult to say precisely when the first example of an SRS surgical procedure using modern medical technology may have occurred. Certainly one early example involved a German child by the name of Martha Baer, an individual born with ambiguous genitalia who was raised as a female. In 1906, at the age of 21, Martha decided that she preferred to live as a male and had a surgical procedure to bring her/his body into conformity with that expectation. As Karl M. (an initial only) Baer, he later became well known both in his native Germany and in his adopted Israel, as a prominent author, social worker, reformer, suffragette, and supporter of Zionism (Funke 2011).

The first SRS of which we know in the United States took place in 1918 and involved a biological female, Lucille Hart, born in Kansas in 1890. Throughout her childhood, Lucille identified more closely as a boy than as a girl. By the time she had completed her medical studies at the University of Oregon in 1917, she was so unhappy as a female that she sought the advice of Dr Joshua Gilbert about having an SRS, and transitioning to male sexuality. Upon completing that process, she became a biological male and lived the rest of her life as Dr Alan L. (for Lucille) Hart. A few months later, he was married to Inez Stark, from whom he was eventually divorced in 1925. He then remarried, to Edna Ruddock, with whom he spent the rest of his life (Moore 2010; a list of some particularly successful transgender individuals in history can be found at "Has Anyone Come across a Transgender Person Who Is Really Successful in Their Life?" 2014).

One of the most important breakthroughs in the history of sex reassignment procedures was the discovery of sex hormones in the 1920s. Researchers had been looking for a very long time for the material(s) present in a woman's body that made her female and that (or those) in a man's body that made him a male. Toward the end of the 19th century, for example, Austrian gynecologist Rudolf Chrobak made up pills containing materials taken from a cow's ovaries for the treatment of complications of ovarian surgery in human females (Sneader 2005, 173). The search for these "female materials" and "male materials" did not achieve success, however, until the 1920s. Then, in 1929, the first of those "materials" was discovered simultaneously and independently by two researchers, American biochemist Edward Adelbert Doisy and German chemist Adolph Friedrich Butenandt. The female "material" turned out to be a hormone, *estrogen* (or *oestrogen*). Only a year later, Butenandt discovered the male counterpart of estrogen, which he named *androsterone* (Sneader 2005, 173–178).

This research eventually proved to be of inestimable value in sex reassignment procedures because it provided a relatively simple method for converting secondary sexual characteristics for one sex into those for another sex. That is, a woman who wished to change her body structure to one more characteristic of a man could simply (relatively speaking) begin taking testosterone (and/or other male sex hormones), which would cause a reduction in the production of female sex characteristics and an increase in the growth of male sex characteristics.

Today, as a consequence, the process by which a person is able to change one's body structure from one sex to that of the other sex (a process known as *transitioning*) involves at least one or, often, two steps: (1) taking sex hormones of the sex to which one wishes to transition and (2) having a surgical procedure (or procedures) in which the sex organs of one sex are removed and the sex organs of the opposite sex added to one's body. (One of the best descriptions of the surgical and hormonal aspects of transitioning can be found at Lovell 2016.)

This brief introduction to the transitioning process does not begin to deal with the wide range of personal, psychological, social, ethical, economic, political, and other issues related to the process of changing one's sex. (For a review of some of these issues, see "Issues" 2016; and "Transgender and Transsexual Road Map" 2015.)

Transgenderism Today

How many transgender people are there? Interestingly enough, researchers have been attempting to answer this question as least as far back as the 1960s when, for example, physician Ira B. Pauly estimated that there were 2,000 transgender women and 500 transgender men living in the United States (Pauly 1968). Over time, more detailed and more sophisticated surveys have been conducted, with increasing reliable data on the number of transgender people living in the United States. For example, the Williams Institute made a prediction in 2011 based on earlier surveys in California and Massachusetts that about 0.3 percent of Americans (700,000 individuals) self-identified as transgender (Gates 2011, figure 5, page 6). A more recent, if somewhat limited, study was conducted in 2013 by the Public

Religion Research Institute. That study suggested that about 1 percent of all respondents to its survey were transgender (Jones and Cox 2013; "PRRI 2014 LGBT Issues & Trends Survey" 2013, 22).

The most recent such survey on this question was produced by the U.S. Census Bureau in 2015. Drawing on an extensive database of official U.S. Census records, researcher Benjamin Cerf Harris estimated that the total number of transgender individuals in the United States between 1936 and 2010 ranged from about 22,000 to 30,000 and the number alive in 2010 was between 16,000 and 21,000 (Harris 2015, tables 4 and 5, page 28; these data are highly conservative since they come from federal census data in which individuals have formally changed both their names and their sex on government records).

A number of factors are involved in the uncertain data on transgenderism numbers. In the first place, there does not appear to be a standard definition as to who is transgender and who is not. Second, some individuals are in the process of transitioning and may not be sure how to classify themselves with regard to "transgender." Finally, social attitudes toward transgenderism are often problematic, and individuals may be unwilling to disclose their status to friends, neighbors, or other members of the community (Chalabi 2014; Miller 2015). (Possibly the best existing information on the demographics of the transgender population can be found in Grant et al. 2011, 16–31.)

Gender Roles

Gender issues extend far beyond one's personal perceptions. Society also has a great deal to say as to what constitutes a "male" and a "female" and what types of activities are appropriate for each gender. These perceptions and proscriptions are known as *gender roles*. For example, the culture in which a person lives may regard the proper form and behavior of a "male" as an individual who speaks loudly, pushes himself forward in social situations, easily takes offense at personal comments, works hard and plays hard, and provides for his family. That description would be considered part of a person's *gender role* in that society. A list of "traditional" gender roles in the United States in the current era might look something like the following. Behaviors expected of men may include:

- a tendency to enjoy playing and/or watching sports;
- greater likelihood of taking on messy or dirty jobs, such as construction work;
- a tendency to take charge of family affairs and other tasks in the community;
- usually better at math and science than are women;
- a tendency to dictate and/or control the behavior of their wives and children;
- attracted to outdoor activities, such as hunting, fishing, and camping; and
- unlikely to be engaged in "soft" activities, such as cooking, homemaking, child care, sedentary jobs (such as secretarial), and the arts and crafts.

By contrast, women might be more likely to:

- be subservient in the house, following directions from the head of the household;
- play a similar role in the community, where they do as male leaders tell them to do;
- work in "clean," helping professions, such as nursing, teaching, or personal care jobs;
- be expected to stay at home and maintain a well-operated family system;
- use their "sexual charms" to achieve goals that they deem important;

- not need and should not expect as much education and training as men; and

- be better and more interested in arts and crafts than men; do not do well in math and the sciences; leave physically diffi-cult and "dirty" jobs to men at home and in the community; and, generally, tend to be less confident and less assertive than men (see also Nesbitt and Penn 2000).

It is critical to observe that the above are general statements, and that a great many women and men deviate from these "standards." The items in the list could more accurately be called *stereotypical gender roles*, roles that are likely to be ex-pected and approved by large numbers of the general public. But other gender roles—*non-stereotypical gender roles*—can also appear. For example, movies, television shows, books, and ad-vertisements can show men who display behaviors that might fit the "female" items in the list above, and women who display supposedly "male" behaviors: a man staying at home taking care of the children while his wife is working at a NASA space station, for example. Such non-stereotypical gender roles al-ways exist in a society, to some extent or another. (One of the most interesting academic studies designed to study this issue has been England, Descartes, and Collier-Meek 2011.)

Also, gender roles differ over time; it seems clear that the list above would have been more accurate 50 years ago than it is today, and it will almost certainly change in the future. Still, it does represent one view of the role that men and women are expected to play in the United States in the modern world today. (Chapter 2 of this book includes a discussion of chang-ing gender roles in the United States today.)

Gender roles are not the same in all cultures. The description of a "male" provided in the list above might be totally inap-propriate for a "male" in some other culture, such as a group of people living in 15th-century England or the upper reaches of the Amazon Valley today. And gender role can be very different from gender identity. In almost any culture, there are biological males and females who do not see themselves in ways that correspond with or fit their society's gender roles. The world is filled with endless examples of men and women who do not fit into the model that society sets for them, resulting in sometimes serious problems for both those individuals and for society at large.

Gender Roles in Human Civilization

When an anthropologist goes out into the field to study a culture (which can be any type of society from the most primitive known to humans to that of the most modern city on the planet), one of the features he or she looks for is the gender roles and types of expectations that society has for males and for females: how does each sex dress; what kinds of language do they use both when to talking to other members of the same sex and when communicating with the opposite sex; what tasks is each sex supposed to perform or avoid; who makes the most important decisions in the community; and to what extent can the two sexes said to be "equal" within the community.

Anthropologists tend to classify societies as either *patriarchal* or *matriarchal* (from the Latin *pater*, for "father," and *mater*, for "mother"). Patriarchal societies are those communities in which males tend to be dominant and matriarchal societies are those in which females are dominant. One of the great ongoing debates among anthropologists is which of these two societal forms is most common, both today and throughout human civilization. Some authors have argued that the very earliest human communities were primarily matriarchal, probably because all humans are born of mothers whose lives are often devoted to the children who grow up within the society. (See, for example, "The Myth of the Myth of Matriarchy" 2016. For a concise review of this question, see Lockard 2015, 88–89.)

The general consensus among anthropologists today appears to be that human societies have probably always been primarily, perhaps almost exclusively, patriarchal. As one expert in the field has written:

> As Western history and the anthropological record have told us, equality between the sexes is rare; in most known societies, females are subordinate. Male dominance is so widespread that it is virtually a human universal; societies in which women are consistently dominant do not exist and have never existed. (Friedl 2003, 101; an interesting view of the rise of patriarchal societies can be found at "Women in Patriarchal Societies" 1992)

This judgment clearly does not say that strong, effective, and powerful women have not appeared throughout human history. The list of such individuals can be staggering, including queens such as Cleopatra of Egypt; Elizabeth I, Victoria, and Anne of England; and Isabella of Spain; warriors such as Zenobia of Palmyra and Joan of Arc; revolutionaries such as Sojourner Truth and Harriet Tubman; and great scientists, such as Marie Curie and Lisa Meitner (for a longer list, see "100 Important Women in History" 2015). The existence of strong women does not negate the fact that the overwhelming majority of human societies are and always have been matriarchal. (The existence of at least some matriarchal cultures remains a point of contention among some experts and on the Internet. For arguments in support of greater presence of matriarchal societies in human history, see, for example, Garrison 2012; Goettner-Abendroth 2012; "Matriarchy around the World" 2014.)

Faced with the apparent dominance of patriarchy in modern and historic cultures, some anthropologists have long asked the question: Why? Why is it that humans have chosen male-dominant ways of creating the communities in which they live, compared to female-dominant ways? As it turns out, that question is not just one of academic interest because male gender traits, like those listed above, are decidedly different from female gender traits: stronger, more aggressive, more assertive, more goal-oriented, more domineering, and so on. The patriarchal model that has evolved, then, is an important factor in determining the kind of world in which we live. Imagine, instead, that a matriarchal model had somehow "won out" in human history and the world today was characterized by matriarchal principles of tenderness, compassion, cooperation, and similar "mothering" traits. How would that change the way that humans live and interact with each other in today's world?

So asking how the world got to be patriarchal rather than matriarchal may have some practical significance in the modern world. One of the many answers that researchers have developed to this question lies in a study of other animal life on Earth, with special emphasis on animals most like humans. Some writers have noted, for example, that many (most?) animal societies are patriarchal. This pattern is especially clear among primates, who are most similar to humans. One author, an evolutionary biologist and feminist, has proposed a number of mechanisms that might explain why evolution resulted in male animals having become dominant in their cultures. She points out, for example, that ethnographic studies show that among primates, males tend to work together to bring females under control while females tend not to support each other in this process. She then goes on to suggest ways in which similar changes took place among early humans (Smuts 1995).

Researchers have also posited many other reasons that patriarchy "won out" over matriarchy in the process of human evolution. They argue, for example, that females have a biological disadvantage because of the fact that they can become pregnant. Pregnancy and the extended period of time required to raise a child (usually a task assigned to the mother) can make it difficult for a female to take on other more authoritative positions in society ("Gender: Why Did More Societies Develop to Be Patriarchal than Matriarchal?" 2014). Also, males tend to be physically stronger than females. A large number of studies have shown that males tend to be more physically adept at a wide array of tasks, making it possible for them simply to control females by physical means ("Sex Differences in Physical Ability" 2014).

Probably the most common explanation provided for the rise of patriarchy is based on some analysis of the changing methods for food production in early human civilization. Most observers have acknowledged that hunter-gatherer societies common among the Neanderthals and other early peoples tended to be free of gender bias; that is, both men and women were equally involved in the collection of food needed for survival. But the development of agriculture changed that equation. Men became free to pursue more aggressively more nutritious types of food available from animals, while women stayed at home to tend the gardens. (This analysis involves a number of considerations that can be explored in more detail in sources such as Iversen and Rosenbluth 2010; Lerner 1986; Mason 2005; and Smuts 1995.)

The Rise of Feminism

One of the ongoing controversies throughout much of human history has focused on patriarchism: What have been and are its effects of human societies? How has it contributed to or damaged the development of individual humans and human institutions? Would matriarchy be a better model for the structure of human societies? Should humans abandon both models entirely and find a middle way that provides equality for both sexes? Is sexual equality even possible in human civilization?

Given the dominance of patriarchy throughout the world, such questions are often framed within the context of a more *feminist* view of human nature. The term *feminism* was probably first used by the French philosopher Charles Fourier in 1837 (*feminism*; "Feminism" 2016). It did not become widely used by English speakers, however, until about 1895, as a way of describing a contrasting view of the relative positions of the sexes in human communities. Feminism has been described in a variety of ways, but one popular definition is a type of "social, cultural and political movements, theories and moral philosophies concerned with gender inequalities and equal rights for women." Feminism, then, tends to represent a way of thinking about the organization of human societies and about gender roles that contrasts with patriarchism ("Feminism" 2016; for an excellent general history of feminism, see Freedman 2002; Hannam 2007; and LeGates 2001).

It seems likely that at least some women from the earliest days of patriarchal society must have asked themselves if there were not another way to live their lives, a way in which women could be treated as equal to men. But such individuals tend to be in the minority, with histories that stand out among the more common lives of women of their time. For example, one website on famous women's rights activists lists only 4 women out of 86 "pioneers" who were born prior to 1790 ("Famous Women's Rights Advocates" 2016).

Historians now suggest that the movement for equal rights for women, sometimes referred to as the *feminist movement*, has taken place in three "waves." They do not agree, however, as to the precise dates on which those "waves" occurred and exactly what change the "waves" represented. By most accounts, however, the first wave involved the demand by women for access to legal equality with men in such areas as access to educational opportunities, the right to divorce, property ownership, and, probably most important of all, the right to vote. Some of the important accomplishments of this first wave of feminism are summarized in Table 1.1. (At the same time that events in Table 1.1 were occurring, feminists were active in many other parts of the world. For more on the international phase of the movement, see, for example, Kirner 2012; Moynagh and Forestell 2011; and Paletschek and Pietrow-Ennker 2004.)

The second wave of the feminist movement is generally dated to the mid-1960s. That wave continued to focus on some issues raised during the first wave, especially those dealing with the legal status of women in society. For example, the Equal Rights

Table 1.1 Some Accomplishments of the First Wave of Feminism in the United States

Date	Accomplishment
1848	Attendees at the Seneca Falls Convention rewrite the Declaration of Independence in the form of the Declaration of Sentiments.
1849	Elizabeth Blackwell becomes the first woman in the United States to earn a medical degree from the Geneva (New York) Medical College, now Hobart College.
1851	Sojourner Truth delivers her famous "Ain't I a Woman" speech at the Ohio Women's Rights Convention.
1869	Elizabeth Cady Stanton and Susan B. Anthony form the National Woman Suffrage Association to lobby for women's right to vote. Wyoming becomes the first (territory at the time) state to allow women to vote.
1873	The Women's Christian Temperance Union, one of the most powerful forces in the feminist movement, is founded.
1896	The National Association of Colored Women is formed by the merging of more than 100 black women's clubs.
1903	The National Women's Trade Union League is formed to advocate for more equitable wages and improved working conditions for women.
1916	Margaret Sanger opens the first family planning clinic in Brooklyn.
1917	Jeanette Rankin (of Montana) becomes the first woman to be elected to the U.S. Congress.
1919	The U.S. Congress passes the Nineteenth Amendment to the U.S. Constitution, giving women the right to vote. The amendment was ratified in 1920 when the state of Tennessee approved the amendment.
1921	Suffragist Alice Paul drafts the first Equal Rights Amendment to the U.S. Constitution. The amendment does not pass, and has never passed in later reincarnations.

Amendment first proposed in 1923 was finally passed by the U.S. Congress almost 50 years later, in 1972. The amendment then went to the states, where it never achieved the majority needed for adoption ("Equal Rights Amendment" 2016). But the second wave also focused on some new issues, many of them dealing with personal and family questions, such as domestic violence and marital rape, reproductive rights, prostitution, pornography, issues of sexual orientation, sexism in workplace and the community in general, and inequality in almost every phase of everyday life (Nicholson 1997).

An important aspect of the second wave was that it occurred during a period in American history of widespread dissent over a whole range of social issues. The 1960s saw the rise of protests against the Vietnam War, calls for racial equality, the rise of an LGBT movement, increased demands for workers' rights, and calls for greater attention to minority issues, among other "liberation" movements (Thompson 2010). As a consequence, multipurpose protest groups became more common, with gay and lesbian groups joining forces with African American organizations, environmental advocates finding common cause with farm worker groups, and feminist organizations joining with almost any other protest group with common concerns and demands.

As with the first wave, the second wave of feminism eventually notched a number of achievements, including the following:

- A presidential commission releases a report on "The Status of Women," which found inequities in every aspect of society and called for a number of basic reforms, such as paid maternity leave and more equitable pay and hiring practices (1961).
- The Equal Pay Act of 1963 is adopted, requiring equal compensation for men and women in many (but not all) jobs.
- The U.S. Supreme Court strikes down state laws banning the use of contraceptives by married couples in 1965 (*Griswold v. Connecticut*).
- The National Organization of Women is founded (1966).
- In 1968, Radical Women, of New York, protested at the Miss America contest as being "sexist and racist" event.
- The National Association for the Repeal of Abortion Laws is founded in 1969.

- The year 1970 sees the publication of one of the most influential books in women's history, *Our Bodies; Ourselves* (whose 40th anniversary edition was published in 2011).
- The U.S. Congress adopts Title IX of the Education Amendments of 1972, making it illegal to discriminate on the basis of sex in any federally funded education program or activity.
- Congress passes the Equal Credit Opportunity Act, prohibiting discrimination in consumer credit practices on the basis of sex, race, marital status, religion, national origin, age, or receipt of public assistance (1974).
- In 1976, Nebraska becomes the first state to pass a law prohibiting a man from raping his wife.
- Congress passes the Pregnancy Discrimination Act of 1978, making it illegal to fire a woman or deny her a job simply on the basis of her being pregnant.

As with the first wave, the second wave arose in many other parts of the world with revolutionary effects on the status of women and their relationship to men in many other countries ("Women's Movements" 2016).

Third wave feminism dates to the early 1990s and is often associated with a classic article by American writer Rebecca Walker that appeared in *Ms.* magazine in 1992. In that article, Walker noted the progress made during the first and second waves, but pointed out some of the deficiencies that remained in the struggle for equality between the sexes in the late 20th century (Walker 1992). Out of that article, and promoted by similar pronouncements among women activists, a third wave developed that, according to some reviewers, was almost unrecognizable to participants in the first and second wave. For one thing, third wave feminists took pride in adopting traditional "feminine" qualities (such as the use of makeup and provocative clothing) that earlier reformers had worked to eliminate. A classic description of this position has long been a statement made by Pinkfloor, a Danish company that at one time produced a game called PowerBabes. The company's website promoted the concept that "it's possible to have a push-up bra and a brain at the same time" (Krotoski 2006). As with other reform movements, third wave feminists chose to pick up on traditionally offensive terms, such as *bitch*, and use them as a way of empowering their efforts (compare with the current use of *nigger* and *queer* by African American and LGBT activists, respectively.) Some third wave women have also chosen to refer to themselves as *womyn* (rather than *women*) and *grrls* (or *grrrrrrls*) as terms of empowerment rather than disparagement ("Grrl" 2005). (For an excellent overview of third wave feminism, see Heywood 2003.)

Another major feature of third wave feminism has been its emphasis on groups of women who have sometimes been ignored in previous waves, such as African American, Asian, and Latino women, as well as lesbians, bisexuals, and other women of nontraditional sexual orientation. As one writer on the subject has observed,

> Feminists can be hairy if they want to be. They can be a size 2, a size 20, lesbian, transgender, male, female, beauty queens, athletes, models, physicists, stay-at-home-moms, CEOs. The whole point of feminism is that women have the right to be whoever they want to be. That means we can decide how we dress, talk, act, and yes, who we do or don't have sex with. (Calcasola 2015)

Almost two decades into the 21st century, some feminists are now looking forward to yet another iteration of the movement, a fourth wave of feminism. The precise focus, strength, and direction of this movement are not yet clear. Some observers suggest that a fourth wave may reflect a dissatisfaction with the accomplishments of the second and third waves, that much was left to be done in the former case, and that attitudes and efforts were insufficiently effective and unfocused in the second case. In the words of one of the keenest observers of feminist waves, Martha Rampton, director of the Center for Gender Equity at Pacific University, says:

The fourth wave of feminism is emerging because (mostly) young women and men realize that the third wave is either overly optimistic or hampered by blinders. . . . Issues that were central to the earliest phases of the women's movement are receiving national and international attention by mainstream press and politicians: problems like sexual abuse, rape, violence against women, unequal pay, slut-shaming, the pressure on women to conform to a single and unrealistic body-type and the realization that gains in female representation in politics and business, for example, are very slight. It is no longer considered "extreme," nor is it considered the purview of rarified intellectuals to talk about societal abuse of women, rape on college campus, Title IX, homo and transphobia, unfair pay and work conditions, and the fact that the US has one of the worst records for legally-mandated parental leave and maternity benefits in the world. (Rampton 2015)

Gender Inequality Today

Inequality between the sexes in the United States (and much of the rest of the world) has undergone a dramatic shift since the early 20th century. Significant changes have occurred in obtaining the right to vote for women, gaining access to formal educational and workplace opportunities, gaining increased respect for one's basic character traits in contrast to the force of stereotyping, greater sharing of domestic chores with one's partner, increased involvement in the political process, greater acknowledgment of one's sexual orientation and options, and a host of other measures. For example, the fraction of married American women with children in the workplace increased from about 20 percent in 1900 to nearly

60 percent in 2007. The percentage of women employed in jobs traditionally thought of as "male occupations" (such as the law, architecture, and law enforcement) rose from 5 percent or less in 1930 to more than 25 percent for most occupations in 2007. And the disparity between male and female hourly earnings for comparable jobs decreased from almost 30 percent in 1973 to about 18 percent in 2005 (Wright and Rogers 2011, chapter 15).

It would be difficult to argue, then, that progress in reducing inequity between the sexes did *not* occur during the 20th century. But much remains to be done. The World Economic Forum issues an annual report on the extent to which 145 nations are taking advantage of their female "talent pool," a measure of the equity between the sexes in those countries. In its 2015 report, the median score was 0.698, meaning that the average disparity between the sexes was about 30 percent. The nation with the greatest level of equality was Iceland with a score of 0.881, making women disadvantaged in the country by a factor of about 10 percent. The lowest ranked country was Yemen, a nation in which 55 percent of women can read, 6 percent attend college, and none are members of the national legislature. (These scores are calculated on the basis of women's relative position on economic participation and opportunity, educational attainment, health and survival measures, and political empowerment ["The Global Gender Gap Index 2015" 2016].)

The United States ranked 28th among the nations included in the survey, a position somewhat lower than it has ranked in previous surveys (see Table 1.2). The factors that contributed to the U.S. ranking were a 6th place ranking for economic participation and opportunity (a score of 0.826), a 40th place ranking in educational attainment (0.999), a 64th ranking in health and survival (0.975), and a 72nd place ranking in political empowerment (0.162; "The Global Gender Gap Index 2015" 2016, table 3, page 8).

Table 1.2   U.S. Ranking, Global Gender Gap Report, 2006–2015

Year	Ranking	Score
2006	23	0.704
2007	31	0.700
2008	27	0.717
2009	31	0.717
2010	19	0.741
2011	17	0.741
2012	22	0.737
2013	23	0.739
2014	20	0.746
2015	28	0.740

Source: "The Global Gender Gap Report 2014," 2015; World Economic Forum and "The Global Gender Gap Index 2015," 2016; World Economic Forum, http://reports.weforum.org/global-gender-gap-report-2015/the-global-gender-gap-index-2015/; and http://www3.weforum.org/docs/GGGR14/GGGR_CompleteReport_2014.pdf, accessed on August 8, 2016.

Affectional Orientation

One of the most striking features about human sexuality is the range of expressions that can occur. As discussed earlier, it is inaccurate to try to fit all human beings into a few neat categories, such as "male" or "female," when talking about sex and gender. One is safer in thinking in terms of a range of possibilities that may also include intersex, transgender, "gender-free," and a host of other categories. Such is the case also with affectional orientation. The term *affectional orientation* as used in this book refers to the range of possibilities experienced by males and females in terms of the biological sex to which they may be sexually attracted. Other terms with a similar meaning are *homosexual orientation, heterosexual orientation, bisexuality,* and *pansexuality.*

Variations in affectional orientation have been observed since the beginning of human civilization. Such variations have almost never, if ever, been dominant or a majority trait in any human society. The fundamental nature of human biology— heterosexual contact for the production of children—would appear to exclude that possibility. But there is certainly no lack of examples of historic figures, and often the behavior of ordinary individuals within a culture, of being sexually attracted to one another.

Perhaps the earliest example of same-sex affectional orientation that we know comes from Sumeria in about 2750 BCE. The example comes from perhaps the greatest of all Sumerian texts, the *Epic of Gilgamesh*. That story concerns the powerful king of that name, a man more god-like than human, with enormous strength and ferocity. At one point in his life, the gods decide to trying "reining in" Gilgamesh by sending him a male companion, Enkidu, to serve as a moderating force in his life. The two soon develop an intense personal relationship, whose precise nature has been the subject of debate for centuries. The language with which the relationship is described in the epic poem certainly seems explicit in many places. Even before Enkidu appears in Gilgamesh's life, the king dreams about his future companion. He imagines that Enkidu falls from the sky in the form of a stone and is aroused and turned into a living human only when Gilgamesh takes him in his arm and caresses him. When asked to explain the dream, the king's mother tells her son that the stone/man who has fallen from the sky stands for a dear friend, a mighty hero. "You will," she says, "take him in your arms, embrace and caress him the way a man caresses his wife." In a battle in which the two men kill the monster Humbaba, Enkidu is mortally wounded, evoking the following response from Gilgamesh:

When he heard the death rattle, Gilgamesh moaned
like a dove. His face grew dark. "Beloved,
wait, don't leave me. Dearest of men,
don't die, don't let them take you from me." (Park 2012)

Such stories are hardly uncommon in human history. One of the classic tales from ancient China, for example, has become known as the "tale of the cut sleeve." According to this tale, Emperor Ai was besotted with a young courtier by the name of Dong Xian, and took him as his lover. On one particular occasion, the two men fell asleep together on a straw mat. When Ai was awakened to deal with a matter of state, he hesitated to wake his sleeping companion and, instead, ordered that his voluminous "butterfly" sleeve be cut off to allow Dong to continue sleeping. Ever since that time, the phrase "passion of the cut sleeve" (duanxiu zhi pi) had been used in Chinese literature to refer to same-sex relationships (Hinsch 1990).

Perhaps the most famous story of same-sex attraction from the ancient world is that of Achilles and Patroclus. This relationship is described in detail in the great Greek classic, the *Iliad*, written about 1100 BC. According to the story, the two men had been friends since childhood, a friendship that may well have been sexual for all or part of their lives. As with the story of Gilgamesh and Endiku, it is virtually impossible for modern analysts to decide how physically extensive this relationship was, but the language used to describe it certainly seems suggestive at some times. In the *Iliad*, for example, Homer writes that Achilles, upon hearing of the death of Patroclus, weeps that

> I could suffer nothing worse than this, not even if I learned my father's died . . . or if I heard my dear son had died. . . . Up to now, the heart in my chest hoped that I alone would perish here in Troy. . . . You'd return to Phthia, taking my child in your swift black ship away from Scyros. (Homer 2004)

(The history of same-sex relationships in history is far too extensive to be covered in this book. For more information on the topic, see, for example, Crompton 2003; and Neill 2009.)

Whatever the historical record, it is obvious that few societies have taken kindly to same-sex affectional orientation. The historical record of such relationships has largely been one of hatred, fear, oppression, abuse, and rejection. Even today, three of the world's largest religions (Islam, Christianity, and, to some extent, Judaism) continue to offer strong condemnations of such relationships. In the vast majority of Islamic-majority nations, the number of people who say they believe that same-sex relationships should be accepted ranges in the single digits (less than 5% in Egypt, Jordan, Tunisia, Indonesia, Pakistan, and Nigeria, for example; "The Global Divide on Homosexuality" 2013). In a number of Islamic nations, such relationships are not only reviled, but also punished severely with imprisonment ranging from a few months to life; physical punishment, such as whipping; fines that may exceed many thousands of dollars; and, in a handful of nations, death. Overall, 75 nations (39% of all UN members) maintain one or more of these penalties against same-sex relationships (Carroll and Itaborahy 2015).

Legal Prohibitions on Same-Sex Acts in the United States

Laws like those in force in many Islamic nations today were largely the rule throughout most of the world until fairly recently. When the American colonies were founded in the 17th century, for example, early settlers brought with them the same type of laws with which they were familiar in England, Germany, France, and other European nations. Such laws generally referred to *sodomy* and called for severe penalties, often the death penalty. (The term *sodomy* originally referred to anal intercourse between two men, although it lost much of its specific meaning throughout most of history and more generally referred to any form of same-sex physical contact. See Painter 1991–2005. For specific instances of the implementation of such laws, see Katz 1976, chapter 1.)

Sodomy laws remained in effect in the United States for more than three centuries after the nation's founding. The penalty for such acts generally ranged from 1 year to 20 years in prison and a fine of $500 to $5,000 or more (Maza 2011).

It was not until 1962 that a sodomy law was repealed in any state, in which year the Illinois legislature took that action. It took almost another decade before a second state (Connecticut) took a similar action in 1971. Nineteen more states followed suit during the 1970s, two more followed in the 1980s, and three more in the 1990s (Painter 1991–2005).

The final blow to sodomy laws occurred in 2003 when the U.S. Supreme Court ruled in *Lawrence v. Texas* (539 U.S. 558) that such acts violated the U.S. Constitution, thus invalidating all state laws on the topic (*Lawrence et al. v. Texas* 2003). (The Court's decision has turned out not to be the final word on punishment for same-sex acts in the United States, however. See Maza 2011 for a discussion of continuing use of legal remedies for the practice of some same-sex acts.)

Civil Rights for LGBT Individuals

By the end of the 20th century, then, criminal penalties for the practice of same-sex acts were largely disappearing in the United States. The same cannot be said, however, for another area of the law: civil rights protections. The Civil Rights Law of 1964 prohibited discrimination in the United States on the basis of race, color, religion, sex, or national origin, but not sexual orientation. That law applied to a variety of activities, most prominently employment, housing, and public accommodation. It meant that a person could not be denied a job or a place to live or access to a public building simply on the basis of his or her race, color, religion, sex, or national origin.

A handful of federal officials were concerned that sexual orientation had been omitted from that act, and, in 1974, two Democratic representatives from New York state, Bella Abzug and Ed Koch, introduced federal legislation to remedy that defect. The Abzug/Koch bill did not pass, nor has any other version of the legislation been adopted since that time ("A History of Federal Non-Discrimination Legislation" 2016). Instead, a number of states have taken action to provide such protection within their own borders, the first of which was Wisconsin in

1982. Today, 30 states and the District of Columbia have some form of anti-discrimination law in place, although the precise nature of those laws differs from state to state. Some laws apply only to employment OR housing OR public accommodation, while some laws apply only to public employment and others apply to both public and private employment (Hunt 2012; "Non-Discrimination Laws" 2016).

Attitudes toward Same-Sex Behaviors in the United States

The preceding discussion suggests that public attitudes about same-sex relationships have evolved somewhat rapidly over the past half century. That conclusion is supported by a review of public opinion polls conducted over that period of time. Probably the best single source of information on this trend is the ongoing review of public opinion surveys conducted on a regular basis by the American Enterprise Institute. In the most recent of those reports currently available (Bowman, Rugg, and Marsico 2013), the trend toward a greater acceptance of same-sex relationships in a wide variety of fields is clear. For example, the question as to whether same-sex relationships are "wrong" or "almost always wrong" produced a "yes" response from 80 percent of respondents in 1973, a number that fell to 63 percent in 2000 and 50 percent in 2010, the latest year for which data are available. A similar trend was observed for questions about civil rights of LGBT individuals. In 1977, 56 percent of those interviewed said that "homosexuals" should have equal rights in terms of job opportunities, and 33 percent said they should not. By 2008, those numbers had changed to 87 percent and 10 percent, respectively (Bowman, Rugg, and Marsico 2013, 4, 14–15).

The Range of Human Affectional Expression

One of the most important events in the study of human sexuality occurred in the 1940s when Alfred Kinsey, then a professor of zoology at Indiana University, decided to initiate a somewhat different line of research: the types of sexual expressions found among American men and women. Kinsey later published two books summarizing the results of his findings, *Sexual Behavior in the Human Male* (1948) and *Sexual Behavior in the Human Female* (1953). Possibly the most important single result of Kinsey's work was his conclusion that affectional expression (or sexual orientation) cannot be neatly classified into one of two categories ("gay" and "straight," for example), but rather on a continuum from "interested only in someone of the same sex" to "interested in equal proportions to the same and opposite sex" to "interested only in someone of the opposite sex."

Kinsey expressed this situation on a scale ranging from 0 (exclusively opposite sex, or "heterosexual") to 6 (exclusively same sex, or "homosexual"). (Kinsey also included a category that he labeled "X" for those who had had "no socio-sexual contacts or reactions." Table 1.3 summarizes his findings for men of various ages for each of the six categories. These findings only confirmed for him and his research team that

[m]ales do not represent two discrete populations, heterosexual and homosexual. The world is not to be divided into sheep and goats. Not all things are black nor all things white. It is a fundamental of taxonomy that nature rarely deals with discrete categories. Only the human mind invents categories and tries to force facts into separated pigeon-holes. . . . The sooner we learn this concerning human sexual behavior the sooner we shall reach a sound understanding of the realities of sex. (Kinsey, Pomeroy, and Martin 1948, 639)

The Kinsey scale is no longer used by researchers today, although variations of it have been developed and are sometimes used in studies of sexuality. One such variation is known as the Klein Sexual Orientation Grid, which measures the degree of

Table 1.3   Frequency of Affectional Orientation, Sample of Kinsey Data

Age	Cases	X	0	1	2	3	4	5	6
10	819	62.9	8.5	2.2	5.1	5.9	1.0	0.5	13.9
14	811	41.2	31.4	1.7	5.3	6.4	2.1	1.4	10.6
18	635	11.5	61.6	4.6	7.9	5.7	2.4	1.7	4.6
22	306	7.8	63.9	4.2	6.9	7.8	2.6	2.6	4.2
26	172	2.3	0.5	5.8	9.9	10.5	3.5	1.7	5.8
30	107	1.9	53.2	6.5	11.2	13.1	4.7	1.9	7.5
34	72	2.8	58.2	1.4	11.1	12.5	2.8	5.6	5.6
38	57	1.8	57.8	1.8	12.3	15.8	0.0	3.5	7.0

Source: Kinsey, Alfred C., Wardell B. Pomeroy, and Clyde E. Martin. 1948. *Sexual Behavior in the Human Male*. Philadelphia: W. B. Saunders Company, table 141, page 640.

affectional orientation, as did the Kinsey scale, in three different time periods: past, present, and an "ideal" situation (see Lovelock 2014 for an explanation and typical data collected with the instrument).

Conclusion

Sex and gender are complex topics that are perhaps too often treated in the most casual and simplistic way. Almost anything that people think they know about these topics is likely to be only partially correct. The nuances involved in a study of sex and gender are not just a matter of academic interest, but issues of profound significance to individuals. Some of those issues, the problems associated with them, and solutions that have been devised to deal with them are the topic of Chapter 2 of this book.

References

Adewale, Heather. 2016. "External Genital Development in Males and Females." Study.com. http://study.com/academy/lesson/external-genital-development-in-males-and-females.html. Accessed on July 17, 2016.

"Ardhanarishvara—The Symbolic Unity of Nature and Knowledge." 2016. Dolls of India. http://www.dollsofindia .com/library/ardhanarishvara-symbolism/. Accessed on July 27, 2016.

"Atrahasis Epic: The Flood Story, 18th Century BCE." 2016. Center for Online Judaic Studies. http://cojs.org/atrahasis_ epic-_the_flood_story-_18th_century_bce/. Accessed on July 23, 2016.

Bauer, J. Edgar. 2015. "Third Sex." GLBTQ. http://www .glbtqarchive.com/ssh/third_sex_S.pdf. Accessed on July 23, 2016.

"Berdache." 2011. Encyclopedia of the Great Plains. http:// plainshumanities.unl.edu/encyclopedia/doc/egp.gen.004. Accessed on July 28, 2016.

Bernstein, Jacob. 2015. "The Bruce Jenner Story Goes from Gossip to News." *The New York Times*. http://www.nytimes .com/2015/02/05/fashion/the-bruce-jenner-story-goes-from-gossip-to-news.html?_r=0. Accessed on July 26, 2016.

Bowen, R. 2003. "Congenital Adrenal Hyperplasia." http:// arbl.cvmbs.colostate.edu/hbooks/pathphys/endocrine/ adrenal/cah.html. Accessed on July 21, 2016.

Bowman, Karlyn, Andrew Rugg, and Jennifer Marsico. 2013. "Polls on Attitudes on Homosexuality & Gay Marriage." American Enterprise Institute. http://www.aei.org/wp-content/uploads/2013/03/-polls-on-attitudes-on-homo sexuality-gay-marriage_151640318614.pdf. Accessed on August 11, 2016.

Brannon, Linda. 2016. *Gender: Psychological Perspectives*, 6th ed. London; New York: Routledge, Taylor & Francis Group.

Brisson, Luc. 2002. *Sexual Ambivalence: Androgyny and Hermaphroditism in Graeco-Roman Antiquity*. Berkeley: University of California Press.

Brown, Christia S. 2014. "The Way We Talk about Gender Can Make a Big Difference." Psychology Today.

https://www.psychologytoday.com/blog/beyond-pink-and-blue/201403/the-waywe-talk-about-gender-can-make-big-difference. Accessed on July 25, 2016.

Burnham, William H. 1889. "Economy in Intellectual Work." *Scribner's Magazine* 5(3): 306–314. Available online at http://ebooks.library.cornell.edu/cgi/t/text/pageviewer-idx? c=scri;cc=scri;rgn=full%20text;idno=scri0005-3;didno=scri 0005-3;view=image;seq=314;node=scri0005-3%3A6;page= root;size=100. Accessed on July 24, 2016.

Calcasola, Lisa. 2015. "The Big Fat F Word Redefined, Feminism." Thought Catalog. http://thoughtcatalog.com/ lisa-calcasola/2015/06/the-big-fat-f-word-redefined-feminism/. Accessed on August 7, 2016.

"California's Trans Rights Collective." 2016. Transpire. https://lynneauraniastuart.wordpress.com/2016/06/10/ californias-trans-rights-collective/. Accessed on July 27, 2016.

Carroll, Aengus, and Lucas Paoli Itaborahy. 2015. "State Sponsored Homophobia: A World Survey of Laws: Criminalisation, Protection and Recognition of Same-sex Love." 10th ed. http://old.ilga.org/Statehomophobia/ ILGA_State_Sponsored_Homophobia_2015.pdf. Accessed on August 10, 2016.

Chalabi, Mona. 2014. "Why We Don't Know the Size of the Transgender Population." FiveThirtyEight. http:// fivethirtyeight.com/features/why-we-don't-know-th-size-of-the-transgender-population/. Accessed on August 1, 2016.

"Chapter 2: Myths of Origins." 2011. Internet Sacred Text Archive. http://www.sacred-texts.com/ane/sum/sum07 .htm. Accessed on July 23, 2016.

Chen, Harold. 2016. "Klinefelter Syndrome." Medscape. http://emedicine.medscape.com/article/945649-overview #a4. Accessed on July 19, 2016.

Cleminson, Richard, and Francisco Vázquez García. 2013. *Sex, Identity and Hermaphrodites in Iberia, 1500–1800.* London: Pickering & Chatto Publishers.

Colapinto, John. 2004. "Gender Gap: What Were the Real Reasons behind David Reimer's Suicide?" Slate. http://www.slate.com/articles/health_and_science/medical_examiner/2004/06/gender_gap.html. Accessed on July 23, 2016.

Coleman, Vernon. 1996. *Men in Dresses: A Study of Transvestism/Crossdressing.* Barnstaple, UK: European Medical Journal. Available online at http://www.vernon coleman.com/mid.htm. Accessed on July 18, 2016.

Consortium on the Management of Disorders of Sex Development. 2006. "Handbook for Parents." Whitehouse Station, NJ: Intersex Society of North America. Available online at http://www.accordalliance.org/dsdguidelines/parents.pdf. Accessed on July 21, 2016.

Conway, Lynn. 2006. "Vaginoplasty: Male to Female Sex Reassignment Surgery." http://ai.eecs.umich.edu/people/conway/TS/SRS.html#anchor41859. Accessed on July 28, 2016.

Crompton, Louis. 2003. *Homosexuality & Civilization.* Cambridge, MA: Belknap Press of Harvard University Press.

Dalley, Stephanie. 2008. *Myths from Mesopotamia: Creation, the Flood, Gilgamesh, and Others,* rev. ed. Oxford, UK: Oxford University Press. https://books.google.com/books?id=0YHfiCz4BRwC&pg=PA305&lpg=PA305&dq=%22who+changed+their+masculinity+into+femininity%22&source=bl&ots=BzC4t1zW8L&sig=wTSAmgc0LY1MWv0SDAL2afKEpTg&hl=en&sa=X&ved=0ahUKEwiFiP-kg5TOAhUBzWMKHV_4ClcQ6AEIIDAB#v=onepage&q=%22who%20changed%20their%20masculinity%20into%20femininity%22&f=false. Accessed on July 27, 2016.

Daniel, Maala S. 2016. "Turner Syndrome." Medscape. http://emedicine.medscape.com/article/949681-overview. Accessed on July 19, 2016.

"David Reimer: The Boy Who Was Raised as a Girl." 2004. http://www.mcrcad.org/reimer.html. Accessed on July 23, 2016.

"Dear Colleague Letter on Transgender Students." 2016. U.S. Department of Justice; U.S. Department of Education. http://www2.ed.gov/about/offices/list/ocr/letters/colleague-201605-title-ix-transgender.pdf. Accessed on July 16, 2016.

DelliSwararao. 2016. "Hijra's and Their Social Life in South Asia." *Imperial Journal of Interdisciplinary Research* 2(4). http://www.onlinejournal.in/IJIRV2I4/099.pdf. Accessed on July 27, 2016.

Dingfelder, Sadie F. 2004. "Gender Bender." American Psychological Association. http://www.apa.org/monitor/apr04/gender.aspx. Accessed on July 25, 2016.

Docter, Richard F., and Virginia Prince. 1997. "Transvestism: A Survey of 1032 Cross-Dressers." *Archives of Sexual Behavior* 26(6): 589-605.

Dreger, Alice D., et al. 2005. "Changing the Nomenclature/Taxonomy for Intersex: A Scientific and Clinical Rationale." *Journal of Pediatric Endocrinology & Metabolism* 18(8): 729–733.

England, Dawn Elizabeth, Lara Descartes, and Melissa A. Collier-Meek. 2011. "Gender Role Portrayal and the Disney Princesses." *Sex Roles* 64(7–8): 555–567.

"Equal Rights Amendment." 2016. http://www.equalrights amendment.org/. Accessed on August 6, 2016.

"Famous Women's Rights Advocates." 2016. Bio. http://www.biography.com/people/groups/activists-womens-rights-activists. Accessed on August 4, 2016.

Feit, Candance. 2016. "Mortal to Divine and Back: India's Transgender Goddesses." *The New York Times.*

http://www.nytimes.com/2016/07/25/world/asia/india-transgender.html?_r=0. Accessed on July 27, 2016.

"Feminism." 2016. New World Encyclopedia. http://www .newworldencyclopedia.org/entry/Feminism. Accessed on August 3, 2016.

Freedman, Estelle B. 2002. *No Turning Back: The History of Feminism and the Future of Women.* New York: Ballantine Books.

Friedl, Ernestine. 2003. "Society and Sex Roles." In Aaron Podolefsky and Peter J. Brown, eds. *Applying Cultural Anthropology: An Introductory Reader.* Boston: McGraw-Hill, 101–105.

Funke, Jana. 2011. "The Case of Karl M.[artha] Baer: Narrating 'Uncertain' Sex." In Ben Davies and Jana Funke, eds. *Sex, Gender and Time in Fiction and Culture.* Houndmills, Basingstoke, UK; New York: Palgrave Macmillan.

Garrison, Laura Turner. 2012. "6 Modern Societies Where Women Literally Rule." Mental Floss. http://mentalfloss .com/article/31274/6-modern-societies-where-women-literally-rule. Accessed on August 2, 2016.

Gates, Gary J. 2011. "How Many People Are Lesbian, Gay, Bisexual, and Transgender?" The Williams Institute. http:// williamsinstitute.law.ucla.edu/wp-content/uploads/Gates-How-Many-People-LGBT-Apr-2011.pdf. Accessed on July 31, 2016.

"Gender: Why Did More Societies Develop to Be Patriarchal than Matriarchal?" 2014. Quora. https://www.quora.com/ Gender-Why-did-more-societies-develop-to-be-patriarchal-than-matriarchal. Accessed on August 3, 2016.

"Gender Identity and Gender Development." 2016. http:// foothill.edu/attach/1474/49_ppt_chapter_8.pdf. Accessed on July 25, 2016.

"Genetic Components of Sex and Gender." Genetic Resource Centre. World Health Organization. http://www.who.int/ genomics/gender/en/index1.html. Accessed on July 19, 2016.

"The Global Divide on Homosexuality." 2013. Pew Research
Center. http://www.pewglobal.org/2013/06/04/the-global-
divide-on-homosexuality/. Accessed on August 10,
2016.

"The Global Gender Gap Index 2015." 2016. World Economic
Forum. http://reports.weforum.org/global-gender-gap-
report-2015/the-global-gender-gap-index-2015/. Accessed
on August 8, 2016.

Goettner-Abendroth, Heide. 2012. *Matriarchal Societies:
Studies on Indigenous Cultures across the Globe.* New York:
Peter Lang Publishing.

Gongala, Sagari. 2016. "Coping with Emotional Changes
during Puberty." Mom Junction. http://www.momjunction
.com/articles/emotional-changes-during-puberty-for-boys-
and-girls_00379793/. Accessed on July 24, 2016.

Grant, Jaime M., et al. 2011. "Injustice at Every Turn:
A Report on the National Transgender Discrimination
Survey." National Gay and Lesbian Task Force and the
National Center for Transgender Equality. Available online
at http://www.transequality.org/sites/default/files/docs/
resources/NTDS_Report.pdf. Accessed on August 12,
2016.

Griffiths, Mark. 2012. "Dressed to Thrill?: A Brief Overview
of Transvestic Fetishism." WordPress.com. https://
drmarkgriffiths.wordpress.com/2012/02/28/dressed-to-
thrill-a-brief-overview-of-transvestic-fetishism/. Accessed
on July 18, 2016.

"Grrl." 2005. Urban Dictionary. http://www.urbandictionary
.com/define.php?term=grrl. Accessed on August 7, 2016.

Hall, G. Stanley. 1904. *Adolescence; Its Psychology and Its
Relations to Physiology, Anthropology, Sociology, Sex, Crime,
Religion and Education.* New York: Appleton.

Hannam, June. 2007. *Feminism.* Harlow, UK; New York:
Pearson/Longman.

Harris, Benjamin Cerf. 2015. "Likely Transgender Individuals in U.S. Federal Administrative Records and the 2010 Census." Working Paper #2015-03. U.S. Census Bureau. https:// www.census.gov/srd/carra/15_03_Likely_Transgender_ Individuals_in_ARs_and_2010Census.pdf. Accessed on July 31, 2016.

"Has Anyone Come across a Transgender Person Who Is Really Successful in Their Life?" 2014. Quora. https://www .quora.com/Has-anyone-come-across-a-transgender-person-who-is-really-successful-in-their-life#!n=12. Accessed on July 30, 2016.

Heywood, Leslie. 2003. *Third Wave Agenda: Being Feminist, Doing Feminism*, 4th ed. Minneapolis: University of Minnesota Press.

Hillman, David C. A. 2013. *Hermaphrodites, Gynomorphs and Jesus: She-Male Gods and the Roots of Christianity*. Oakland, CA: Ronin Publishing.

Hinsch, Bret. 1990. *Passions of the Cut Sleeve: The Male Homosexual Tradition in China*. Berkeley: University of California Press.

"A History of Federal Non-Discrimination Legislation." 2016. http://hrc-assets.s3-website-us-east-1.amazonaws.com// files/assets/resources/History_of_Non-Discrimination_ Legislation_4_12_16_ChartOnly.pdf. Accessed on August 11, 2016.

Hockenbury, Don H., and Sandra E. Hockenbury. 2016. *Discovering Psychology*, 7th ed. New York: Worth Publishers.

Homer. 2004. *The Iliad*. Translated by Ian Johnston. http:// www.mlahanas.de/Greeks/Texts/Iliad/iliad19.htm. Accessed on August 8, 2016.

"How Common Is Intersex?" 2016. http://www.isna.org/faq/ frequency. Accessed on July 21, 2016.

Hughes, I. A., et al. 2006. "Consensus Statement on Management of Intersex Disorders." *Archives of Disease in Childhood* 91(7): 554–563.

"Human Heredity." 2016. SlideShare. http://www.slideshare .net/jpollack13/chromosome-number-and-karyotype. Accessed on July 16, 2016.

Hunt, Jerome. 2012. "A State-by-State Examination of Nondiscrimination Laws and Policies." Center for American Progress. https://www.americanprogress.org/wp-content/ uploads/issues/2012/06/pdf/state_nondiscrimination.pdf. Accessed on August 11, 2016.

Hutcheson, Joel. 2016. "Disorders of Sex Development." Medscape. http://emedicine.medscape.com/article/1015520- overview. Accessed on July 19, 2016.

"Indian History Sourcebook: The Laws of Manu, c. 1500 BCE Translated by G. Buhler." 1998. Fordham University. https:// legacy.fordham.edu/halsall/india/manu-full.asp. Accessed on July 23, 2016.

"Intersex Conditions." 2016. Intersex Society of North America. http://www.isna.org/faq/conditions. Accessed on July 21, 2016.

"Issues." 2016. National Center for Transgender Equality. http://www.transequality.org/issues. Accessed on July 30, 2016.

Iversen, Torben, and Frances McCall Rosenbluth. 2010. *Women, Work, and Politics: The Political Economy of Gender Inequality*. New Haven, CT: Yale University Press.

Jarne, Philippe, and Josh R. Auld. 2006. "Animals Mix It up Too: The Distribution of Self-fertilization among Hermaphroditic Animals." *Evolution* 60(9): 1816–1824. Available online at http://www.bioone.org/doi/abs/10.1554/ 06-246.1. Accessed on July 20, 2016.

Jones, Robert P., and Daniel Cox. 2013. "How Race and Religion Shape Millennial Attitudes on Sexuality and Reproductive Health." Public Religion Research Institute. http://www.prri.org/wp-content/uploads/2015/03/PRRI-Millennials-Web-FINAL.pdf. Accessed on July 31, 2016.

Katz, Jonathan. 1976 *Gay American History*. New York: Thomas Y. Crowell.

Kinsey, Alfred C., Wardell B. Pomeroy, and Clyde E. Martin. 1948. *Sexual Behavior in the Human Male*. Philadelphia: W. B. Saunders Company.

Kirner, Joan. 2012. "The Three Waves of Feminism." Australian Centre for Leadership for Women. http://www .leadershipforwomen.com.au/empowerment/joan-kirner-the-three-waves-of-feminism. Accessed on August 4, 2016.

Krotoski, Aleks. 2006. "European Companies Recognised." *The Guardian*. https://www.theguardian.com/technology/gamesblog/2006/feb/02/europeancompan. Accessed on August 7, 2016.

Lawrence et al. v. Texas. 2003. U.S. Supreme Court. https://supreme.justia.com/cases/federal/us/539/558/case.pdf. Accessed on August 10, 2016.

LeGates, Mariene. 2001. *In Their Time: A History of Feminism in Western Society*. New York: Routledge.

Lerner, Gerda. 1986. *The Creation of Patriarchy*. New York; Oxford, UK: Oxford University Press.

Linden, M. G., B. G. Bender, and A. Robinson. 1995. "Sex Chromosome Tetrasomy and Pentasomy." *Pediatrics* 96(4) Pt 1: 672–682.

Lockard, Craig A. 2015. *Societies, Networks, and Transitions: A Global History*, 3rd ed. Stamford, CT: Wadsworth, Cengage Learning.

Long, Kathleen P. 2006. *Hermaphrodites in Renaissance Europe*. Aldershot, Hampshire, England; Burlington, VT: Ashgate Publishers.

Lopes, Sandra M. 2016. "Is Crossdressing a Psychological Disorder?" Quora. https://www.quora.com/Is-crossdressing-a-psychological-disorder. Accessed on July 18, 2016.

Lovell, Rose. 2016. "Trans 101 for Trans People." Open-Minded Health. http://openmindedhealth.com/transgender-101-trans-people/#phalloplasty. Accessed on July 30, 2016.

Lovelock, James M. 2014. "Using the Klein Sexual Orientation Grid in Sociological Studies." *Journal of Bisexuality* 14(3-4): 457–467.

Mason, Jim. 2005. *An Unnatural Order: The Roots of Our Destruction of Nature*. New York: Lantern Books.

"Matriarchy around the World." 2014. Maps of the World. http://www.mapsofworld.com/around-the-world/matriarchy.html. Accessed on August 2, 2016.

Maza, Carlos. 2011. "State Sodomy Laws Continue to Target LGBT Americans." Equality Matters. http://equalitymatters.org/blog/201108080012. Accessed on August 10, 2016.

McCarthy, Julie. 2014. "A Journal of Pain and Beauty: On Becoming Transgender in India." Parallels. NPR. http://www.npr.org/sections/parallels/2014/04/18/304548675/a-journey-of-pain-and-beauty-on-becoming-transgender-in-india. Accessed on July 27, 2016.

Merriam-Webster. 2016. http://www.merriam-webster.com/dictionary/sex. Accessed on July 16, 2016.

Miller, Claire Cane. 2015. "The Search for the Best Estimate of the Transgender Population." *The New York Times*. http://www.nytimes.com/2015/06/09/upshot/the-search for-the-best-estimate-of-the-transgender-population.html?_r=1. Accessed on August 1, 2016.

Miller, Margaret C. 1999. "Reexamining Transvestism in Archaic and Classical Athens: The Zewadski Stamnos." *American Journal of Archaeology* 103(2): 223–253.

Money, J., J. G. Hampson, and J. L. Hampson. 1955. "An Examination of Some Basic Sexual Concepts: The Evidence of Human Hermaphroditism." *Bulletin of the Johns Hopkins Hospital* 97(4): 301–319.

Moore, Michelle. 2010. "TG History: The Measure of a Man—Dr. Alan L. Hart." TG Forum. http://www.tgforum.com/wordpress/index.php/tg-history-the-measure-of-a-man-d. Accessed on January 30, 2017.

Moynagh, Maureen, and Nancy Forestell, eds. 2011. *Documenting First Wave Feminisms Volume 1: Transnational Collaborations and Crosscurrents*. Toronto; Buffalo; London: University of Toronto Press.

"The Myth of the Myth of Matriarchy." 2016. Chapel of Our Mother God. http://www.mother-god.com/matriarchy.html. Accessed on July 31, 2016.

Navoti, D. A. 2016. "Then and Now: 7 Amazing, Two Spirit, LGBTQ Natives You Should Know." Indian Country. http://indiancountrytodaymedianetwork.com/2016/06/23/then-and-now-7-amazing-two-spirit-lgbtq-natives-you-should-know-164909. Accessed on July 28, 2016. This essay continues at http://indiancountrytodaymedianetwork .com/2016/06/30/then-and-now-7-more-amazing-two-spirit-lgbtq-native-people-you-should-know-164982. Accessed on July 28, 2016.

Neill, James. 2009. *The Origins and Role of Same-Sex Relations in Human Societies*. Jefferson, NC; London: McFarland & Company.

Nesbitt, Muriel N., and Nolan E. Penn. 2000. "Gender Stereotypes after Thirty Years: A Replication of Rosenkrantz et al." *Psychological Reports* 87: 493–511. http://prx.sagepub .com/content/87/2/493.full.pdf+html. Accessed on August 2, 2016.

Nicholson, Linda J., ed. 1997. *The Second Wave: A Reader in Feminist Theory*. New York: Routledge.

"Non-Discrimination Laws." 2016. Movement Advancement Project. http://www.lgbtmap.org/equality-maps/non_ discrimination_laws. Accessed on August 11, 2016.

Norton, Rictor. 2008. "A Critique of Social Constructionism and Postmodern Queer Theory." http://rictornorton.co.uk/ social14.htm. Accessed on July 23, 2016.

"100 Important Women in History." 2015. Angelfire. http://www.angelfire.com/anime2/100import/. Accessed on August 2, 2016.

O'Neil, Dennis, 2013. "Sex Chromosome Abnormalities." http://anthro.palomar.edu/abnormal/abnormal_5.htm. Accessed on July 19, 2016.

"OtherWise Elders and Saints." 2016. Angelfire. http://www .angelfire.com/on/otherwise/saints.html. Accessed on July 28, 2016.

Painter, George. 1991–2005. "The Sensibilities of Our Fathers: The History of Sodomy Laws in the United States." Sodomy Laws. http://www.glapn.org/sodomylaws/ sensibilities/introduction.htm. Accessed on August 10, 2016.

Paletschek, Sylvia, and Bianka Pietrow-Ennker, eds. 2004. *Women's Emancipation Movements in the Nineteenth Century: A European Perspective.* Stanford, CA: Stanford University Press.

Park, Chris. 2012. "The World's First Gay Love Story?" LGBT History Project. http://lgbthistoryproject.blogspot.com/ 2012/02/worlds-first-gay-love-story.html. Accessed on August 8, 2016.

Pauly, Ira B. 1968. "The Current Status of the Change of Sex Operation." *Journal of Nervous and Mental Disease* 147(5): 460–471.

Platine, Cathryn. 2003. "We Are an Old People; We Are a New People." Maetreum of Cybele, Magna Mater. http:// gallae.com/His2.html. Accessed on July 27, 2016.

"Posts from the 'Transgender' Category." 2016. The Hieron. https://thehieron.wordpress.com/category/transgender/. Accessed on July 27, 2016.

"PRRI 2014 LGBT Issues & Trends Survey." 2013. http://www.prri.org/wp-content/uploads/2014/02/2014-LGBT-Topline-FINAL.pdf. Accessed on July 31, 2016.

Rampton, Martha. 2015. "Four Waves of Feminism." Pacific University Oregon. http://www.pacificu.edu/about-us/news-events/four-waves-feminism. Accessed on August 7, 2016.

Reis, Elizabeth. 2009. *Bodies in Doubt: An American History of Intersex.* Baltimore: Johns Hopkins University Press.

Roscoe, Will. 2015. "Native Americans." LGBTQ. http://www.glbtqarchive.com/ssh/native_americans_S.pdf. Accessed on July 28, 2016.

Schultz, Rachael. 2014. "3 Signs You Started Out as a Girl." Men's Health. http://www.menshealth.com/health/3-signs-you-started-as-a-girl. Accessed on July 17, 2016.

Schmidt-Hori, Sachi. 2009. "The New Lady-in-Waiting Is a Chigo: Sexual Fluidity and Dual Transvestism in a Medieval Buddhist Acolyte Tale." *Japanese Language and Literature* 43(2): 383–423.

"Sex Differences in Physical Ability." 2014. Science v. Feminism. http://www.sciencevsfeminism.com/the-myth-of-equality/sex-differences-physical-ability/#fn1-965. Accessed on August 3, 2016.

"Sexual Differentiation." 2016. https://courses.washington.edu/conj/bess/differentiation/differentiation.htm. Accessed on July 17, 2016.

Smuts, Barbara. 1995. "The Evolutionary Origins of Patriarchy." *Human Nature* 6(1): 1–32. http://isites.harvard.edu/fs/docs/icb.topic1001965.files/Course%20Materials_Week%205/Evolution%20of%20Patriarchy%20Smuts%201995.pdf. Accessed on August 2, 2016.

Sneader, Walter. 2005. *Drug Discovery: A History.* Hoboken, NJ: Wiley.

Sokol, Andrew I., and Eric R. Sokol. 2007. *General Gynecology: The Requisites in Obstetrics and Gynecology*. Philadelphia: Mosby.

Swaab, Dick F., and Alicia Garcia-Falguereas. 2009. "Sexual Differentiation of the Human Brain in Relation to Gender Identity and Sexual Orientation." *Functional Neurology* 24(1): 17–28. http://www.functionalneurology.com/materiale_cic/389_XXIV_1/3373_sexual/. Accessed on July 25, 2016.

Thompson, Heather Ann. 2010. *Speaking Out: Activism and Protest in the 1960s and 1970s*. Boston: Prentice Hall.

"Transgender and Transsexual Road Map." 2015. http://www.tsroadmap.com/index.html. Accessed on July 30, 2016.

"Transvestic Fetishism." 2016. Encyclopedia of Mental Disorders. http://www.minddisorders.com/Py-Z/Transvestic-fetishism.html. Accessed on July 18, 2016.

"20 Most Historically Famous Crossdressers." 2012. In the Mind of a Crossdresser. http://paulmitchellrabell.blogspot.com/2012/12/20-most-historically-famous.html. Accessed on July 18, 2016.

"Two Spirit 101." 2016. Native Out. http://nativeout.com/twospirit-rc/two-spirit-101/. Accessed on July 28, 2016.

"The Two-Spirit Tradition." 2013. http://androgyne.0catch.com/2spiritx.htm. Accessed on July 28, 2016.

"Understanding Transgender." 2009. National Center for Transgender Equality. http://www.transequality.org/sites/default/files/docs/resources/NCTE_UnderstandingTrans.pdf. Accessed on July 16, 2016.

"United States District Court for the District of Nebraska." 2016. http://www.michigan.gov/documents/ag/Complaint_528927_7.pdf. Accessed on July 16, 2016.

"Urning: Etymology." 2016. Liquid Search. http://www.liquisearch.com/urning/etymology. Accessed on July 23, 2016.

Utiger, Robert D. 2016. "Pseudohermaphroditism." *Encyclopedia Britannica*. https://www.britannica.com/science/pseudohermaphroditism. Accessed on July 20, 2016.

Vedeler, Harold Torger. 2008. "Reconstructing Meaning in Deuteronomy 22:5: Gender, Society, and Transvestitism in Israel and the Ancient near East." *Journal of Biblical Literature*. 127(3): 459–476.

Vitelli, Romeo. 2013. "Storming into Adulthood." Psychology Today. https://www.psychologytoday.com/blog/media-spotlight/201309/storming-adulthood. Accessed on July 24, 2016.

Walker, Rebecca. 1992. "Becoming the Third Wave." *Ms. Magazine* 11(2): 39–41.

"What to Expect." 2016. http://www.whattoexpect.com/pregnancy/week-by-week/week-6.aspx. Accessed on July 17, 2016.

"What's the History behind the Intersex Rights Movement?" 2008. Intersex Society of North America. http://www.isna.org/faq/history. Accessed on July 23, 2016.

Whitaker, Brian. 2016. "Transgender Issues in the Middle East." http://al-bab.com/sites/default/files/trans.pdf. Accessed on July 27, 2016.

"Why Be a TV?" 2008. http://ybatv.blogspot.com/. Accessed on July 18, 2016.

"Why Are Hijras Worshiped in India?" 2015. Quora. https://www.quora.com/Why-are-hijras-worshipped-in-India. Accessed on July 27, 2016.

Williams, Rhiannon. 2016. "Facebook's 71 Gender Options Come to UK." *The Telegraph*. http://www.telegraph.co.uk/technology/facebook/10930654/Facebooks-71-gender-options-come-to-UK-users.html. Accessed on August 21, 2016.

Williams, Walter L. 1986. *The Spirit and the Flesh*. Boston: Beacon Press.

"Women in Patriarchal Societies." 1992. International World History Project. http://history-world.org/Civilization,%20 women_in_patriarchal_societies.htm. Accessed on August 3, 2016.

"Women's Movements." 2016. Encyclopedia.com. http://www .encyclopedia.com/topic/womens_movement.aspx. Accessed on August 6, 2016.

Wright, Erik Olin, and Joel Rogers. 2011. *American Society: How It Really Works*. New York: W.W. Norton & Company.

2 Problems, Issues, and Solutions

Introduction

The Jonesboro County fairground was packed with people. Officer Stanley had plenty to do watching for pickpockets and other petty criminals. But the husky man entering the women's restroom caught his attention. The man was easily 6 feet 4 inches tall and probably weighed about 240 pounds. What was he doing in a women's restroom?

Carlos knew he would draw attention at the fair. He certainly did not look female. But, of course, that is how he was born. These days he carried his birth certificate wherever he went. The state law made that necessary. Since he was born female, he was required to use a women's restroom; his muscular build and heavy beard made no difference. To the state, he was a woman.

Officer Stanley was even more puzzled when he confronted Carlos. The man's birth certificate confirmed that he was born a female, so he was correct according to state law in using the women's restroom. Was this really the way the law was supposed to work? Were the young girls in the women's restroom really safer under the new law than they had been before it was passed?

South Africa's Caster Semenya celebrates after winning the gold medal in the women's 800-meter final during the athletics competitions of the 2016 Summer Olympics at the Olympic stadium in Rio de Janeiro, Brazil, August 20, 2016. Semenya has been subjected to severe debate as to the true status of her biological sex. (AP Photo/Matt Slocum)

Transgender Discrimination

Of all the issues associated with sex and gender in the United States during the second decade of the 21st century, none seems quite as complex and contentious as the increase in attention to transgenderism. The concept that a person might want—often very badly—to change from being a man into a woman or a woman into a man seems to some individuals to violate the most basic facts that we know about human biology. After all, a person born with a penis and testicles is a male, right? And someone born with a vagina is a female. What could be more basic than those facts of life?

As noted in Chapter 1 of this book, transgender individuals have existed in human civilization for centuries. Yet, efforts to bring transgender issues before the general public and, most important of all, to ensure the civil rights of transgender people are very new phenomenon. Prior to the 1990s, any discussion of transgenderism focused on a handful of particularly notable individuals, such as Christine Jorgensen, Renee Richards, and Brandon Teena. A few governmental districts had begun to recognize and protect the rights of transgender individuals, but they were few and far between: the city of Minneapolis adopted an ordinance protecting transgender individuals in 1975 and the state of Minnesota followed suit 18 years later in 1993. It then took another eight years before another state, Rhode Island, adopted similar legislation ("Milestones in the American Transgender Movement" 2015).

Today, 18 states and the District of Columbia have laws banning discrimination against transgender people, generally in the areas of employment, housing, and public accommodation ("Know Your Rights: Transgender People and the Law" 2016). There is of yet no federal law with such an intent. The first mention of gender identity as an issue involving discrimination came in the 2007 version of the Employment Non-Discrimination Act (ENDA), introduced by Representative Barney Frank (D-MA). The bill included transgender people along with gays, lesbians, and bisexuals in offering protection by federal legislation. Reaction to Frank's inclusion of transgender people was so strong, however, that he removed "gender identity" from his original version of the bill and introduced a second bill devoted specifically to that topic. In the end, that action did not help, as neither bill passed the U.S. Congress. "Gender identity" was included in the 2009 version of ENDA, and has been a part of the bill every time it has been introduced since that time (although it still has not been passed by the Congress; Eleveld 2007; "A History of Federal Non-Discrimination Legislation" 2016).

The debate over ENDA and similar types of nondiscrimination legislation at the state and federal level often focuses on the question as to whether such action is even necessary. On the one side, proponents of the legislation point to the record of discrimination against transgender people in the United States. Among the findings of the 2011 National Transgender Discrimination Survey:

- 78 percent of respondents reported harassment, 35 percent reported physical assault, and 12 percent reported sexual violence.

- 90 percent reported some form of harassment at work, including 47 percent who said they were fired or denied a promotion for being transgender.

- 19 percent said they were denied a home or an apartment because of their gender identity and 11 percent were evicted when their sexuality was discovered.

- 32 percent reported that they had been denied equal treatment at a retail store, 24 percent had the same claim for a doctor's office or hospital, 22 percent had the same complaint for a government office, and 19 percent reported similar treatment from a restaurant or hotel.

- 50 percent claimed that they found it necessary to instruct medical providers about technical aspects of transgender issues and 19 percent were refused any type of medical care when their sexual status became known (Grant 2011, 2–6).

Given that the federal government already guarantees equal treatment for almost every class of Americans, such as race, sex, color, religion, national origin, affiliation, physical or cultural traits or clothing, perception, or association ("Employment Discrimination Based on Religion, Ethnicity, or Country of Origin" 2016), one might ask why providing equal treatment for gender identity might be controversial. Opponents of such legislation make the following arguments:

- Such laws interfere with the operation of the free market, in which individual and businesses have the right to decide whom they will and will not serve.
- They undermine the right of businesses to set certain dress and grooming standards.
- Gender identity laws violate the privacy of others by allowing individuals to make use of facilities (such as bathrooms) not appropriate for their birth sex.
- Such laws are unnecessary because most businesses already have adequate policies to prevent discrimination.
- They also result in reverse discrimination, in which citizens are not allowed to act on their own moral precepts.
- Gender identity laws provide a fruitful field of legal action, vastly increasing the financial risk for companies (Anderson 2015; Sprigg 2016).

The focal point of the debate over transgenderism in the 2010s was the Department of Education/Department of Justice's letter to schools and colleges throughout the United States in May 2016. That letter (Chapter 1, page 1, of this book) was motivated by a bill adopted by the North Carolina legislature two months earlier, on March 23, 2016, specifying that individuals in the state could use only those bathrooms, changing rooms, and similar facilities in public buildings (such as schools and colleges) that correspond to the sex stated on their birth certificate ("House Bill 2" 2016). Thus, a person who had transitioned from male to female could use only a men's bathroom or locker room. And a female-to-male transsexual (such as "Carlos" at the beginning of this chapter) was required to use a women's facility only, no matter what his or her current biological features appeared to be.

One justification for the adoption of House Bill 2 appeared to be the simple desire to protect the privacy of individuals who use the state's bathrooms, locker rooms, and similar facilities. In a public statement on the issue, Governor Pat McCrory said that the bill was intended to do no more than maintain the "basic expectation of privacy" that people had when they used such facilities (Campbell 2016). But another motivation appeared to be based on fears of the threat that transgender individuals might pose to children and young adults using the same facilities. In an earlier statement on the issue, Governor McCrory had argued that "This shift in policy [the use of public facilities by transgender individuals] could also create major public safety issues by putting citizens in possible danger from deviant actions by individuals taking improper advantage of a bad policy" (Harrison 2016). Implicitly, McCrory's argument was that transgender individuals would pose a security threat to children in the state if they were allowed to use a bathroom or locker room of their own choice. McCrory's statement was echoed by that of the state's lieutenant governor, Dan Forest, who tweeted at the time:

> If our action in keeping men out of women's bathrooms and showers protected the life of just one child or one woman from being molested or assaulted, then it was worth it. North Carolina will never put a price tag on the value of our children. ("Lt. Governor Forest Responds to PayPal Decision" 2016)

At least 17 other states considered "bathroom bills" similar to that of North Carolina's House Bill 2: Illinois, Indiana, Kansas, Kentucky, Louisiana, Massachusetts, Minnesota, Missouri, Mississippi, New York, Oklahoma, South Carolina, South Dakota, Tennessee, Virginia, Washington, and Wisconsin. Other states that considered such a bill included Colorado, Florida, Nevada, and Texas (all in 2015) and Arizona (in 2013). None of these bills was ever adopted, leaving North Carolina as the only state having such a law as of late 2016 (Kralik 2016).

One possible explanation for the failure of other states to pass "bathroom bills" has been the strong response against the North Carolina bill by major corporations, entertainers, sports figures, politicians, and other individuals. One of the first businesses to take such an action was the online payment system PayPal, which announced on April 5, 2016, that it was canceling plans to build a new operations center in Charlotte, North Carolina, because of the state's position on transgender issues (Rothacker, Portillo, and Peralta 2016). A May 2016 report by the Williams Institute at the University of California at Los Angeles, School of Law, estimated that the cost to the state of having adopted this legislation was likely to amount to:

• Loss of $4.8 billion in federal funding, almost all of which would come from grants and contracts to schools and colleges in the state

• Loss of $60 million in business investment and 1,800 jobs

• Loss of an unestimated amount from unrealized travel and tourism

• "Significant costs" of litigation in defending the provisions of the bill against a variety of law suits (Mallory and Sears 2016)

At the end of 2016, the question remains as to whether and, if so, how states and local communities can and will respond to the increased demands for equal treatment of transgender individuals in the United States.

LGBT Discrimination

The civil rights issues with which transgender individuals are currently dealing are a reflection of the same battle previously fought by gays, lesbians, and bisexuals over the past century. Some historians trace the origin of the "gay rights movement" to a series of events, starting with the Stonewall Riot, that took place in New York City on June 28, 1969, and ensuing weeks (Teal 1971). But efforts by gay men and lesbians to achieve equality in American society actually date to a much earlier period. Probably the first such effort dates to 1924 when a small group of single and married men formed a club they called the Society for Human Rights. The club lasted only a short while, until one of the men's wives reported the activity to the local police (Chrislove 2012).

A more permanent organization intended for gay men, the Mattachine Society, was founded in Los Angeles in 1951 and has survived in one form or another until the present day (Chibbaro 2014; Sears 2006). A similar organization for women, the Daughters of Bilitis, appeared in San Francisco four years later, but survived for a much shorter time than did Mattachine (Gallo 2006).

By the mid-1960s, gay men and lesbians were also beginning to think of more ambitious organizing projects, the first of which was the East Coast Homophile Organizations, consisting of representatives of gay and lesbian organizations in New York City, Philadelphia, and Washington, D.C. The group had its first meeting in Philadelphia in January 1963 and eventually had few concrete achievements to its credit. But it did serve an essential function in bringing together some of the most enthusiastic activists of the gay and lesbian movement of the time. It was succeeded three years later by a similar, but more broad-based organization, the North America Conference of Homophile Organizations (NACHO). NACHO consisted of representatives from 15 gay and lesbian groups from around the country. Among NACHO's projects were the creation of a national legal fund to finance gay- and lesbian-related court cases, challenges to bar closings and bans on gay and lesbian immigration, and the rights of gay and lesbian service personnel (D'Emilio 1983, 197–199).

Through efforts such as these, a variety of local, regional, and national gay and lesbian groups began to break through the wall of discrimination that existed in the United States. Over time, often quite slowly, new breakthroughs occurred at the local, state, and national levels, such as those listed in Table 2.1. (A complete history of the gay and lesbian rights movement is, of course, far beyond the range of this book. For more details, see Newton 2009, especially chapter 4.)

Arguably the most significant event in the history of the gay and lesbian movement was the decision by the U.S. Supreme Court in 2015 in the case of *Obergefell v. Hodges* that legalized same-sex marriage in the United States. At that point in time, a number of indicators suggested that Americans had become more accepting of same-sex relationships in both public and

Table 2.1   Some Important Events in the Recognition of LGBT Civil Rights

1961	The state of Illinois becomes the first state to decriminalize same-sex acts.
1972	East Lansing, Michigan, becomes the first city in the United States to ban discrimination against gays and lesbians in hiring.
1973	The American Psychiatric Association removes "homosexuality" from its list of mental disorders.
1980	Rhode Island high school senior Aaron Fricke takes his boyfriend to the school's senior prom.
1981	Wisconsin becomes the first state to adopt antidiscrimination legislation for gay and lesbian individuals.
1983	Congressman Gary Studds (D-MA) becomes the first such person to "come out" as being gay.
1984	Berkeley, California, becomes the first city to provide domestic partnership benefits to its employees.
1985	New York City creates the first high school designed exclusively for gay and lesbian students, the Harvey Milk High School.
1993	An estimated 750,000–1,000,000 people attend the first March on Washington for Lesbian, Gay, and Bi Equal Rights and Liberation.
2000	Vermont becomes the first state to recognize same-sex domestic partnerships (civil unions).

private lives. A Gallup poll conducted in May 2016, for example, found that 60 percent of respondents agreed with the statement that gay and lesbian relationships are "morally acceptable" (compared to 40% who agreed with that statement in May 2001). Also, 68 percent of respondents said that they thought that relationships between gay and lesbian couples should receive the same legal recognition as those between opposite-sex couples (compared to 43% who took that stance in a June 1977 poll; "Gay and Lesbian Rights" 2016).

That having been said, it is certainly *not* the case that all people in the United States now hold favorable views about the morality or legal status of same-sex relationships. After all, nearly a third of those polled in 2016 disapproved of same-sex marriage and more than a third said that such relationships were "immoral." The reactions to the Supreme Court's decision only confirmed that reality and made it clear that objections to equal rights for gay men and lesbians would continue at least into the near future.

The most immediate of those reactions took one of two forms. First, some individuals argued that the Supreme Court decision was simply wrong, that it was legally flawed and could be ignored at least in some ways. For example, Roy Moore, chief justice of the Alabama Supreme Court, announced in January 2016 that state probate judges were still under a state court order forbidding them to conduct same-sex marriage. He based his order on a belief that the U.S. Supreme Court's decision applied only to the states covered by the appeal court—Kentucky, Michigan, Ohio, and Tennessee—where the *Obergefell* case originated, the Sixth District ("Alabama Supreme Court Dismisses Gay Marriage Challenge" 2016).

A handful of legal authorities in other states agreed with Judge Moore's position. In 2016, nearly identical bills calling for the nullification of the Supreme Court's decision were filed in Tennessee and South Carolina. Nullification is a political philosophy that permits any state to declare null and void any federal law that the state believes to be unconstitutional. The author of the Tennessee bill, Representative Mark Body, explained that he was only carrying out God's instructions in filing the legislation, that he was "speaking to the unsaved, to the people that are performing same-sex marriages, to the people involved in same-sex marriage, it is wicked, it is wrong and I am doing the best I can to warn them." South Carolina representative Bill Chumley pointed to the close 5-to-4 vote on the Court and said that the vote "sends a message, it's not cut and dry" (Wright 2016). These efforts eventually proved to be fruitless, as neither the Tennessee bill nor the South Carolina bill was adopted, and Judge Moore was tried by the Alabama Court of the Judiciary for violating judicial ethics in announcing his order to state probate judges (Chandler and Reeves 2016).

Another approach for expressing one's objection to the Supreme Court decision on same-sex marriage has had a somewhat more successful result. That approach argues that the possibility of same-sex marriage places two basic American rights in conflict with each other: the right of same-sex couples to marry and the right of individuals to oppose such actions based on their religious beliefs. The government must ensure, many people say, that one's religious freedoms are not denied by forcing them to acknowledge a practice that violates their religious beliefs. This position does *not* argue that same-sex marriage is still illegal; it *does* argue that individuals do not have to become complicit with the practice.

An example of the issue involved dates to July 2012, when two men, David Mullins and Charlie Craig, visited the Masterpiece Cakeshop in Lakewood, Colorado, asking to have a cake made for their forthcoming wedding (which was, at the time, legal in the state). The owner of the shop, Jack Philips, declined to take the order, explaining that his religion taught that same-sex marriage was immoral and sinful. Mullins and Craig brought a claim against Philips at the Colorado Civil Rights Division (CCRD), claiming that Philips's action violated the state antidiscrimination law. The CCRD, confronted with the conflict of state antidiscrimination law and the rights of religious freedom, eventually decided in favor of Mullins and Craig, a ruling that was later affirmed by the Colorado Court of Appeals in 2015 ("*Charlie Craig and David Mullins v. Masterpiece Cakeshop*" 2015).

Possibly the best-known example of the claim of religious freedom against the acknowledgment of same-sex marriage involved Kim Davis, county clerk of Rowan County, Kentucky. After the Supreme Court decision in *Obergefell*, Davis declined to issue marriage licenses to same-sex couples, explaining that such an action violated her religious beliefs. Following a somewhat drawn out dispute over Davis's decision (during which she spent a short time in jail), an accommodation was reached and the county began issuing the marriage licenses in question (Neugold 2016).

The "religious freedom" position has, however, resonated with many lawmakers and ordinary citizens across the nation. For example, two states, Arkansas and Indiana, adopted so-called religious freedom restoration bills in 2015. These bills were modeled on a federal law of the same name, the Religious Freedom Restoration Act of 1993, which stated that "[g]overnment shall not substantially burden a person's exercise of religion even if the burden results from a rule of general applicability." When the Supreme Court ruled in 1997 that the law applied only to the federal government, and not to individual states, some states began passing their own versions of the law. As of 2015, 21 states had adopted religious freedom laws, and a year later, 10 more states had begun consideration of such laws ("2016 State Religious Freedom Restoration Act Legislation" 2016).

The Arkansas and Indiana laws drew special scrutiny because they were passed so soon after the *Obergefell* decision and appeared to be designed quite specifically to allow business owners to reject requests for services from same-sex couples (Gjelten 2016). In fact, the uproar from many large businesses, nonprofit organizations, other state and municipal governments, and ordinary citizens grew to such a point that Indiana eventually passed a second law specifically protecting the rights of gay men and lesbians (Cook, LoBianco, and Eason 2015).

The debate over same-sex marriage, LGBT (lesbian, gay, bisexual, and transgender) discrimination, and religious liberty laws is not likely to go away any time soon. In August 2016, for example, a federal appeals court continued an injunction against a religious freedom act adopted in Mississippi four months earlier, an injunction state officials vowed to contest (Lavers 2016).

Sex Education

Should public schools in the United States offer classes in human sexuality? In one sense, that question might seem absurd; sexuality is one of the most fundamental and relevant topics that young adults should learn about. It would seem to be considerably more important than, for example, algebra or Latin. But the issue is not that simple. While many people *do* argue for the importance of sex education in formal classrooms, others disagree, saying that the topic of sexuality is one that parents should deal with in their own homes. They insist that sexuality is a very personal issue involving moral judgments, involving the kind of instruction that belongs only within the nuclear family ("Sex Education" 2016). But critics also offer stronger arguments against sex education classes. For example, they worry that such classes only increase an individual's interest in sex and will encourage that person to become sexually active earlier in life. Some opponents who claim special expertise in sex education offer other arguments, such as that they "block the development of compassion [and] weaken the mental barriers controlling base sexual instincts, thereby making the child vulnerable to perversions in later life," as well as "separat[ing] them from their parents and their values" (Anchell 1985; Mahoney 2016; for a recent review of this debate, see "Parents, Schools Divided as Sex Ed Controversy Erupts" 2016).

Proponents of sex education in schools argue that school-based instruction is more likely to provide unbiased, accurate scientific information about sexual issues than that available at home. They also say that schools attempt to provide students with an ethical context within which to make judgments about their own sexual behavior. Finally, they often point to research studies that indicate that formal sex education classes tend to have favorable effects on the attitudes and behaviors of students who complete such classes.

The history of sex education in the United States dates to 1892, when the National Education Association first recommended that such a course be part of a national curriculum. Seven years later, the national Parent–Teacher Association added its endorsement to the inclusion of sex education for children who have not yet reached the age of puberty. Over the following century, a wide variety of governmental and nongovernmental organizations added their names to the support of sex education ("History of Sex Education" 2008).

As of late 2016, every state required at least some form of sex education in its public schools, most commonly instruction about HIV/AIDS (33 states and the District of Columbia). Twenty-four states required some form of sex education beyond HIV/AIDS instruction, in most cases (20 states) adding that such instruction be "medically accurate" as determined by some recognized medical source, such as the state department of health ("State Policies on Sex Education in Schools" 2016). As a consequence of these laws, almost half (49.0%) of all students in the United States currently receive some form of sex education, 34.0 percent in elementary school, 54.9 percent in middle school, and 73.6 percent in high school ("Results from the School Health Policies and Practices Study 2014" 2015). Eighty-eight percent of schools in the country that offer sex education classes also allow parents to have their children "opt out" (not take) such classes. The most common topics taught in American sex education classes are listed in Table 2.2.

Table 2.2 Most Common Topics Included in U.S. Sex Education Classes (percentage)

Topic	Total	Elementary	Middle	Secondary
Abstinence	37.0	7.2	49.6	76.3
Condom efficacy	46.2	NA	26.7	65.7
Dating and healthy relationships	35.3	5.4	48.8	73.8
How students can influence, support, or advocate for others to make healthy decisions related to sexual behaviors	32.3	3.9	44.8	69.4
How to correctly use a condom	22.8	NA	10.4	35.3
How to obtain condoms	33.6	NA	17.0	50.3
Human development issues (e.g., reproductive anatomy and puberty)	39.5	20.6	45.3	66.4
Marriage and commitment	27.9	6.1	29.7	64.0
Resisting peer pressure to engage in sexual behavior	35.5	6.4	46.8	74.8
Risks associated with having multiple sexual partners	55.8	NA	38.5	73.2
Sexual identity and sexual orientation	36.5	NA	21.5	51.5
Social or cultural influences on sexual behavior	30.0	1.5	41.4	68.3
The importance of using a condom at the same time as another form of contraception to prevent both STDs and pregnancy	40.4	NA	25.9	54.9
The importance of using condoms consistently and correctly	39.4	NA	19.0	59.9
The influence of families on sexual behavior	27.0	1.5	36.6	61.7
The influence of peers on sexual behavior	34.9	6.6	45.0	74.3
The influence of the media on sexual behavior	32.4	5.6	42.6	68.8
The relationship among HIV, other STDs, and pregnancy	33.2	3.6	44.3	73.5
The relationship between alcohol or other drug use and risk for HIV, other STDs, and pregnancy	34.1	3.8	44.7	76.1

Source: "Results from the School Health Policies and Practices Study 2014." 2015. Centers for Disease Control and Prevention, table 1.19, page 21. http://www.cdc.gov/healthyyouth/data/shpps/pdf/shpps-508-final_101315.pdf. Accessed on August 15, 2016.

One feature of Table 2.2 deserves special attention. Notice that the most common topic included in sex education classes is "abstinence." The call for "abstinence-only-until-marriage" sex education dates to 1981, when the U.S. Congress began providing funds to states to support sex education programs that taught exclusively about abstinence, with no other topics included. Those topics became very popular among teachers, government officials, and parents at least partly because they avoided the discussion of more controversial issues, such as contraception and sexual orientation. Over the next two decades, the Congress continued to provide money for such programs, eventually reaching a total of $1.5 billion spent on them.

The only problem with this trend is that numerous studies have found that such programs had essentially no effect on the sexual behavior of students who took them. For example, unwanted pregnancy rates and time-of-first-sexual-encounter data for girls who had taken abstinence-only programs were no different from those who had taken traditional sex education programs or who had taken no sex education courses at all in school ("A History of Federal Funding for Abstinence-Only-under-Marriage Programs" 2016). Finally, in 2016, President Barack Obama removed from the federal 2017 budget an appropriation of $10 million for the continuation of grants for abstinence-only programs. For the present, in any case, it appears that such programs may become less popular in the country (Marrone 2016).

Gender Dysphoria

Issues related to individuals whose gender identity differs from their biological sex were first formally recognized by the medical profession in 1980 with the publication of the American Psychiatric Association's third edition of its *Diagnostic and Statistical Manual of Mental Disorders* (*DSM-III*). That book included a new category of disorders called *genetic identity disorders*, defined as an incongruence between one's biological sex and his or her gender identity. The fourth and fifth revisions of

DSM produced modified versions of this concept, and the category was finally given the new name of *gender dysphoria* (GD) in *DSM-5*, released in 2013. (*Dysphoria* means a state of unease or generalized dissatisfaction with one's life.) An important feature of the current definition of GD is that it does not, in and of itself, refer to a medical condition; a person is not "sick" if he or she displays GD (Vitale 2005).

GD can occur at any age; a 50-year-old woman who decides to transition to a man can be said to have GD. That decision is generally loaded with questions and problems, both for the individual involved and for his or her loved ones. The situation is quite different when a child at the age of 6 or a young adult 14 years old decides that he or she would like to transition to the opposite sex. The question then arises as to whether that person's wishes should be acceded to. In the United States (or some other parts of the world) in the 2010s, the question of GD has been discussed with increasing frequency by the media (e.g., see Talbot 2013). Very commonly, children and adolescents confronted with this dilemma are said to be *gender nonconforming*, meaning that the gender to which they feel they belong differs from their biological gender.

Data on the prevalence of GD in young people are scarce. The limited evidence available suggests that less than—probably substantially less than—1 percent of boys and girls under the age of 18 express symptoms of GD and an even smaller number actually express the desire for sex reassignment surgery (Zucker and Lawrence 2009, table 1, page 10).

The fundamental question about GD children and young adults is what steps can and should be taken to assist such individuals with the turmoil over their gender status. Many experts note that the human brain does not mature to the point that it can make a full assessment of risks and benefits until one reaches his or her twenties (Cretella 2016). It may not be realistic, then, to allow a 12-year-old or a 16-year-old to make decisions about permanent changes in his or her sexuality. The question becomes, then, what choices a parent or guardian can or should make about a child's or adolescent's desire to change his or her gender.

Experts in the field of GD come to their work with a variety of presuppositions about how gender identity develops and how GD evolves. So they also have differing views as to how the condition should be treated. Generally, they recommend different options for different age levels—one type of treatment for prepubescent children and one for postpubescent adolescents.

Most commonly, treatment for children takes some form of "talk therapy." *Talk therapy* is the common name for psychotherapy, a type of treatment in which an individual spends time with an expert in the field, discussing the nature of his or her problem and possible ways of dealing with that problem. (Note that many people who are classified with GD and/or their friends and loved ones object to calling GD a "problem," preferring to think of it as a naturally occurring condition in a person's life with which one has to deal.) Talk therapy used for the treatment of GD is sometimes called *therapeutic intervention*, a term that reflects a therapist's efforts to interrupt and/or prevent some pattern of behavior (such as GD). Therapeutic interventions can occur in one-on-one sessions between a therapist and an individual child, in meetings with some or all family members, and in groups of individuals dealing with the same problem. Therapeutic interventions as a way of dealing with GD have been available since the 1980s (Koh 2012).

The primary objective of therapeutic intervention is to help a child avoid the trauma involved in feeling that he or she is "living in the wrong body." It does so by devising a series of exercises that help the child to become more comfortable with his or her own body, reducing the felt need to switch his or her biological sex. This goal has been promoted perhaps most clearly by one of the deans of research on GD in young people, psychologist Kenneth Zucker, formerly psychologist-in-chief and head of the Gender Identity Service at the Centre for Addiction and Mental Health in Toronto.

In recent years, Zucker's approach to the treatment of GD has come under attack by specialists who have an alternative view about the treatment of the condition. These individuals suggest that a better approach for dealing with GD children is to listen to and accept the feelings and thoughts held by those children. In such cases, the option for a change in one's sex may become more reasonable and more practical than trying to help a child accept his or her biological sex. Some individuals and organizations that have adopted this view have argued against the use of therapeutic interventions with fervor. For example, in the seventh edition of its "Standards of Care for the Health of Transsexual, Transgender, and Gender Nonconforming People," the World Professional Association for Transgender Health said that therapeutic intervention is "no longer considered ethical" ("Standards of Care for the Health of Transsexual, Transgender, and Gender Nonconforming People" 2016, 16). The debate also had a very personal side that resulted in Zucker's being fired from the position he held in Toronto, at least partly because of his advocacy of therapeutic intervention for the treatment of GD (Singal 2016).

Another approach to dealing with GD has been called the *gender affirmative model.* As the name suggests, therapists who use this approach to working with GD children try to understand the basic feelings such children have with regard to their gender and support the decisions they are making about their sexuality and gender presentation. As one therapist has written about this approach, "[o]ur goals within this model are to listen to the child and decipher with the help of parents or caregivers what the child is communicating about both gender identity and gender expressions. . . . In this model, gender health is defined as a child's opportunity to live in the gender that feels most real or comfortable to that child and to express that gender with freedom from restriction, aspersion, or rejection" (Hidalgo et al. 2013).

The onset of puberty produces a whole new set of issues for nonconforming individuals and, thus, new questions as to what form of therapy, if any, is appropriate. The new problems arise because puberty is accompanied by the appearance of concrete and specific changes that clearly label a person as a "male" or a "female." At that point, the perhaps somewhat vague feelings that a child may have had about belonging to the opposite sex is confronted with bodily changes that say quite clearly, "no, you belong to the male/female sex." That situation may prove to be profoundly troubling for the nonconforming child. As one person with experience has said, "To force trans children go through with their biological puberty—do you have any idea what that means? Hell is a picnic compared to that" (Reardon 2016).

One popular proposal for dealing with this issue involves the use of certain hormones (analogues of gonadotropin-releasing hormone; GnRH) to inhibit the process of puberty, a process known as *puberty blocking* or *puberty suppression*. These hormones delay the appearance of the classic signs of puberty and allow a child a greater period of time to think about his or her sexual and gender feelings. The hormones can be discontinued at any time and puberty will then begin. For those children/adolescents who still wish to consider transitioning to the opposite sex, puberty blocking is followed by a second step involving the use of *cross-sex hormones*, that is, hormones that initiate the appearance of sex traits of the opposite sex (Gibson and Catlin 2010; Olson-Kennedy et al. 2016). The physical, social, psychological, and ethical issues associated with this set of procedures are, of course, profound and are the subject of an ongoing debate among professionals in the field (Shumer and Spack 2013; Vrouenraets et al. 2015).

Perhaps the key question to this debate is what actually happens to gender nonconforming children and adolescents when they have one or another type of treatment. Unfortunately, the answer to this question is not yet available. Little research has been conducted on the outcomes for individuals who have been through one or another of these treatments, or no treatment at all. One of the most frequently cited studies found that most children (80% to 95%) who demonstrate GD during childhood do not remain in that condition once puberty occurs (Wallien and Cohen-Kettenis 2008).

These data can be viewed in light of studies on the effect of puberty suppression and cross-sex hormone treatment for GD children and adolescents. In one study on the use of this procedure, researchers found that *all individuals* in the study who had been given puberty-suppressing hormones requested the next step also, using cross-sex hormones. But that means, if both studies are correct, that 80 to 95 percent of children who would *not* have continued being gender dysphoric were then actually on the path of transitioning to the opposite sex (De Vries et al. 2011; for a commentary on this phenomenon, see Cretella 2016).

Obviously, more study is needed, and in 2016, the National Institutes of Health announced that it would fund the largest study ever conducted on gender nonconforming youth and the effects of treatments available to deal with this issue (Reardon 2016).

Gender Testing in Athletics

Women's canoeing should not be allowed in the 2020 Olympics, according to some male competitors in the sport. In the first place, women are just not good enough to compete in the Olympics. Besides, can you imagine what they would look like after practicing for the Games? "Canoeists are always like one shoulder up, one shoulder down . . . Imagine all the girls walking like that." Those were the opinions of Erik Vicek of Slovakia and Josef Dostal of the Czech Republic, both medal winners in kayaking in the 2016 Olympic Games. Their comments came after the announcement that the Olympic Committee was considering adding canoeing for women to the program for the 2020 Games in Tokyo (Ritter 2016).

The inclusion of women in the Olympics and other major international events has long been a matter of contention.

The founder of the modern Olympic Games, French historian and educator Baron de Coubertin, observed that including women in the first of the modern games in 1896 would be "impractical, uninteresting, unaesthetic, and incorrect." He was supported by medical experts who were convinced that taking part in sports would damage a woman's ability to have children and might well lead to promiscuity and prostitution (Williams 2016).

Even though some events were opened to women in the 1900 Games, the debate over their participation in most sports continued throughout the century. After a classic race between Stella Walsh of Poland and Helen Stephens of the United States at the 1936 Games, for example, a number of voices were raised as to whether the two contestants even *were* women or, perhaps, men in disguise. No woman could, the argument went, be such a successful athlete (Raga 2016).

Ongoing disputes such as the Walsh-Stephens debate eventually led to the introduction of a simple method for determining who could and who could not compete in an athletic contest: the visual inspection of a person's genitalia. It was on this basis that Olympic officials had concluded that Walsh, the winner of the race, actually was a biological female. The discovery at the autopsy following her death in 1980, however, produced a very different result: she was, in fact, an intersex individual with ambiguous genitalia (Raga 2016).

Officials then decided on another criterion for determining the legitimacy of participants in women's athletics: a chromosomal test. They argued that this was a clear and unambiguous standard because anyone who had a Y chromosome in their genetic makeup was obviously "male." The first person for whom this test made a significant difference was Polish sprinter Ewa Klobukowska, who won a gold medal at the 1964 Olympics. Her genetic test found that she had an unusual chromosomal composition, XX/XY, which made her, apparently, at least partially "male" biologically. She was stripped of her medal for competing in a women's event when she was actually a male.

Klovukowska's response to the decision was that "It's a dirty and stupid thing to do to me. I know what I am and how I feel" (Ghorayshi 2016).

International sports authorities were gradually coming to recognize the challenges posed by trying to place an individual into one of two neat categories: male or female. Cases such as that of Walsh and Klobukowska demonstrated what scientists had long known: it is almost impossible to place people into binary boxes; in other words, authorities could not draw a line between the sexes "that nature itself refused to draw" (Padawer 2016). Still faced with the challenge of deciding who could and could not compete in women's events, however, authorities tried yet another approach: measuring testosterone blood content. The basis for the test was the presumption that a major reason that men tend to be taller, heavier, stronger, faster, and generally better at sports skills was that their bodies produce testosterone. If a woman's body produced testosterone at the same level as found in a man's body, then perhaps she could be considered a "male" for athletic purposes, so the argument went.

The first person to receive a "testosterone test" was South African middle-distance runner Caster Semenya who swept most of the races in which she competed as a young woman. Because of her nontraditional female appearance, a number of complaints were raised about her biological sex. Measurements of her blood testosterone level showed that she was, indeed, hyperandrogenic, with testosterone levels significantly higher than normal for her sex. Confronted with this evidence, however, she was not banned from competition by either the International Association of Athletics Federations (IAAF) or the International Olympic Committee. That decision was based on the fact that scientists have yet to completely determine the effect of hyperandrogenism on athletic performance. Semenya competed in the 2016 Olympics and won a gold medal in the 800-meter competition. At that point, Sebastian Coe, president of the IAAF, announced that his organization would reintroduce a complaint against the race results based on Semenya's biological sex (Bull 2016).

One of the interesting features of this long story is the degree it focuses on the sexual status and its relationship to athletic achievement *among women*. The point appears to be that individuals with somewhat different chromosomes, abnormal levels of testosterone, or nontypical physical characteristics should not be allowed to compete with women who do not have these traits. But scientists and sports authorities have known for some time that there is a fairly significant difference *among men* on a number of these characteristics. Perhaps most obvious is the fact that some men have been taking illegal substances to improve their athletic performance, a practice that dates back at least a century and probably much longer (Newton 2014). Yet, some sports administrators and officials have largely ignored this practice and allowed those athletes to compete with non-substance-using peers. (Perhaps the best example of this practice was the banning of large number of potential competitors from the 2016 Olympics because of failed drug tests that had been ignored for many years; see Aisch and Lai 2016.)

Indeed, some observers have argued that all types of activities are permitted to allow one competitor to develop skills that will allow them to win in a contest with his or her peers, including special nutrition programs, high quality coaching, special training equipment and programs, and the use of legal substances that improve athletic performance. And little or no attention is paid to the effect of varying testosterone levels among male competitors. If testosterone really does affect a person's athletic performance (as assumed with the testosterone testing of female athletes), then why is not also conducted with male athletes to determine if some are "better prepared" to compete than their peers? So, the question might be asked, why women are subjected to specific types of gender testing, which, in most cases, have yet to be definitively associated with improved athletic performance? (For an extended discussion of this point, see Elsas et al. 2000; Heggie 2010; Pieper 2016.)

Gender Inequality

Gender inequality—meaning almost without exception that males have been dominant—has been essentially a given in most societies throughout human history. Most people would probably agree that that situation has changed in many (but, by no means, all) cultures throughout the world during the 20th century. Indeed, gender inequality remains an ongoing issue in the United States and most other parts of the world.

Politics

One of the most visible examples of gender inequality is the relative absence of women in politics. As of late 2016, no woman has ever been elected president or vice president of the United States, and only one, Hillary Rodham Clinton, has ever been nominated for the highest post. A total of 104 women overall served in the 113th Congress (2015–2016), of whom 84 were members of the House and 20 were members of the Senate. (An additional four women were Delegates of territories.) That number was the highest ever and represented one-fifth (20%) of the total membership of the Congress, 20 percent of the Senate, and 19.3 percent of the House (Manning 2016). These numbers pale in comparison to the fact that women make up just over half (50.8%) of the American population. Similar figures hold true for individual states, where women make up anywhere from 0.0 percent of U.S. representatives (18 states) to 100.0 percent (South Dakota and Wyoming; Hess et al. 2015, table B1.1, p. 24).

The United States ranks in about the middle of the world's nations in terms of the fraction of women in the national legislature. The nations with the best record in this regard are Rwanda (68.8% women in the lower house; 38.5% in the upper house), Bolivia (53.1% and 47.2%, respectively), and

Cuba (48.9% in a unicameral legislature), compared to nations with no women in the lower house of the legislature (0.0% for Haiti, Micronesia, Palau, Qatar, Tonga, Vanuatu, and Yemen; "Women in National Parliaments" 2016).

Concern about equal representation of the sexes in government is to be expected in democratic institutions, where policy decisions are supposed to represent the views of *all* citizens, not just males. But critics also suggest other reasons that gender equality is a desirable condition for any government. They point out that women are perceived to be at least as good as, and often better than, men on a number of traits that people look for in individuals in positions of political leadership. For example, a 2008 Pew Research Center poll found that women were considered to be more honest than men (by 50% to 20%), more intelligent (38% to 14%), more compassionate (80% to 5%), more outgoing (47% to 28%), more creative (62% to 11%), and equally hardworking and ambitious. In terms of specific political skills, women were also preferred over men in working out compromises (42% to 16%), keeping government honest (34% to 10%), representing a citizen's interests (28% to 18%), standing up for what they believe in (23% to 16%), and dealing with education and health care (52% to 7%; ("Men or Women: Who's the Better Leader?" 2008, 1–2).

So why then do more women not get elected to public office? Respondents to the Pew poll provided some revealing answers to that question. The most common reason supplied was that Americans are simply "not ready" to elect women to political office. That answer, which is actually nonresponsive, appears simply to confirm the fact that women are in some way inferior to men with regard to the skills needed for political leadership, although those same respondents had just provided a diametrically opposite response to this line of thinking (as reflected in the data in the previous paragraph). The next two most popular responses were that women in politics "get held back by men" and that women face discrimination in all aspects of life, and politics is no exception. In other words, women do not get elected to political leadership because their paths are blocked by male privilege and tradition ("Men or Women: Who's the Better Leader?" 2008, 4; also see "Chapter 2: What Makes a Good Leader, and Does Gender Matter?" 2015).

A number of programs for promoting the participation of women in national politics exist on the international level, including those sponsored by the International Center for Research on Women (http://www.icrw.org/), Commonwealth Women Parliamentarians (http://www.cpahq.org/cpahq/), National Democratic Institute (https://www.ndi.org/gender-women-democracy), UN Women (http://www.unwomen.org/en/what-we-do/leadership-and-political-participation), and U.S. Agency for International Development (https://www.usaid.gov/what-we-do/gender-equality-and-womens-empowerment/addressing-gender-programming/strengthening-womens).

A handful of U.S. organizations also place the promotion of women in politics at the top of their agendas. As an example, the National Women's Political Caucus (http://www.nwpc.org/) offers training programs for women interested in running for office or working as organizers for such campaigns. These sessions include instruction in fund-raising, communication, field organization, voter contact, and general campaign basics. They also offer advice and training for individuals interested in working in support functions for women candidates at all levels of political office. The Center for American Women and Politics at Rutgers University also offers a program called Ready to Run® that offers training for women who are interested in becoming involved in the political process through seminars and training sessions in specific states ("Ready to Run" 2016).

Employment

Women have always played an essential role in the work that needs to be done within a community. Generally speaking, that role has been one that could be conducted at home, where women were also responsible for child-rearing, maintenance of the home, and other domestic activities. If she could also contribute to the family economy by taking in washing or weaving baskets, so much the better for everyone (except, in many cases, the woman herself).

The Industrial Revolution that arose in the mid-18th century produced a dramatic change in the nature of work in many parts of the world. Instead of providing for their basic needs on farms and in the fields around one's home, either the man or the woman in the household, or both, left home to work in a factory, mill, or other establishment, where they earned money that could be used to buy food and other basic necessities. Generally speaking, and for a variety of reasons, the contributions of men and women were not considered equal in such work settings. Women were generally paid less for their contributions, even though they might perform tasks equal in difficulty to those of at least some men.

Gender inequality in employment remains a fact of life in the United States in the 21st century and in essentially every other nation of the world. According to the most recent data, women earn overall in the United States about 79 percent the pay rate of men for comparable types of jobs ("The Simple Truth about the Gender Pay Gap" 2016, 3). That number has changed gradually over time, increasing from about 46 percent in 1890 to a maximum of about 62 percent in 1955 before falling to 56 percent in 1975 and rising again to its current level in the mid-2010s (Goldin 2002). The "gender gap" in wages varies considerably for various demographic and geographic factors. The gender gap was smallest for the District of Columbia (10%), New York (13%), Hawaii (14%), and Maryland (15%) and largest for Louisiana (35%), Utah (33%), Wyoming (31%), and West Virginia (30%; "The Simple Truth about the Gender Pay Gap" 2016, 7). Some other factors that affect pay differential between the genders are summarized in Table 2.3.

Table 2.3   Demographic Factors Related to Gender Pay Gap

Demographic Variable	Gender Pay Differential (%)
Race/Ethnicity	
African American	90
Hispanic or Latina/o	89
Native Hawaiian or Pacific Islander	88
American Indian or Alaska Native	85
Asian American	79
White (non-Hispanic)	78
Age (years)	
20–24	92
16–19	91
25–34	90
35–44	81
45–54	77
55–64	76
65 and older	79
Educational Level	
Less than high school diploma	80
High school diploma	77
Some college or associate degree	75
Bachelor's degree	75
Advanced degree	74
Occupation	
Counselors	94
Registered nurses	90
Secondary school teachers	89
Pharmacists	87
Computer programmers	87
Secretaries	84
Lawyers	83
Medical scientists	79
Financial managers	67

Source: "The Simple Truth about the Gender Pay Gap." 2016. American Association of University Women, figure 3, page 10; figure 5, page 12; figure 6, page 13; and figure 9, page 17. http://www.aauw.org/files/2016/02/SimpleTruth_Spring2016.pdf. Accessed on August 24, 2016.

The magnitude of the gender pay gap problem is illustrated by a series of studies by economists that attempt to predict how long it will take for women to reach parity with women in the United States. One such study predicts that the first states to reach the level are likely to be Florida, in 2038; Maryland and California, in 2042; and Arizona and Nevada, in 2044. The last states to reach this point are predicted to be Utah (2102), North Dakota (2104), Louisiana (2106), and Wyoming (2159; Hess et al. 2015, figure 2.2, page 45).

A logical question to ask about the gender pay gap at this point is what the forces are that are responsible for this situation. Studies on this question have produced a variety of answers, typical of which is one conducted in 2007 by Francine Blau and Lawrence Kahn for the National Bureau of Economics Research. The researchers found that they could account for about 60 percent of the difference between men's and women's pay because of differences in race or ethnicity, labor force experience, the industry in which one worked, and the specific occupation of an employee (Blau and Kahn 2007). One review of this study pointed out the significance of the 40 percent "unexplainable" cause(s) of the pay gap, suggesting that this difference may be caused by any number of factors ranging from "overt sexism to unintentional gender-based discrimination to reluctance among women to negotiate for higher pay" (Farrell and Glynn 2013).

Another analysis of the gender pay gap attempted to explicate some of these "unexplainable" causes. The primary theme that ran through this analysis was that "discrimination is intangible, but it's there," probably to a large extent because "old stereotypes die hard." That is, some of the age-old attitudes about the inferiority of women may well remain in the workplace, as they do in politics and other aspects of everyday life ("Top 10 Reasons for the Wage Gap" 2016).

Legislative and administrative bodies at all levels have made attempts to deal with the gender pay gap. The most important piece of legislation on the federal level thus far has been the Equal Pay Act of 1963. In that act, Congress declared that gender-based pay differentials

- depress wages and living standards for employees necessary for their health and efficiency;
- prevent the maximum utilization of the available labor resources;
- tend to cause labor disputes, thereby burdening, affecting, and obstructing commerce;
- burden commerce and the free flow of goods in commerce; and
- constitute an unfair method of competition ("An Act" 1963; Cho and Kramer 2016).

Most observers seem to agree that the act was instrumental in reducing the gender pay gap from 59 to 79 percent, but the rate of improvement in that measure has slowed and considerable progress is needed ("Fifty Years after the Equal Pay Act" 2013). For that reason, a new version of the act has been introduced into the U.S. Congress, the Paycheck Fairness Act. That act was first offered on June 24, 1997, was not adopted, and has been reintroduced in every Congress since that time. As of 2016, the act had become something of a political "football," with nearly every Democratic legislator favoring and cosponsoring the legislation, and essentially no Republican representative or senator ever voting in favor of the bill. It was introduced again into the 114th Congress in March 2015 but, as of late 2016, has not even been referred to committee ("S. 862.: Paycheck Fairness Act" 2016).

As is often the case, progress at the state and local levels in adopting legislation to promote the reduction of the gender pay gap has been more successful. As of late 2016, all but six states (Alabama, Mississippi, North Carolina, South Carolina, Utah, and Wisconsin) and the District of Columbia have enacted equal pay laws that, in general, require that employers pay equal wages for men and women who perform similar jobs ("State Equal Pay Laws—August 2016" 2016).

Inequality in the workplace can extend beyond issues of pay. Women may also be subject to discrimination in ease of hiring and promotion, working conditions, leave time for various reasons, physical and/or emotional harassment in the workplace, accommodation for special conditions (such as pregnancy and child-rearing), and other situations. At the present time, all such forms of gender inequality are prohibited under federal and most state laws ("Federal Laws Prohibiting Job Discrimination Questions and Answers" 2009).

Some of these forms of discrimination have been described as constituting for women a *glass ceiling*. That term was first suggested in 1979 by Katherine Lawrence, who was then working at Hewlett-Packard. By the term, Lawrence meant that "in corporate America, the official policy is one way—the sky's the limit—but in actuality, the sky had a glass ceiling for women" (Zimmer 2015). She chose "glass" for the ceiling because people (women) striving to achieve were given a good look at the opportunities available to them, even if they had few realistic opportunities to attain those goals.

More than a decade later, the U.S. Department of Labor decided to study the concept of a glass ceiling in more detail by appointing a committee it called the Glass Ceiling Commission. For a period of five years, experts studied the problems posed by a glass ceiling and some ways in which those problems could be overcome. The commission sponsored 19 papers on topics such as barriers for African American women and for women with disabilities; the effects of downsizing on women employees; a review of selection, promotion, and compensation policies; family-friendly policies; and some successful programs for breaking the glass ceiling (all Glass Ceiling Commission papers are available at Glass Ceiling Commission [1991–1996] 2008).

The argument on which the glass ceiling concept is based is that women find it more difficult to get a job in competition with equally qualified men seeking the same job, are promoted less easily and less commonly, and less often reach the highest level of management and leadership, compared to their male counterparts. Concrete evidence for this argument is somewhat limited and generally comes from two sources. One source is legal action taken by women who believe they have been discriminated against and choose to sue their employer (or former employer) for relief from this action (or lack of action). One of the best-known most recent cases is *Pao v. Kleiner Perkins Caufield & Byers*, in which the plaintiff, Ellen Pao, sued her former employer. Pao was a former partner in the firm who was unable to receive promotions she thought were due to her because, according to her suit, she was being discriminated against as a woman. Pao lost her case, but its very existence increased public scrutiny of the way in which women were or were not treated in large professional firms (Streitfeld 2015; "Pao v. Kleiner Perkins Caufield & Byers" 2013).

Another basis for the claim of gender discrimination is a variety of experiments that have been conducted by academics. One of the classical examples of this research focused on tryouts by male and female artists for positions on a number of symphony orchestras. Researchers found that women did significantly better on such tryouts when they were conducted behind a screen, without the jury knowing the sex of the performer (Goldin and Rouse 2000).

In fact, the empirical evidence for the existence of gender discrimination in hiring and promotion tends to be somewhat thin (Petersen and Togstad 2004). Instead, commentators are more likely to make mention of the paucity of women at the highest levels of business and industry. In a recent fact sheet, for example, the Center for American Progress noted that: (1) women make up 50.8 percent of the U.S. population, but constitute only 14.8 percent of executive officers, 8.1 percent of top earners, and 4.6 percent of Fortune 500 chief executive officers in the country; make up 54.2 percent of the labor force of the financial services industry, but only 12.4 percent of executive officers and 18.3 percent of boards of directors; constitute 78.4 percent of the labor force in the health care and social assistance industries, but make up only 14.6 percent of executive officers and 14.4 percent of boards of directors; and comprise 34.3 percent of all physicians and surgeons in the country, but only 15.9 percent of medical school deans (Warner 2014). Data of this kind, some critics say, make it difficult to argue that at least some amount of gender discrimination is not taking place in the American workplace.

Perhaps the most common response to that observation, however, is that yes, gender discrimination in the workplace is still a problem in the United States. But the nation's businesses are making impressive progress in dealing with this problem; women are far better off today than they were a half century ago with regard to hiring, promotion, accommodation, and other aspects of the workplace. Maybe concerns over gender discrimination in the workplace are being overblown ("My Verdict on Gender Bias in the Workplace" 2015). One of the most intriguing responses to that view can be found in a book by sociologists Kevin Stainback and Donald Tomaskovic-Devey, *Documenting Desegregation: Racial and Gender Segregation in Private Sector Employment since the Civil Rights Act*. In their book, the authors say that concern about gender discrimination in the 1970s led to some very real and significant progress in dealing with that problem (Stainback and Tomaskovic-Devey 2012). But the early 1980s saw a change in approach to the topic, with businesses beginning to spend more time justifying unequal outcomes, denying their existence, and/or pointing to progressive policies designed to deal with gender discrimination in the workplace. The authors summarized their research by pointing out that "[t]oday only about 1 in 6 firms hold their managers accountable for the progress of women or minorities in their workplaces. Instead, most firms rely on symbolic public commitments to equal opportunity, occasional diversity training, and defensive legal responses to discrimination complaints as their core diversity practices" (Stainback and Tomaskovic-Devey 2013; also see Steir and Yaish 2014).

The challenge posed by gender discrimination in the workplace today, then, is that many women continue to sense and to argue that important employment decisions made in the workplace are influenced by nonrelevant, discrimination-based factors. The vast majority of companies agree that such forms of discrimination are harmful and wrong. But they tend to be less vigorous in finding and implementing ways of reducing or eliminating those forms of discrimination in their own work settings.

Body Image

One of the most challenging issues for many people, of both sexes and at almost all ages, is one's body image. The term *body image* refers to the perception that one has of his or her own body: "I'm too fat;" "I wish my arms were more muscular;" "My nose is too crooked" are all examples of one's body image.

Many people around the world have negative body images to one extent or another. In the United States, research suggests that

- about four out of five women do not like the way they look;
- about one-third of men are dissatisfied with their body;
- more than half of all Americans are concerned about their weight;
- more than 80 percent of 10-year-olds are concerned about being overweight;
- just over half (53%) of all 13-year-olds are unhappy with some feature of their body, a number that increases to three-quarters (78%) by the age of 17;
- about half of all teenage girls and a third of all teenager boys follow some type of regimen to control their weight, such as fasting or smoking cigarettes (Gallivan 2014; "Body Image Statistics" 2016).

Individuals begin to think about and develop body images when they are still quite young. One research study found that children as young as 3 to 6 years of age had some image of their own bodies and expressed interest in changing that image. A third of the sample studied could name at least one feature they would like to change and about half thought that they might be "too fat" ("Children, Teens, Media and Body Image" 2015, 5; Hayes and Tantleff-Dunn 2010).

A number of factors appear to be associated with development of one's body image, including the influence of beliefs and actions by family members, peers, racial and/or ethnic background, community standards, and other social standings. Many researchers in the field, however, emphasize the significant influence of images presented by television, print media, movies, magazines, social media, and advertising of all kinds. An abundance of research evidence exists to confirm that children, adolescents, young adults, and even older adults may be strongly influenced by images of the "ideal" body expected of both women and men from these sources. In a meta-analysis of 77 studies on this issue, researchers found that media

> exposure is linked to women's generalized dissatisfaction with their bodies, increased investment in appearance, and increased endorsement of disordered eating behaviors. These effects appear robust: They are present across multiple outcomes and are demonstrated in both the experimental and correlational literatures. Thus we can see that media exposure appears to be related to women's body image negatively regardless of assessment technique, individual difference variables, media type, age, or other idiosyncratic study characteristics. (Grabe, Ward, and Hyde 2008, 471; a meta-analysis is a summary of a number of research studies on some particular topic)

Research indicates that similar effects occur among men, whose body images tend to be affected by media factors in much the same way as is the case for women (Barlett, Vowels, and Saucier 2008).

Issues related to poor body images are not simply a matter of academic interest; they can have profound, and often harmful, effects on individuals who develop those images. Among females, one of the most common responses to a poor body image is either an effort to lose weight or a demand for cosmetic surgery to gain the attributes one hopes for. Among males, a strong tendency is to turn to chemical supplements (such as anabolic steroids) that are reputed to add muscle mass and increase other desired traits, such as speed and endurance.

One way of dealing with a person's body image issues is with cosmetic surgery, any medical procedure designed to change the size, shape, or appearance of some part of the body. According to the 2015 report of the American Society of Plastic Surgeons, women accounted for 92 percent of all cosmetic procedures, 1.4 million of which were actual surgical procedures and 12.5 million of which were minimally invasive procedures. Cosmetic procedures were least common among adolescents, accounting for less than 1 percent of all such surgeries, with 40- to 54-year-olds accounting for the largest fraction (7.4 million procedures). The most common minimally invasive procedures performed in 2015 were botulinum injections (6.7 million procedures), soft tissue fillers (2.4 million), chemical peels (1.3 million), and laser hair removal (1.1 million). The most popular full surgical procedures were breast augmentation (279,000 procedures), liposuction (225,000), nose reshaping (218,000), and eyelid surgery (204,000). The most common surgical procedures performed on adolescent boys and girls were gynecomastia (breast reduction in males), accounting for 26 percent of all such procedures in 2015; otoplasty (ear surgery), accounting for 28 percent of such procedures among both sexes; and rhinoplasty (nose reshaping), 14 percent of all such procedures. The only noninvasive procedures used among adolescents accounting for more than 1 percent of all such procedures were laser treatment of veins (9%), laser hair removal (6%), and laser skin resurfacing (5%; all data from "2015 Plastic Surgery Statistics Report" 2016).

As with all forms of surgery, certain risks and complications are associated with the procedures listed here. No single source of data is available for the side effects of all forms of cosmetic surgery, but data on otoplasty may be illustrative. In one study on the procedure, essentially no deaths were attributed to the procedure itself, although some were associated with the anesthetic used. The most common side effects were asymmetrical ears (18.4% of procedures), skin irritation (9.8%), increased sensitivity to cold (7.5%), soreness when touched (5.7%), abnormal shape of ear (4.4%), and loss of feeling in the ear (3.9%; "Otoplasty" 2016). In general, it might be safe to say that most cosmetic procedures are associated with a variety of inconvenient, but not life-threatening, side effects.

Another approach adopted by some individuals with concerns about their body image is modification of eating patterns in order to lose weight. The two most popular of these practices are anorexia nervosa and bulimia nervosa. Anorexia nervosa is an obsessive disorder characterized by a person's refusal to eat, usually as a way of losing weight. Bulimia nervosa is a somewhat similar condition in which a person engages in a series of eating and self-inducing vomiting or refusal to eat, with the same objective as anorexia nervosa. Whatever success they may produce in terms of weight loss, both anorexia and bulimia are associated with serious, including life-threatening, health consequences, as summarized in Table 2.4.

Anorexia and bulimia are both medical and emotional problems that can, if untreated, take over a person's life and cause death. According to the most recent statistics available, anywhere from 0.5 to 3.7 percent of females experience anorexia at some time in their life, as do between 1.1 and 4.2 percent of females who experience bulimia. The condition is largely one affecting females, with only 10 to 15 percent of those with one of the two conditions being a male. The vast majority of individuals who experience an eating disorder (about 90%) are

Table 2.4 Health Consequences Associated with Anorexia and Bulimia

Anorexia	Abnormally slow heart rate
	Low blood pressure
	Increased risk for heart failure
	Severe hydration leading to possible kidney failure
	Fatigue, fainting, and overall body weakness
	Muscle loss
	Osteoporosis
	Dry skin and hair
	Growth of lanugo, a layer of downy hair on all parts of the body
	Bluish tint of fingertips
	Reduction in brain mass
	Infertility
Bulimia	Electrolyte imbalance, leading to irregular heart rate and possible heart failure
	Dehydration, leading to weakness, fatigue, fainting, and possible kidney damage
	Inflammation and/or tears of the esophagus
	Irritation of the mouth, resulting in increased risk for cavities and gum disease
	Swollen salivary glands
	Osteoporosis
	Low blood pressure
	Reduced body temperature
	Potential gastric rupture
	Peptic ulcers and pancreatitis
	Irregular bowel movement

females between the ages of 12 and 25. And just over one out of ten (11%) of high school students have been clinically diagnosed with some type of eating disorder (all statistics from "Eating Disorder Statistics" 2016). Anorexia is now thought to have the highest fatality rate of any type of mental disorder, with an estimated 5.86 percent of individuals with the condition eventually dying as a result of it, 20 percent by sui-cide. With bulimia, the mortality rate from the condition was estimated to be 1.93 percent (Arcelus et al. 2011).

Males also have body image issues (although, perhaps not surprisingly, those "ideal" images differ widely from country to country; see Vagianos 2016). In the United States, that "ideal" image is likely to be modeled on successful athletes, motion picture stars, or other men prominent in advertising and the media (Kurtz 2010; Martin 2010). These models of the ideal male body tend in the United States today to promote a low BMI (body mass index) with extensive musculature. Adolescent and adult males whose own bodies do not meet these standards sometimes turn to chemical means to obtain these results, spe-cifically the use of androgenic anabolic steroids, which tend to encourage the growth of muscle tissue. According to one re-cent study, 2.3 percent of 1,307 boys interviewed said that they sometimes used steroids to improve their bodies, and 0.8 per-cent said they did so frequently. An additional 4.0 percent said they used other types of performance-enhancing substances occasionally and 2.4 percent said that they do so often. (Inter-estingly, the rates in all of these categories was higher for girls than it was for boys; Eisenberg, Wall, and Neumark-Sztainer 2012, table 1.)

As with the use of dieting and purging for dealing with body image issues, so does reliance on anabolic steroids present a host of risky side effects, including hair loss; severe acne; oily skin and hair; possible kidney, liver, and heart disease; develop-ment of breasts (in men) and shrunken testicles; impotence; prostate gland disorders; increased levels of "bad" cholesterol and decreased levels of "good" cholesterol; high blood pressure; and a host of psychological and emotional disorders, such as anxiety and feelings of violence (so-called roid rage; "Anabolic Steroids" 2013).

Eating disorders and the use of steroids for changing body characteristics are largely psychological and emotional prob-lems that are most effectively treated by some form of behavioral therapy. In some cases, however, medications may be valuable for dealing with the symptoms of these problems. For example, people who decide to stop using anabolic steroids may enter an extended period of withdrawal during which they may experience a variety of troublesome physical symptoms, such as headache, nausea, severe depression, and anxiety attacks. These symptoms can be treated by antidepressant drugs and other medications designed to reduce pain, feelings of nausea, and fatigue. Resolving the underlying issues that lead to eating disorders or inappropriate steroid use cannot, however, be treated with drugs. The best approach in such cases is cognitive behavioral therapy, a form of so-called talk therapy in which an individual meets with a therapist in one-on-one or group sessions to discuss the reasons for the person's behaviors and ways in which they can be changed (Kanayama et al. 2010).

The basic issue that underlies essentially all eating disorder problems, such as anorexia and bulimia, and other types of body image disorders is the disconnect between the bodies that the vast majority of people have in everyday life and the "ideal" bodies they see displayed in advertisements, on television, in films, on social media, and in other public settings. When a person strives to make his or her body match those "ideal" models, eating disorders and the use of steroids are likely to develop. The challenge of dealing with these problems, then, is to reduce or eliminate this disconnect between "the real" and "the ideal" of body images.

As noted above, the standard treatment for such conditions is usually some form of behavioral therapy that aims to help people understand the nature of this problem and the issues relating to their efforts to meet some unrealistic standard of body image. But more and more, experts in the area are beginning to recognize that these problems are created not primarily by boys and girls, men and women, trying to reach some ideal standard; they are a problem caused by companies who create those standards in the first place. When an advertiser chooses to show a shirtless "hunk" or a scantily clad supermodel in its advertisements, it must take some responsibility for creating unrealistic body image standards for individuals who view that ad.

A handful of companies have now taken on this challenge, foremost of which is Dove soap. In 2004, the company decided to make a specific and aggressive attempt to acknowledge that women's bodies could have any of a number of shapes and sizes, all of which were legitimate in and of itself. It created a campaign called the Dove Campaign for Real Beauty that featured photographs and videos of women of every kind. Over the years, the company has created other campaigns to further promote this concept, including a 2013 video called "Real Beauty Sketches," said to be the most-watched video advertisement of all time (Bahadur 2014; Campaigns 2016; "Children, Teens, Media and Body Image" 2015). Other companies that have created similar campaigns include Nike (Real Women), Athleta (Power to the She), Aeire (Aerie Real), and Mattel and Sports Illustrated (Barbie#unapologetic; "Children, Teens, Media and Body Image" 2015, table 2, page 26).

Conclusion

Sex and gender are the basis for a host of issue for individuals at every stage of one's life, but perhaps most of all during adolescence. During puberty, boys and girls begin to change into men and women, raising a variety of questions as to what one's new body looks like and how it can and should behave. These questions relate not only to how a person sees herself or himself, but also to the variety of ways in which he or she can and should interact with others. These problems arise for almost every human being, if not during adolescence, at some other point in one's life. And as overwhelming as they may seem to be at the time, they are eventually resolved with greater or less success by most of us.

References

"An Act." 1963. Equal Employment Opportunity Commission. https://www.eeoc.gov/eeoc/history/35th/thelaw/epa.html. Accessed on August 25, 2016.

Aisch, Gregor, and K. K. Rebecca Lai. 2016. "At Least 120 Athletes at the Rio Olympics Have Previously Been Suspended for Doping." *The New York Times.* http://www.nytimes.com/interactive/2016/08/18/sports/olympics/athletes-at-the-rio-olympics-who-were-previously-suspended-for-doping-.html. Accessed on August 21, 2016.

"Alabama Supreme Court Dismisses Gay Marriage Challenge." 2016. *The Guardian.* http://www.theguardian.com/us-news/2016/mar/04/alabama-supreme-court-gay-marriage-challenge-dismissal. Accessed on August 14, 2016.

"Anabolic Steroids." 2013. Center for Substance Abuse Research. http://www.cesar.umd.edu/cesar/drugs/steroids.asp. Accessed on August 29, 2016.

Anchell, [Melvin]. 1985. "A Psychoanalytic Look at Today's Sex Education." American Life League's STOPP. http://www.stopp.org/article.php?id=7206. Accessed on August 15, 2016.

Anderson, Ryan T. 2015. "Sexual Orientation and Gender Identity (SOGI) Laws Threaten Freedom." The Heritage Foundation. http://www.heritage.org/research/reports/2015/11/sexual-orientation-and-gender-identity-sogi-laws-threaten-freedom. Accessed on August 12, 2016.

Arcelus, Jon, et al. 2011. "Mortality Rates in Patients with Anorexia Nervosa and Other Eating Disorders: A Meta-Analysis of 36 Studies." *JAMA Psychiatry* 68(70): 724–731. http://archpsyc.jamanetwork.com/article.aspx?articleid=1107207. Accessed on August 28, 2016.

Bahadur, Nina. 2014. "Dove 'Real Beauty' Campaign Turns 10: How a Brand Tried to Change the Conversation about Female Beauty." http://www.huffingtonpost .com/2014/01/21/dove-real-beauty-campaign-turns-10_n_4575940.html. Accessed on August 29, 2016.

Barlett, Christopher P., Christopher L. Vowels, and Donald A. Saucier. 2008. "Meta-Analyses of the Effects of Media Images on Men's Body-image Concerns." *Journal of Social and Clinical Psychology* 27(3): 279–310. http://public .gettysburg.edu/~cbarlett/index/08bvs.pdf. Accessed on August 27, 2016.

Blau, Francine D., and Lawrence M. Kahn. 2007. "The Gender Pay Gap: Have Women Gone as Far as They Can?" *Academy of Management Perspectives* 21(1): 7–23.

"Body Image Statistics." 2016. Statistic Brain. http://www .statisticbrain.com/body-image-statistics/. Accessed on August 27, 2016.

Bull, Andy. 2016. "Caster Semenya Wins Olympic Gold but Faces More Scrutiny as IAAF Presses Case." *The Guardian.* https://www.theguardian.com/sport/2016/aug/21/caster-semenya-wins-gold-but-faces-scrutiny. Accessed on August 21, 2016.

"Campaigns." 2016. Dove. http://www.dove.com/us/en/ stories/campaigns.html. Accessed on August 29, 2016.

Campbell, Colin. 2016. "McCrory Distances Himself from Sexual Predators Claims Backing House Bill 2." *Charlotte Observer.* http://www.charlotteobserver.com/news/politics-government/article74649942.html. Accessed on August 12, 2016.

Chandler, Kim, and Jay Reeves. 2016. "Panel Sends Chief Justice Roy Moore's Ethics Case to Trial." *The Gadsden Times.* http://www.gadsdentimes.com/news/20160809/ panel-sends-chief-justice-roy-moores-ethics-case-to-trial. Accessed on August 14, 2016.

"Chapter 2: What Makes a Good Leader, and Does Gender Matter?" 2015. Pew Research Center. http://www.pew socialtrends.org/2015/01/14/chapter-2-what-makes-a-good-leader-and-does-gender-matter/. Accessed on August 23, 2016.

"Charlie Craig and David Mullins v. Masterpiece Cakeshop." 2015. ACLU. https://www.aclu.org/cases/charlie-craig-and-david-mullins-v-masterpiece-cakeshop. Accessed on August 14, 2016.

Chibbaro, Lou, Jr. 2014. "New Mattachine Society of D.C. Uncovers LGBT History." Washington Blade. http://www .washingtonblade.com/2014/05/14/new-mattachine-society-d-c-uncovers-lgbt-history/. Accessed on August 13, 2016.

"Children, Teens, Media and Body Image." 2015. Common Sense Media. https://www.commonsensemedia.org/ research/children-teens-media-and-body-image. Accessed on August 27, 2016.

Cho, Rosa, and Abagail Kramer. 2016. "Everything You Need to Know about the Equal Pay Act." Re: Gender. http:// regender.org/EqualPayAct1. Accessed on August 25, 2016.

Chrislove. 2012. "Top Comments: Remembering Early Gay History: Henry Gerber and the Society for Human Rights Edition [sic]." Daily Kos. http://www.dailykos.com/ story/2012/4/28/1087143-Top-Comments-Remembering-Early-Gay-History-Henry-Gerber-and-the-Society-for-Human-Rights-Edition. Accessed on August 13, 2016.

Cook, Tony, Tom LoBianco, and Brian Eason. 2015. "Gov. Mike Pence Signs RFRA Fix." IndyStar. http://www .indystar.com/story/news/politics/2015/04/01/indiana-rfra-deal-sets-limited-protections-for-lgbt/70766920/. Accessed on August 24, 2016.

Cretella, Michelle. 2016. "Gender Dysphoria in Children." American College of Pediatricians. https://www.acpeds.org/ the-college-speaks/position-statements/gender-dysphoria-in-children. Accessed on August 17, 2016.

De Vries, Annelou L. C., et al. 2011. "Puberty Suppression in Adolescents with Gender Identity Disorder: A Prospective Follow-Up Study." *The Journal of Sexual Medicine* 8(8): 2276–2283.

D'Emilio, John. 1983. *Sexual Politics, Sexual Communities*. Chicago; London: University of Chicago Press.

"Eating Disorder Statistics." 2016. The Alliance for Eating Disorders Awareness. https://www.ndsu.edu/fileadmin/counseling/Eating_Disorder_Statistics.pdf. Accessed on August 28, 2016.

Eisenberg, Maria E., Melanie Wall, and Dianne Neumark-Sztainer. 2012. "Muscle-enhancing Behaviors among Adolescent Girls and Boys." *Pediatrics* 130(6): 1019–1026.

Eleveld, Kerry. 2007. "ENDA to be Separated into Two Bills: Sexual Orientation and Gender Identity." Advocate. http://www.advocate.com/news/2007/09/29/enda-be-separated-two-bills-sexual-orientation-and-gender-identity. Accessed on August 12, 2016.

Elsas, Louis J., et al. 2000. "Gender Verification of Female Athletes." *Genetics in Medicine* 2(4): 249–254.

"Employment Discrimination Based on Religion, Ethnicity, or Country of Origin." 2016. U.S. Equal Employment Opportunity Commission. https://www.eeoc.gov/laws/types/fs-relig_ethnic.cfm. Accessed on August 12, 2016.

"Fifty Years after the Equal Pay Act." 2013. National Equal Pay Task Force. https://www.whitehouse.gov/sites/default/files/equalpay/equal_pay_task_force_progress_report_june_2013_new.pdf. Accessed on August 25, 2016.

Farrell, Jane, and Sarah Jane Glynn. 2013. "What Causes the Gender Wage Gap?" Center for American Progress. https://www.americanprogress.org/issues/labor/news/2013/04/09/59658/what-causes-the-gender-wage-gap/. Accessed on August 25, 2016.

"Federal Laws Prohibiting Job Discrimination Questions and Answers." 2009. U.S. Equal Employment Opportunity

Commission. https://www.eeoc.gov/facts/qanda.html. Accessed on August 26, 2016.

Gallivan, Heather R. 2014. "Teens, Social Media and Body Image." Park Nicollet Melrose Center. http://www.macmh .org/wp-content/uploads/2014/05/18_Gallivan_Teens-social-media-body-image-presentation-H-Gallivan-Spring-2014.pdf. Accessed on August 27, 2016.

Gallo, Marcia M. 2006. *Different Daughters: A History of the Daughters of Bilitis and the Rise of the Lesbian Rights Movement.* New York: Carroll & Graf Publishers.

"Gay and Lesbian Rights." 2016. Gallup. http://www.gallup .com/poll/1651/gay-lesbian-rights.aspx. Accessed on August 14, 2016.

Ghorayshi, Azeen. 2016. "These Women Athletes Were Barred from Competing because They Weren't 'Female' Enough." BuzzFeedNews. https://www.buzzfeed.com/ azeenghorayshi/sex-testing-olympians?utm_term=.mp2 qngpEW#.uyed80Arq. Accessed on August 21, 2016.

Gibson, Bethany, and Anita J. Catlin. 2010. "Care of the Child with the Desire to Change Gender—Part I." *Pediatric Nursing* 36(1): 53–59. http://www.medscape .com/viewarticle/718619_1. Accessed on August 20, 2016.

Gjelten, Tom. 2016. "State Religious Freedom Laws Surface in Opposition to Same-Sex Marriage." NPR. http://www .npr.org/2016/05/12/477835915/state-religious-freedom-laws-surface-in-opposition-to-same-sex-marriage. Accessed on August 14, 2016.

Glass Ceiling Commission (1991–1996). 2008. Cornell University ILR School. http://digitalcommons.ilr.cornell .edu/glassceiling/. Accessed on August 26, 2016.

Goldin, Claudia. 2002. "The Rising (and Then Declining) Significance of Gender." National Bureau of Economic Research. https://www.researchgate.net/publication/ 5196887_The_Rising_and_then_Declining_Significance_ of_Gender. Accessed on August 24, 2016.

Goldin, Claudia, and Cecilia Rouse. 2000. "Orchestrating Impartiality: The Impact of Blind Auditions on Female Musicians." *American Economic Review* 90(4): 715–741.

Grabe, Shelly, L. Monique Ward, and Janet Shibley Hyde. 2008. "The Role of the Media in Body Image Concerns among Women: A Meta-Analysis of Experimental and Correlational Studies." *Psychological Bulletin* 134(3): 460–476. https://www.researchgate.net/profile/Shelly_Grabe/publication/5259131_The_Role_of_the_Media_in_Body_Image_Concerns_Among_Women_A_Meta-Analysis_of_Experimental_and_Correlational_Studies/links/54302c850cf27e39fa9dca4b.pdf. Accessed on August 27, 2016.

Grant, Jaime M., et al. 2011. "Injustice at Every Turn: A Report on the National Transgender Discrimination Survey." National Gay and Lesbian Task Force and the National Center for Transgender Equality. http://www.transequality.org/sites/default/files/docs/resources/NTDS_Report.pdf. Accessed on August 12, 2016.

Harrison, Steve. 2016. "If Charlotte Approves LGBT Protections, 'Immediate' State Response Likely." *The Charlotte Observer*. http://www.charlotteobserver.com/news/politics-government/article61307857.html. Accessed on August 12, 2016.

Hayes, Sharon, and Stacey Tantleff-Dunn. 2010. "Am I Too Fat to Be a Princess? Examining the Effects of Popular Children's Media on Young Girls' Body Image." *The British Journal of Developmental Psychology* 28(2): 413–426.

Heggie, Vanessa. 2010. "Testing Sex and Gender in Sports; Reinventing, Reimagining and Reconstructing Histories." *Endeavour* 34(4): 157–163.

Hess, Cynthia, et al. 2015. "The Status of Women in the States." Institute for Women's Policy Research. http://www.iwpr.org/publications/pubs/the-status-of-women-in-the-states-2015-full-report. Accessed on August 22, 2016.

Hidalgo, M. A., et al. 2013. "The Gender Affirmative Model: What We Know and What We Aim to Learn." *Human Development* 56(5): 285–290. https://www.karger.com/Article/FullText/355235. Accessed on August 19, 2016.

"A History of Federal Funding for Abstinence-Only-under-Marriage Programs." 2016. Sexuality Information and Education Council of the United States. http://www.siecus.org/index.cfm?fuseaction=page.viewpage&pageid=1340&nodeid=1. Accessed on August 15, 2016.

"A History of Federal Non-Discrimination Legislation." 2016. http://hrc-assets.s3-website-us-east-1.amazonaws.com//files/assets/resources/History_of_Non-Discrimination_Legislation_4_12_16_ChartOnly.pdf. Accessed on August 11, 2016.

"History of Sex Education." 2008. Advocates for Youth. http://www.advocatesforyouth.org/serced/1859-history-of-sex-ed. Accessed on August 15, 2016.

House Bill 2. 2016. General Assembly of North Carolina. http://www.ncleg.net/Sessions/2015E2/Bills/House/PDF/H2v4.pdf. Accessed on August 12, 2016.

Kanayama, Gen, et al. 2010. "Treatment of Anabolic-Androgenic Steroid Dependence: Emerging Evidence and Its Implications." *Drug and Alcohol Dependence* 109(1–3): 6–13.

"Know Your Rights: Transgender People and the Law." 2016. American Civil Liberties Union. https://www.aclu.org/know-your-rights/transgender-people-and-law. Accessed on August 12, 2016.

Koh, J. 2012. "The History of the Concept of Gender Identity Disorder." *Psychiatria et Neurologia Japonica* 114(6): 673–680.

Kralik, Joellen. 2016. "'Bathroom Bill' Legislative Tracking." National Conference of State Legislatures. http://www.ncsl.org/research/education/-bathroom-bill-legislative-tracking635951130.aspx. Accessed on August 12, 2016.

Kurtz, Sara. 2010. "Adolescent Boys' and Girls' Perceived Body Image and the Influence of Media: The Impact of a Media Literacy Education on Adolescents' Body Dissatisfaction." Carroll University Library. http://archives.carrollu.edu/cdm/ref/collection/edthesis/id/72. Accessed on August 28, 2016.

Lavers, Michael K. 2016. "Injunction against Miss. Religious Freedom Law to Remain in Place." Washington Blade. http://www.npr.org/2016/05/12/477835915/state-religious-freedom-laws-surface-in-opposition-to-same-sex-marriage. Accessed on August 14, 2016.

"Lt. Governor Forest Responds to PayPal Decision." 2016. State of North Carolina. http://ltgov.nc.gov/content/lt-governor-forest-responds-paypal-decision. Accessed on August 12, 2016.

Mahoney, William. 2016. "The Meeting Point . . . between Planned Parenthood and the Pontifical Council for the Family." American Life League's STOPP. http://www.stopp.org/wsr.php?wsr_dt=2016-08-03. Accessed on August 15, 2016.

Mallory, Christy, and Brad Sears. 2016. "Discrimination, Diversity, and Development: The Legal and Economic Implication of North Carolina's HB2." The Williams Institute. http://williamsinstitute.law.ucla.edu/wp-content/uploads/Discrimination-Diversity-and-Development_The-Legal-and-Economic-Implications-of-North-Carolinas-HB2.pdf. Accessed on August 12, 2016.

Manning, Jennifer. 2016. "Membership of the 114th Congress: A Profile." Congressional Research Service. https://www.fas.org/sgp/crs/misc/R43869.pdf. Accessed on August 22, 2016.

Marrone, Katherine. 2016. "The Future of American Sex-Ed May Not Include Abstinence-Only Funding." Alternet. http://www.alternet.org/sex-amp-relationships/future-american-sex-ed-may-not-include-abstinence-only-funding. Accessed on August 15, 2016.

Martin, Jeanne B. 2010. "The Development of Ideal Body Image Perceptions in the United States." *Nutrition Today* 45(3): 98–110. http://wkhpe-co-app6.wkhpe.com/files/TheDevelopmentofIdealBodyImagePerceptionsinthe UnitedStates-1370279139122.pdf. Accessed on August 28, 2016.

"Men or Women: Who's the Better Leader?" 2008. Pew Research Center. http://www.pewsocialtrends.org/2008/08/25/men-or-women-whos-the-better-leader/. Accessed on August 23, 2016.

"Milestones in the American Transgender Movement." 2015. http://www.nytimes.com/interactive/2015/05/15/opinion/editorial-transgender-timeline.html?_r=0. Accessed on August 12, 2016.

"My Verdict on Gender Bias in the Workplace." 2015. Scott Adams' Blog. http://blog.dilbert.com/post/114055529676/my-verdict-on-gender-bias-in-the-workplace. Accessed on August 26, 2016.

Neugold, Cassie. 2016. "Religious Exercise and Objections to Performing Same-Sex Marriage: An Analysis of Kim Davis." Law School Student Scholarship. Paper 829. http://scholarship.shu.edu/cgi/viewcontent.cgi?article=1831&context=student_scholarship. Accessed on August 14, 2016.

Newton, David E. 2009. *Gay and Lesbian Rights: A Reference Handbook*, 2nd ed. Santa Barbara, CA: ABC-CLIO.

Newton, David E. 2014. *Steroids and Doping in Sports: A Reference Handbook*. Santa Barbara, CA: ABC-CLIO.

Olson-Kennedy, Johanna, et al. 2016. "Health Considerations for Gender Non-conforming Children and Transgender Adolescents." Center of Excellence for Transgender Health. http://transhealth.ucsf.edu/trans?page=guidelines-youth. Accessed on August 20, 2016.

"Otoplasty." 2016. Encyclopedia of Surgery. http://www.surgeryencyclopedia.com/La-Pa/Otoplasty.html. Accessed on August 28, 2016.

Padawer, Ruth. 2016. "The Humiliating Practice of Sex-Testing Female Athletes." *The New York Times*. http://www.nytimes.com/2016/07/03/magazine/the-humiliating-practice-of-sex-testing-female-athletes.html. Accessed on August 21, 2016.

"Pao v. Kleiner Perkins Caufield & Byers." 2013. Court of Appeals of California. https://scholar.google.com/scholar_case?case=6358765039056938777&q=pao+v.+kleiner&hl=en&as_sdt=6,38&as_vis=1. Accessed on August 26, 2016.

"Parents, Schools Divided as Sex Ed Controversy Erupts." 2016. CBSNews. http://www.cbsnews.com/news/sex-education-controversy-erupts-in-omaha/. Accessed on August 15, 2016.

Petersen, Trond, and Thea Togstad. 2004. "Getting the Offer: Sex Discrimination in Hiring." Institute for Research on Labor and Employment. http://www.irle.berkeley.edu/workingpapers/104-04.pdf. Accessed on August 26, 2016.

Pieper, Lindsay Parks. 2016. *Sex Testing: Gender Policing in Women's Sports*. Urbana: University of Illinois Press.

Raga, Suzanne. 2016. "How Olympic Sprinter Stella Walsh Nearly Lost Her Medals because of Her Autopsy." Mental Floss. http://mentalfloss.com/article/69911/how-olympic-sprinter-stella-walsh-nearly-lost-her-medals-because-her-autopsy. Accessed on August 21, 2016.

"Ready to Run." 2016. Center for American Women in Politics. http://www.cawp.rutgers.edu/education_training/ready_to_run/overview. Accessed on August 23, 2016.

Reardon, Sara. 2016. "Largest Ever Study of Transgender Teenagers Set to Kick Off." *Nature* 531(7596): 560.

"Results from the School Health Policies and Practices Study 2014." 2015. Centers for Disease Control and Prevention. http://www.cdc.gov/healthyyouth/data/shpps/pdf/shpps-508-final_101315.pdf. Accessed on August 15, 2016.

Ritter, Karl. 2016. "Kayak Men Assail Plans for Women Canoe in Next Olympics." AP. *The Big Story*. http://bigstory .ap.org/article/bab636b70b7c4d389cc3dab0fc206c65/kayak-men-assail-plans-womens-canoe-next-olympics. Accessed on August 21, 2016.

Rothacker, Rick, Ely Portillo, and Katherine Peralta. 2016. "PayPal Withdraws Plans for Charlotte Expansion over HB2." *The Charlotte Observer*. http://www.charlotteobserver .com/news/business/article70001502.html. Accessed on August 12, 2016.

"S. 862.: Paycheck Fairness Act." 2016. GovTrack.US. https://www.govtrack.us/congress/bills/114/s862/summary. Accessed on August 25, 2016.

Sears, James T. 2006. *Behind the Mask of the Mattachine: The Hal Call Chronicles and the Early Movement for Homosexual Emancipation*. New York: Harrington Park Press.

"Sex Education." 2016. American Life League. http://www .all.org/learn/sex-education/. Accessed on August 15, 2016.

Shumer, Daniel E., and Norman P. Spack. 2013. "Current Management of Gender Identity Disorder in Childhood and Adolescence: Guidelines, Barriers and Areas of Controversy." *Current Opinion in Endocrinology, Diabetes, and Obesity* 20(1): 69–73.

"The Simple Truth about the Gender Pay Gap." 2016. American Association of University Women. http://www .aauw.org/files/2016/02/SimpleTruth_Spring2016.pdf. Accessed on August 24, 2016.

Singal, Jesse. 2016. "How the Fight over Transgender Kids Got a Leading Sex Researcher Fired." Science of Us. http:// nymag.com/scienceofus/2016/02/fight-over-trans-kids-got-a-researcher-fired.html. Accessed on August 19, 2016.

Sprigg, Peter. 2016. "Sexual Orientation and Gender Identity (SOGI) Laws: A Threat to Free Markets and Freedom of Conscience and Religion." Family Research Council.

http://www.frc.org/issuebrief/sexual-orientation-and-gender-identity-sogi-laws-a-threat-to-free-markets-and-freedom-of-conscience-and-religion. Accessed on August 12, 2016.

Stainback, Kevin, and Donald Tomaskovic-Devey. 2012. *Documenting Desegregation: Racial and Gender Segregation in Private Sector Employment since the Civil Rights Act.* New York: Russell Sage Foundation.

Stainback, Kevin, and Donald Tomaskovic-Devey. 2013. "Research: Your Firm Probably Isn't an Equal Opportunity Employer." *Harvard Business Review.* https://hbr.org/2013/06/is-your-firm-really-an-equal-o. Accessed on August 26, 2016.

"Standards of Care for the Health of Transsexual, Transgender, and Gender Nonconforming People," 7th edition. 2016. https://s3.amazonaws.com/amo_hub_content/Association140/files/Standards%20of%20Care%20V7%20-%202011%20WPATH%20(2)(1).pdf. Accessed on August 19, 2016.

"State Equal Pay Laws—August 2016." 2016. National Conference of State Legislatures. http://www.ncsl.org/research/labor-and-employment/equal-pay-laws.aspx. Accessed on August 25, 2016.

"State Policies on Sex Education in Schools." 2016. National Conference of State Legislatures. http://www.ncsl.org/research/health/state-policies-on-sex-education-in-schools.aspx#1. Accessed on August 15, 2016.

Steir, Haya, and Meir Yaish. 2014. "Occupational Segregation and Gender Inequality in Job Quality: A Multi-level Approach." *Work, Employment, and Society* 28(2): 225–246. http://soc.haifa.ac.il/~yaish/papers/Stier&Yaish.pdf. Accessed on August 26, 2016.

Streitfeld, David. 2015. "Ellen Pao Loses Silicon Valley Bias Case against Kleiner Perkins." *The New York Times.*

http://www.nytimes.com/2015/03/28/technology/ellen-pao-kleiner-perkins-case-decision.html?_r=1. Accessed on August 26, 2016.

Talbot, Margaret. 2013. "About a Boy." *The New Yorker*. http://www.newyorker.com/magazine/2013/03/18/about-a-boy-2. Accessed on August 17, 2016.

Teal, Donn. 1971. *The Gay Militants*. New York: Stein and Day.

"Top 10 Reasons for the Wage Gap." 2016. National Committee on Pay Equity. http://www.pay-equity.org/info-top10.html. Accessed on August 25, 2016.

"2015 Plastic Surgery Statistics Report." 2016. American Society of Plastic Surgeons. http://www.plasticsurgery.org/Documents/news-resources/statistics/2015-statistics/plastic-surgery-statsitics-full-report.pdf. Accessed on August 28, 2016.

"2016 State Religious Freedom Restoration Act Legislation." 2016. National Conference of State Legislatures. http://www.ncsl.org/research/civil-and-criminal-justice/2016-state-religious-freedom-restoration-act-legislation.aspx. Accessed on August 14, 2016.

Vagianos, Alanna. 2016. "What the 'Ideal' Man's Body Looks Like in 19 Countries." *The Huffington Post*. http://www.huffingtonpost.com/entry/what-the-ideal-mans-body-looks-like-in-19-countries_us_56c5d65de4b08ffac127c485. Accessed on August 28, 2016.

Vitale, Anne. 2005. "Rethinking the Gender Identity Disorder Terminology in the Diagnostic and Statistical Manual of Mental Disorders IV." Transhealth. http://www.trans-health.com/2005/rethinking-gid-terminology-dsm/. Accessed on August 17, 2016.

Vrouenraets, Lieke Josephina Jeanne Johanna, et al. 2015. "Early Medical Treatment of Children and Adolescents with Gender Dysphoria: An Empirical Ethical Study." *Journal of Adolescent Health* 57(4): 367–373.

Wallien, Madeleine S. C., and Peggy T. Cohen-Kettenis. 2008. "Psychosexual Outcome of Gender-dysphoric Children." *Journal of the American Academy of Child and Adolescent Psychiatry* 47(12): 1413–1423.

Warner, Judith. 2014. "The Women's Leadership Gap." Center for American Progress. https://cdn.american progress.org/wp-content/uploads/2014/03/Women Leadership.pdf. Accessed on August 26, 2016.

Williams, John. 2016. "Has the Olympic Games Caught up with the Modern World?" University of Leicester. http://www2.le.ac.uk/offices/press/think-leicester/arts-and-culture/2016/has-the-olympic-games-caught-up-with-the-modern-world. Accessed on August 21, 2016.

"Women in National Parliaments." 2016. Inter-Parliamentary Union. http://www.ipu.org/wmn-e/classif.htm. Accessed on August 23, 2016.

Wright, John. 2016. "GOP Lawmakers in Two Southern States File Bills Comparing Same-Sex Marriage to Forced Sterilization." The New Civil Rights Movement. http://www.thenewcivilrightsmovement.com/johnwright/anti_gay_bills_compare_same_sex_marriage_to_forced_sterilization_japanese_internment. Accessed on August 14, 2016.

Zimmer, Ben. 2015. "The Phrase 'Glass Ceiling' Stretches Back Decades." *Wall Street Journal.* http://www.wsj.com/articles/the-phrase-glass-ceiling-stretches-back-decades-1428089010. Accessed on August 26, 2016.

Zucker, Kenneth J., and Anne A. Lawrence. 2009. "Epidemiology of Gender Identity Disorder: Recommendations for the Standards of Care of the World Professional Association for Transgender Health." *International Journal of Transgenderism* 11(1): 8–18.

https://www.researchgate.net/profile/Kenneth_Zucker3/
publication/247509801_Epidemiology_of_Gender_
Identity_Disorder_Recommendations_for_the_Standards_
of_Care_of_the_World_Professional_Association_for_
Transgender_Health/links/56c4879108aeeeffa9e5ba54.pdf.
Accessed on August 17, 2016.

Introduction

Discussions of sex and gender depend very much on understanding the factual issues involved in such topics. However, they are also laden with a variety of opinions and emotional views. The essays in this chapter provide both types of perspectives about a variety of topics in the field of sex and gender.

"Come Out! Come Out!": A Battle Cry for Change
Philip Bockman (with Paul Feiler)

When I discovered, upon entering kindergarten, that I was deeply attracted to other boys and indifferent to girls, I knew that I could never tell anyone, not even my parents. In the Midwest in the 1940s, I knew nothing about sexuality or sexual identity. Nobody did.

At fourteen, I remember my father returning from a business trip to Saugatuck, Michigan, which I would learn years later was a resort frequented by gay people. I was shocked when he tried to visually describe them. "They go like this," he said, waving his wrists flamboyantly, "and talk like this" (lisping and

---

A Utah Highway Patrol trooper arrests a protester who blocked the doors to the higher education committee hearings at the Utah State Capitol, in Salt Lake City on February 10, 2014. The protesters called for a statewide anti-discrimination law that protects sexual or gender orientation. (AP Photo/Rick Bowmer)

fluttering his eyelids in a way that made him look strangely grotesque for such a down-to-earth man). I've never forgotten the surge of emotions I experienced when he did that—my own father! I felt betrayed. I felt naked and confused.

In those days, homosexuality was deemed a disgusting sin and a sign of mental illness. Parents could have their own children locked up in psych wards for life if such a thing was suspected. Worse yet, anyone who touched another person of the same sex might be sent to prison.

Aside from vague innuendos, I had never heard of anyone else being gay. My own strong urges frightened me, but I felt them so deeply that I came to realize that they were a very important part of who I was. Sometime during my senior year I came to a resolution: If I was to be defined as an outlaw, a sinner and a degenerate—then so be it!

With a profound sense of defiance, I entered the University of Michigan in 1960. There I finally met a few other men who shared my strange propensity. One of them even fell in love with me and sent me a letter to that effect. It meant a lot to me, and I put it where I thought it would be safe—under the bottom drawer of my bedroom dresser. My defiance had caused me to be careless. My mother, on one of her cleaning binges, found it. Too distraught to confront me, she gave it to my father and insisted that he do it. He struggled to find the right words, but they wouldn't come. All he could think of was to make me promise to see a psychiatrist at the university.

The doctor was no help, but the visit did please me. No sooner had I walked into his office than we exchanged a glance of instinctive recognition. Was the doctor "that way" too? Then maybe it wasn't so bad after all. I began to feel more confident.

One night, as I was walking across campus, a policeman lurched out of the dark behind the lighted path. He grabbed me and threw me against his car. "You're one of those perverts, aren't you?" When I hesitated, he became threatening. "Give me the names of all your friends who are queer like you," he ordered, "or you'll be very sorry. I'll tell your parents what you are!" "They already know," I quickly replied, my inner defiance leaping forward. He pushed me up hard against the car, hurting my elbows. He took my wallet out of my back pocket and looked at the ID cards inside. Then, to my surprise, he let me go, repeating his warning, "Remember, you'll be sorry!"

The next morning I got a call from the dean, ordering me to meet him in his office right away. I never got calls like this, so I braced for the worst. When I arrived, there were no pleasantries. He got right to it, red in the face. "I heard about last night. I suggest you don't bother to reregister. We don't need your kind in our program." I was stunned, but surprisingly not intimidated. I found myself answering, "Then I guess I'll go somewhere else, where I'm wanted."

I had already been thinking about moving to New York City, which I had heard might be a safe haven for anyone who was different. When I got there in 1963, I found a gay life more complex than the one in Michigan. Many of the new friends I made were angry and defiant like me. The police had been raiding the bars on a regular basis, and some of us started the practice of forming a circle around the raiding officers. We made them uncomfortable, but did not push it further. Exposure as a gay person could mean jail, the loss of your job, your family—everything.

But there was a spirit of rebellion in the air, and it came to a head at the Stonewall Uprising.

I remember the early morning of June 28, 1969. The drag queens were fed up. They defied the police and locked them in the bar that they'd raided—The Stonewall Inn. I happened to walk by soon after the raid, just as a small but boisterous group of them was spreading out across the street, and joined hands with them, kicking and singing and laughing at the police. For days the rebellion went on, and during that time my friends and I ran up and down the streets of our neighborhood, Greenwich Village, encouraging people to "Come out, come out!" dozens turned to hundreds, and looking over the huge crowd, I felt a release of all my old anger, fear and sadness—and immense relief. "Look how many of us there are!" I shouted to my comrades. At that moment I felt the beginnings of a community, and realized that as a group we could have tremendous power.

Since then we've formed our own social, political and advocacy organizations. As more of us have come out, more families have realized we're part of them, and not perverts or degenerates. Because we dared to be ourselves, it's easier for many people now. Attitudes have begun to change. Even my father, in spite of his struggles, came to accept and respect me as a gay man.

Philip Bockman is a writer, gay activist, and psychotherapist. He has written articles and stories for Christopher Street, *the* New York Native *and collections such as* Boys Like Us, *as well as many letters to the editor on LGBT issues. During the AIDS crisis, he was clinical coordinator for GMHC, and today he continues his private practice of psychotherapy in New York City.*

Paul Feiler has been a New York City psychotherapist for the past 20 years. His practice has included working with individuals, couples, and groups. He is now focusing on life coaching and clinical supervision. He also enjoys writing and is planning to write a book based on his experiences as a psychotherapist.

Intersex Human Rights Abuse
Veronica Drantz

Intersex people have always been and will always be among us. Their existence proves that sex is a spectrum, not binary. Nevertheless, doctors have assumed that intersex bodies are disordered rather than just different. Many intersex infants and children have been subjected to nonconsensual, unnecessary, irreversible, and harmful genital surgeries and/or hormonal treatments to force their bodies to resemble binary sex expectations.

Moreover, doctors often guess the gender identity incorrectly. A United Nations report on abuse in health-care settings characterized such medical interventions as "unscientific, potentially harmful and contributing to stigma" with damaging long-term outcomes including "scarring, loss of sexual sensation, pain, incontinence and lifelong depression" (Mendez 2013, 18). Accordingly, this report calls on the world's nations to outlaw "genital normalizing" surgeries on intersex individuals without their free and informed consent. Four intersex people tell their stories here.

> I am 20 years old and intersex. My hormones and chromosomes are characterized as male, but my genitals are not. When I was born I was anatomically ambiguous. I presented with penoscrotal 3rd stage hypospadias and severe chordee. I also had penoscrotal transposition. I was assigned male and underwent multiple surgeries at age one to "fix" my genital variations to fit society's expectations to be a man. Those surgeries left me with genitals that tear and bleed when aroused. I have immensely struggled with being comfortable in my body because my sense of self has been compromised. Being intersex has contributed to my depression and continued feelings of trauma for being surgically assigned a sex without my consent. My family and pediatric surgeons assumed my life would be hard if my genitalia did not look male. If only they knew that what they had done to me has played a major part in multiple attempts to take my life, then maybe they could have reconsidered before making a permanent and irreversible change to my body that I would have to live with for the rest of my life.
>
> *Avery Capaldi*

> When I was born the doctor said I was a boy, then changed his mind and said "girl". Surgery was done on my genitals to make me look more female. I have a condition called

Congenital Adrenal Hyperplasia. I was never told about the surgery; I had to find out on my own decades later. The surgery left me with very little feeling in my clitoris. I was raised as a girl and was miserable. I battled with depression and eventually alcoholism. I was hospitalized three times in my early twenties for suicidal ideation. I got sober in my late thirties and finally had to really deal with all that had happened to me. I was hospitalized eight more times in the first five years I was sober. It was at this point I was able to convince my doctor to start me on testosterone. Everything shifted for me when I started living my truth as a man. That was eight years ago and I haven't been hospitalized again. Not that everything is always fantastic, I am still human after all, but generally I am much happier.

Alex McCorry

When I was born, the doctor asked "would you like a boy or a girl?" My parents responded "boy," and the surgeries to "correct" my ambiguous genitalia and cloacal exstrophy began. I remember most of the surgeries. A few I expressed I didn't want. No one listened. Doctor visits every 3–6 months, surgery every year or two. Ultrasounds, "inspections" of my genitalia, blood work and urinalysis. Questions about my ability to "orgasm"; if any "ejaculate" was present. Therapist appointments. I was told I had nothing to worry about. I was normal. Just born with my kidney and bladder on the outside. I knew something was different. I felt like I was being lied to. I would compare my genitals to those of neighbor boys and girls and wonder why mine were different. Throughout high school, when everyone was exploring their sexual identity, I was having sexual fears. Constant worries someone would find out. What, I didn't know. See, I never even knew the truth. Not until age 19. I was at my mom's for the weekend when I was finally told the story. It all made sense. During the next 10 years, I tried to kill myself, lost faith in humanity, trust in doctors, parents, anyone with authority, and tried almost every drug. And then I changed my gender to who I felt I should be. All of this could have been avoided if I had simply been told the truth instead of being pushed into one gender, forced to grow up that gender, and having my genitals mutilated to "conform." There are surgeries that sometimes need to be performed; however no doctor should ever mutilate a child's genitalia without their consent. And all intersex children deserve the truth.

Alexis Mickler

I was born in the Philippines with the help of both a midwife and a doctor. The doctor recognized that I was born with ambiguous genitalia, but did not explain this to my family. I assume this was because the term "intersex" was not widely understood, and the doctor did not want to alarm my mother. While my mother realized my genitalia was different from other "girls" (which the doctor said I was), since I was a healthy baby, she never asked any questions. Therefore, no surgeries were performed to "correct" my genitalia. Culturally, the Philippines is very accepting of both sexual orientation and gender choices. This gave me the freedom to be myself. I was often taken for being a "boy" throughout my childhood, though gender seemed fluid to me. I experienced puberty as a male, with all of the sexual preoccupations that boys have. I attribute this to my high level of testosterone as an intersex person. At age 36, I was diagnosed with Congenital Adrenal Hyperplasia and XXY chromosomes. I was mistakenly given estrogen by my doctor and it feminized me and made me very ill. It took years for doctors to realize I needed testosterone, but once I received the correct hormone, my physique went back to normal and I felt much better. I do not suffer from any mental illness, which I attribute largely to the fact that I was allowed to "be me" growing up, and I am happy with who I have become.

Crixs Haligowski

Reference

Mendez, Juan E. 2013. "Report of the Special Rapporteur on Torture and Other Cruel, Inhuman or Degrading Treatment or Punishment." United Nations General Assembly Human Rights Council, February 1, 2013. Available online at http://www.ohchr.org/Documents/HRBodies/HRCouncil/RegularSession/Session22/A.HRC.22.53_English.pdf. Accessed on October 21, 2016.

Dr. Veronica Drantz has taught physiology and related sciences to medical professionals most of her life. She also educates the public about the scientific evidence accumulated over the last fifty-plus years on gender identity, sexual orientation, and intersexuality.

Feminisms Coming and Going
Mel Ferrara

The first time I heard the word "patriarchy," I was seventeen and sitting in the passenger seat of one of my best friend's cars in the parking lot of our conservative Catholic school's parking lot listening to a poem by the spoken word artist Andrea Gibson. I remember this moment viscerally, astounded by the impact that this word had on me even though I was not yet fully sure of its meaning. It was not until about a year later when I entered college and took my first feminist theory class that I began to understand why this moment was so significant to me. As I began to delve deeper into the canonical texts—works by thinkers such as Judith Butler, bell hooks, and Audre Lorde—I found myself finally having the words to describe the social and cultural arrangements of gender and sexuality that I had observed and experienced. Lauren Zuniga encapsulates the transformative power of language in her poem "Confessions of an Uneducated Queer," when she describes first hearing the word "heteronormative" and feeling "like being handed a corkscrew after years of opening the bottle with my teeth" (Vancouver Poetry Slam 2012). To this day, I am continually discovering ways in which feminist and queer theory has given me unique forms of access to my own narrative as a queer and non-binary transgender person.

Yet access to these words is so limited. Since the field of women's studies was first introduced as an academic discipline in the 1960s, it has experienced on-going critique from those both inside and outside of academia for the ways in which it has become situated within the "Ivory Tower," given that access to higher education is limited and often excludes people of color and those without certain amount of class privilege (hooks 2000). Personally, as a first generation college student from a lower middle-class background, there have been times where I have felt uncomfortable in spaces of higher education because I have experienced the stigmatization of those who are less formally educated or from a lower socioeconomic status as "backwards" or in need of enlightening by those with degrees. Even outside of its institutionalization, feminist movements have been known for explicitly and implicitly marginalizing members of their community, especially women of color, women from the Global South, and trans women.

So where do we go from here? How can we reconcile the transformative capacities of theory with the ways in which it also functions as a source of marginalization?

I certainly do not have the answers to these questions and instead allow them to orient me as I continue to unpack my identities as both a scholar and an activist. That said, I do have some thoughts that hopefully can spur some on-going dialogue as we consider the state of feminism today.

First of all, that there is a "state of feminism" is in itself a bit misleading. A firm definition of feminism is one that is difficult to ascertain without inaccurately conflating different branches of its theories and praxis. I find that it is often more appropriate to frame the discourse around feminisms as multiplicitous, related (albeit sometimes contradictory) ideologies and methodologies. It is also perhaps easier to begin by teasing out what feminism is not, or at the very least, not quite.

In addition, it is not quite just a movement centered on gender equality. When considering feminist theories and practices, it is vital to consider the complex inter-relationships between gender and other social identities and markers. Black feminist theorist Patricia Hill Collins, for one, underscores the importance of this multifaceted understanding of power and oppression with her theory of the matrix of domination, which she describes as replacing an additive model of identity with a paradigm that examines the "interlocking systems of oppression" (Collins 2000, 223). In other words, we cannot consider sexism without simultaneously considering racism, classism, heterosexism, and other hierarchies of power. Only in attending to these various dynamics can their integral relationship with one another be attended to and collapsed.

Feminism is not just thought. Black feminist theory, womanism, and post-colonial feminism have been at the forefront of critiquing the way in which some feminisms value intellectual knowledge more than embodied knowledge—a move that only reifies hegemony. Instead, feminism is situated at the crux of theory and praxis, the speculative and the experiential.

Nor can feminism be characterized as stagnant. Some understanding of this activity has been explained by the wave metaphor, in which the first-wave was a rights-based movement for women's equality beginning in the 19th century, the second wave was the radical and cultural movement of the 1960s–1980s, and the third-wave is the product of 1990s identity politics. Some propose that a fourth-wave of feminism has started because of the unique ways in which the Internet has come to play a role in social justice advocacy (Munro 2013). The wave model, while useful, inaccurately depicts different feminisms as having clear contextual start and end points, which fails to represent their dynamic ideological interactions still today. Further, it fails to examine the nuances of an even greater variety of feminist theories and practices, including liberal, radical-libertarian, radical-cultural, Marxist, socialist, psychoanalytic, care-focused, existentialist, postmodern, women of color, queer, trans, and ecofeminisms (Tong 2009; Kolmar and Bartkowski 2010).

Where does this leave us? What does it mean to complicate our understanding of feminism in a way that makes pinning it down its definition much more difficult? While there are of course certain risks to such an approach, I also find this that it allows for an interrogation of the relationships of sex, gender, and other social identities as situated within systems of power and difference. The complexities of feminism are vital in the continual production of new ways of thinking and of acting in a world of (im)permenances.

References

Collins, Patricia Hill. 2000. *Black Feminist Thought*. New York: Routledge.

hooks, bell. 2000. *Feminism Is for Everybody: Passionate Politics*. Cambridge: South End Press.

Kolmar, Wendy K., and Frances Bartkowski. 2010. *Feminist Theory: A Reader*, 4th ed. New York: McGraw Hill.

Munro, Ealasaid. 2013. "Feminism: A Fourth Wave?" *Political Studies Association* 4(2): 22-25. doi: 10.1111/2041-9066.12021.

Tong, Rosemary. 2009. *Feminist Thought: A More Comprehensive Introduction*. Boulder, CO: Westview Press.

Vancouver Poetry Slam. 2012. "Lauren Zuniga—Confessions of an Uneducated Queer." YouTube video. https://www.youtube.com/watch?v=bGCXJqn6DRg. October 23, 2016.

Mel Ferrara is a graduate student at the University of Arizona pursuing her MA/PhD in Gender and Women's Studies. Mel is a Point Foundation Scholar and received her BA from Muhlenberg College. Her research focus is in transgender and intersex studies, queer theory, new materialisms, somatechnics, and medicalization.

Bringing Feelings to the Diagnostic Criteria of Gender Dysphoria
Dean A. Haycock

Films and television programs can both reflect and influence our perception of history and social issues. For decades, transgender persons were portrayed in inaccurate and insulting ways. Films released before 1960 depicted few true transgender characters and instead featured transvestites or cross-dressers. These characters were frequently clown-like, deviant, or disturbed individuals. Understanding, sympathetic portrayals of characters who did not identify with the biological sex assigned to them at birth, or who did not conform to society's generally accepted gender roles, have appeared on screen only relatively recently.

Films like *Boys Don't Cry* and *Normal*, for example, released in 1999 and 2003 respectively, reveal increased understanding of transgender issues and are consistent with the fact that biology plays an indisputable role in determining identity. These films highlight the struggles some individuals experience by honestly treating specific issues of transgender dysphoria. The dialog in these films gives viewers a sense of the raw feelings and emotions behind the clinical, diagnostic criteria the American Psychiatric Association uses to diagnose this dysphoria.

The criteria are listed in the fifth edition of the *Diagnostic and Statistical Manual of Mental Disorders* (*DSM-5*). The nine pages it devotes to gender dysphoria include seven criteria. One in particular must be present, and at least two of the remaining six are required for a formal diagnosis.

Tom Wilkinson plays Roy Applewood, a 50+-year-old Midwesterner, in *Normal*. Roy has been married for 25 years and has, on the surface, a happy life with his wife and daughter. Soon after celebrating his 25th wedding anniversary, however, he announces his long internal struggle trying to reconcile his true female identity with his male persona. When he says "I've been hiding it for years. It has been an agony. I can't go on living my life like this. I'd rather die," he clearly satisfies the prime criterion of "significant distress" associated with a person's gender identity. Roy's distress is related to the pressure and pain he's felt his entire life as he hid his true identity.

Brandon Teena (played by Hilary Swank) in *Boys Don't Cry* illustrates a different aspect of the primary criterion. His transgender struggle causes significant distress related to his impaired ability to function in society. He deceives girls into believing he is biologically male, that he is not transgender. It gets him in trouble with his associates and leads to a tragic end. He indicates his distress when he tells his cousin, "Lonny, my life is a f**kin' nightmare."

Had Roy and Brandon been able to deal with their transgender issues in a supportive community while experiencing little distress, they would not meet the criteria for gender dysphoria. A transgender person who is fortunate enough to accept and realize his or her true sexual identity without significant distress does not, by definition, suffer from gender dysphoria, according to American Psychiatric Association.

Both Roy and Brandon face discrimination, and lack of understanding and sympathy, from the people in their lives. Roy makes the transition to Ruth and eventually achieves acceptance from her family, if not from many of his former friends and co-workers. Brandon—whose story is based on true events—never does. He is tormented, raped and eventually murdered by transphobic bigots as a direct result of his struggle to reconcile his biologically assigned gender with the gender he accepts for himself.

Both figures need to meet only two additional criteria, in addition to some form of significant distress, for a diagnosis of gender dysphoria.

I. When Roy declares, "I was born in the wrong body. I'm a woman. I've known it all my life," she indicates a strong desire not to have the primary and/or secondary sex characteristics she had been assigned at birth. When Brandon, born with female anatomy, assumed the identity of a male as a young adult, he says "Then I was more like . . . a boy-girl . . . Finally, everythin' felt right."

II. A strong desire to have the sexual characteristics of the opposite sex one was assigned at birth is another factor that can contribute to a diagnosis of gender dysphoria. Roy moves towards meeting this criterion when she says, "I'd like to have the operation to change my sex." Brandon would like to undergo hormone and other medical treatments but realizes that ". . . it costs a f**kin' fortune. I'm gonna be an old man by the time I get that kinda money."

III. When Roy announces that "I'm a woman born in a man's body," she, like Brandon, is acknowledging another feeling that is recognized as a feature of gender dysphoria. Both characters clearly live with the sense that there is little or no satisfying fit between the gender they identify with and the sex listed on their birth certificates.

IV. Brandon demonstrates his desire to be treated like someone who is the opposite of the gender he was assigned at birth when, as a 21-year-old male, he befriends the male acquaintances of his girlfriend.

V. "I've been hiding it for years," Roy says, and strongly suggests he is convinced he has the feelings, personality and outlook of a female, although he was born with male physical traits.

VI. And finally, Brandon demonstrates the strong conviction that he feels, acts and reacts to situations as if he is male. "I'm gonna ask her to marry me," he announces about his girlfriend. "Before or after your sex-change operation?" his cousin and confidant asks, "Before or after you tell her you're a girl?" Brandon is not interested in a same sex marriage. He intends to propose as a man would propose to a woman despite his concealed female anatomy.

In the final scenes, Roy writes to his son, "I'm a woman born in a man's body and I'll be getting a sex change. I hope you'll understand that I would like to find some peace and happiness in my life." The real life Brandon, murdered by his transphobic peers, found little of the peace and happiness that even fictional characters like Roy hope to find.

References

American Psychiatric Association. 2013. *Diagnostic and Statistical Manual of Mental Disorders*, 5th ed. Arlington, VA: American Psychiatric Association, pp 451–459.

Peirce, K., and A. Bienen (screenwriters). 1999. *Boys Don't Cry*. Fox Searchlight Pictures.

Anderson, J. (screenwriter). 2003. *Normal*. HBO Films.

Dean A. Haycock, PhD, is a science and medical writer. He is the author of Murderous Minds: Exploring the Criminal Psychopathic Brain, Characters on the Couch: Exploring Psychology through Literature and Film, *and* The Everything Health Guide to Adult Bipolar Disorder.

Intersex: Beyond the Sex Binary
Axel Keating

When a baby is born, someone will usually announce "it's a boy" or "it's a girl." That announcement leads to a designation, assigning the newborn as male or female. This announcement is primarily dependent on external genitalia, leading to a classification of the newborn's sex based on these organs. In most countries, children need to be assigned as either male or female at birth or shortly thereafter for legal and statistical purposes. From that initial assignment, it is assumed that a child will grow up, experience the world and oneself, and identify in a certain way. However, this is not always the case and this assumption can have dramatic repercussions. In particular, when some infants are born, it is not as easy to make an assignment of sex based on our current model. Some babies are born with sex characteristics that have been deemed "ambiguous," or not conforming to current prevailing binary notions of male and female bodies.

Intersex people are born with sex characteristics, including genital, gonadal, and chromosomal patterns, that do not fit constructed binary notions of what male or female bodies should look like. Intersex is an umbrella term used to describe a wide range of variations in sex traits. In some cases, intersex traits are visible at birth while in others, they are not apparent until puberty or later in life. Some chromosomal intersex variations may not be physically apparent at all. While there is no formal statistic about the number of people born intersex, it's presumed that 0.05% to 1.7% of the population is born with intersex traits, with the upper estimate being similar to the number of natural red haired people ("Free & Equal"). However, some experts argue that a more accurate number is actually higher, with an upwards of 1 in 150 or 200 people ("Brief Guide"). Being intersex relates to one's sex characteristics and is distinct from a person's gender or sexuality. An intersex person may identify with a wide range of sexual orientations, including straight, gay, lesbian, bisexual, asexual, or many other sexualities, and may identify with a wide range of genders, including woman, man, non-binary, genderqueer, agender, and many more ("Free & Equal"). Intersex people may identify as cisgender, transgender, or simply intersex.

We are often taught—from doctors, our schools, the government, the media, and many more—that sex is simple and binary: everyone is male or female. Sex is also often conflated with gender, with the same assumptions: everyone is born male or female and is a man or woman. However, the category of sex refers to a combination of genital, gonadal, hormonal, and chromosomal patterns that varies from person to person. Furthermore, there are often more similarities in these traits than differences: all bodies have testosterone and estrogen at a variety of different levels, the tissue for body parts such as the penis and clitoris are homologous, and testes and ovaries both develop as gonads. There are a multitude of ways that sex traits can line up. But there is no one concrete marker of sex that clearly distinguish bodies labeled male or female ("Defining: Intersex"). Additionally, the current distinction and classification of male, female, and intersex bodies are unstable and bodily meaning of sex traits have been perceived differently throughout history and within different contexts.

However, there are still deeply ingrained assumptions around the sex dichotomy and what is assumed to be medical and social norms for male and female bodies. The idea of male and female bodies is seen as a natural fact, rather than something that has become naturalized over time. Intersex bodies are often seen as different and intersex children and adults are often stigmatized, discriminated against, and most pressingly, face cosmetic medical interventions and surgeries used to "normalize," which have been deemed by advocates and various international bodies as human rights violations, mutilation, and torture ("Free & Equal"; "Standing Up"; "Brief Guide"). Intersex people often face unnecessary medical interventions, including a common practice of subjecting intersex children to unnecessary and irreversible surgical and other medical procedures for the purpose of trying to make their appearance conform to binary sex stereotypes ("Free & Equal"). Doctors will often advise parents to have these surgical and other medical interventions on intersex newborns and children to make their bodies seemingly conform to stereotypical male or female characteristics ("Standing Up"). These medical interventions are often performed without the full, free and informed consent of the intersex person involved, who is often too young to comprehend the decision or be part of the decision-making process, as well as without peer support or information from intersex communities ("Free & Equal"). In most cases, such interventions are not medically necessary and can have extremely negative consequences on intersex children as they grow older ("Standing Up").

Often times, these irreversible procedures can cause pain, scarring, urinary incontinence, permanent infertility, loss of sexual sensation, lifelong mental suffering, including depression, anxiety, and post-traumatic stress disorder (PTSD), can lead to lifelong hormone replacement therapy in order to regulate hormones that the removed gonads would have naturally regulated, and risk surgically assigning intersex people into sex/gender categories that do not fit them ("Free & Equal"). These physical and emotional effects can lead to shame and stigma towards one's own body and emotional distress. It undermines one's physical integrity, bodily autonomy, and self-determination.

Instead of focusing on the needs of intersex people, the medicalization of intersex, along with the binary notions of sex, assumes that all intersex people will have conflict with their gender identity formation. This leads to intersex bodies being considered "medical problems" and "psycho-social emergencies" that need intervened upon in order to be fixed, usually through medical or psychological means ("Standing Up"). However, there is no evidence that children who grow up with intersex traits are worse off psychologically than those who have surgical, hormonal, or other medical interventions. In fact, there is evidence that children with intersex traits without these interventions do well psychologically. Many intersex people are in more distress due to non-consensual medically unnecessary interventions done by doctors. This can create huge distrust towards doctors and medical establishments, which can further jeopardize intersex people's health ("What's Wrong").

But in the past twenty years, a rise in intersex activism has occurred. The fight to end irreversible non-consensual medically unnecessary interventions on intersex people has been taken up by many intersex advocates across the world. Intersex advocates and their allies, as well as international agencies such as the United Nations and the World Health Organization, have challenged medical establishments throughout the world to end medical interventions and fight for the human rights and bodily integrity of intersex people. Great strides have been made in the past few years: South Africa became the first country to explicitly add protections for intersex people to legislation in 2006, with Australia adding protections of intersex status in 2013, and in 2015, Malta became the first country in the world to protect intersex people on the basis of sex characteristics, with Chile joining shortly thereafter in early 2016, ordering the suspension of medically unnecessary interventions for intersex people ("Judicial Matters"; "Sex Discrimination"; "Standing Up"; "Chilean Ministry of Health"). Since then, several other cities and countries have passed measures to protect intersex people. But there is still much more work to be done. Advocacy organizations, such as interACT, which uses innovative strategies to advocate for the legal and human rights of intersex children, or OII, a decentralized global network of intersex organizations, and community and peer support organization throughout the world are gaining traction in their efforts, including an end to non-consensual medical interventions, end to discrimination, legal recognition, greater awareness and acceptance, and overall human rights, among countless other efforts. And there are many things anyone can do to promote intersex justice: further education about intersex variations, integrating intersex equality in their own work and lives, checking binaristic language and offering intersex-inclusive language instead, and supporting intersex advocates and organizations fighting for justice ("Brief Guidelines"; "Standing Up").

References

Astorino, Claudia, and Hida Viloria. 2012. "Brief Guidelines for Intersex Allies." OII-USA. http://oii-usa .org/wp-content/uploads/2012/10/Brief-Guidelines-for-Intersex-Allies.pdf. Accessed on October 25, 2016.

Carpenter, Morgan. 2016. "Chilean Ministry of Health Issues Instructions Stopping 'Normalising' Interventions on Intersex Children." OII Australia. https://oii.org .au/30250/chilean-ministry-stops-normalising/. Accessed on October 25, 2016.

Davis, Georgiann. 2016. "Defining: Intersex." My Kid Is Gay. Everyone Is Gay. http://mykidisgay.com/defining-intersex/. Accessed on October 25, 2016.

"Free & Equal Campaign Fact Sheet: Intersex." 2015. United Nations Office of the High Commissioner for Human Rights. https://unfe.org/system/unfe-65-Intersex_ Factsheet_ENGLISH.pdf. Accessed on October 25, 2016.

Ghattas, Dan Christian. 2015. "Standing Up for the Human Rights of Intersex People—How Can You Help." http:// www.ilga-europe.org/sites/default/files/how_to_be_a_ great_intersex_ally_a_toolkit_for_ngos_and_decision_ makers_december_2015_updated.pdf. Accessed on October 25, 2016.

"Judicial Matters Amendment Act, No. 22 of 2005, Republic of South Africa, Vol. 487, Cape Town." 2006. http://www .justice.gov.za/legislation/acts/2005-022.pdf. Accessed on October 25, 2016.

"Sex Discrimination Amendment (Sexual Orientation, Gender Identity and Intersex Status) Act 2013, No. 98, 2013, C2013A00098." 2013. ComLaw. https://www .legislation.gov.au/Details/C2013A00098. Accessed on October 25, 2016.

"What's Wrong with the Way Intersex Has Traditionally Been Treated?" 2016. Intersex Society of North America. http:// www.isna.org/faq/concealment. Accessed on October 25, 2016.

Axel Keating is a recent graduate of New York University and a youth advocate for the organization Advocates for Youth.

Living with Gender Dysphoria
Whitney McKnight

Were Emma to stand before you, sporting hair that is cropped military-style atop her tall, athletic frame that is draped in a black, baggy hoodie, most likely you would be certain: This person is a young man. This "fact" would be so obvious, you probably would not be conscious of the process your mind has gone through to reach this conclusion. In Emma's mind, however, you would be wrong.

"In public, I still look male. I haven't socially transitioned yet," says Emma, whose name at birth was Ethan. Emma tends to present herself monochromatically: black jeans, black tee shirts, black hoodies, black boots. She keeps her hair short and neat, worn like the paramedic she aspires to become. She has begun hormone therapy to help bring her body into alignment with her emotional and mental reality: Her voice is gaining a higher timbre; she has started to grow breasts. "I see myself in my future as a pretty woman," she says.

"Gender dysphoria" is the medical term for people who identify as the gender opposite from their biological one. That a person experiences what psychiatrists also call "gender nonconformity" is not considered a mental disorder. Instead, what clinicians seek to treat in this population is the resulting "clinically significant distress" (*DSM-5* 2013) that adolescents and young adults like Emma experience as they work to resolve the misalignment between their physical, mental, and emotional realities.

Studies have shown that between 0.17% and 1.3% (Shields 2013; Diemer et al. 2015) of youth identify themselves as transgender, also referred to by some as "gender nonbinary." The causes for a person to be transgender have not been identified by science. Compared with their peers, young persons with gender dysphoria are at a higher risk than their "binary gender" peers for having depression, committing acts of self-harm, developing eating disorders, or having suicidal thoughts (Connolly 2016).

Emma herself suffers from anxiety, clinical depression, and has been hospitalized several times for suicidal depression. Because Emma's version of who she is challenges how society expects her to think of herself, she says is fearful that she is being judged and ostracized. This, Emma says, contributes to her "intense anxiety" and fuels her depression, capturing her in a vicious cycle. Indeed, ostracism has been linked to depression and anxiety, two mental states that often lead a person to feel isolated (Kendler et al. 2003; Fung 2016). Feeling separated from others—particularly if it is the result of being bullied, a risk that is higher for nonbinary gender youth than binary gender ones—can lead to a fear of others (Levinson et al. 2013), which further separates a person from the group, intensifying the risk of suicide and depression (Slavich et al. 2010).

Therapy does seem to help (Connolly 2016), as has been Emma's experience. "The transgender people in my [therapy] group who are at ease with themselves inspire me," Emma says. Belonging to this group has been a bulwark against Emma's loneliness, exacerbated when her girlfriend ended their relationship. "It was hard for me to be loving because of my depression, so we broke up."

Although it might seem counterintuitive, gender nonconformity does not overlap with sexual preference. In Emma's case, she remains attracted to young women, just as she was before at age 19 when she began to identify as male. Again comes Emma's anxiety: "If I am attracted to girls, I will have to date a lesbian who will date trans-girls. I don't know if I am ever going to be able to find someone like that. It contributes to my feeling hopeless."

Although Emma says her family—unlike the families of some of her gender nonbinary friends—has not abandoned her, Emma is frightened that she will always be an outsider, essentially alone. "There's a lot of hate out there. Sometimes I feel like I don't have the energy to get through all that."

Whether Emma will have her penis surgically removed after her hormone therapy is complete over the next two years, she has yet to decide; however, she is certain she will not ever return to identifying as male. "I think if ten years from now I were to try and go back to being Ethan, it wouldn't last. It would always give me discomfort because it doesn't match how I feel inside."

Emma says she relies on her "warrior spirit" when her fears of isolation come on, and tries to remember she is connected to others, even though she is different. "There aren't a whole lot of positives in being transgender; the world isn't built for us. But being transgender does give me the sense that I am unique, even though I am a normal person, too. I go through the same everyday stuff others do. It's not some weird, perverted thing."

References

Connolly, Maureen D., et al. 2016. "The Mental Health of Transgender Youth: Advances in Understanding." *Journal of Adolescent Health*. http://www.jahonline.org/article/S1054-139X(16)30146-X/abstract. Accessed on October 20, 2016.

Diemer, Elizabeth W., et al. 2015. "Gender Identity, Sexual Orientation, and Eating-Related Pathology in a National Sample of College Students." *Journal of Adolescent Health*. http://www.jahonline.org/article/S1054-139X(15)00087-7/abstract. Accessed on October 20, 2016.

DSM-5 Fact Sheet. 2013. *Diagnostic and Statistical Manual of Mental Disorders*. http://www.dsm5.org/documents/gender%20dysphoria%20fact%20sheet.pdf. Accessed on October 20, 2016.

Fung, Kenneth P., et al. "Once Hurt, Twice Shy: Social Pain Contributes to Social Anxiety." 2016. Emotion. http://psycnet.apa.org/?&fa=main.doiLanding&doi=10.1037/emo0000223. Accessed on October 20, 2016.

Kendler, Kenneth S., et al. 2003. "Life Event Dimensions of Loss, Humiliation, Entrapment, and Danger in the Prediction of Onsets of Major Depression and Generalized Anxiety." *JAMA Psychiatry*. http://jamanetwork.com/journals/jamapsychiatry/fullarticle/207719. Accessed on October 20, 2016.

Levinson, Cheri A., et al. "Reactivity to Exclusion Prospectively Predicts Social Anxiety Symptoms in Young Adults." 2013. *Behavior Therapy*. https://www.ncbi.nlm.nih.gov/pubmed/23768673. Accessed on October 20, 2016.

Shields, John P., et al. 2013. "Estimating Population Size and Demographic Characteristics of Lesbian, Gay, Bisexual, and Transgender Youth in Middle School." *Journal of Adolescent Health*. http://www.jahonline.org/article/S1054-139X(12)00258-3/abstract. Accessed on October 20, 2016.

Slavich, George M., et al. 2010. "Targeted Rejection Predicts Hastened Onset of Major Depression." *Journal of Social and Clinical Psychology*. http://guilfordjournals.com/doi/abs/10.1521/jscp.2009.28.2.223. Accessed on October 20, 2016.

Whitney McKnight is a freelance medical writer and a member of National Association of Science Writers and the Association of Health Care Journalists.

Feminism: Where We've Been and Where We're Going
Martha Rampton

It has long been common to speak in terms of three waves of feminism, but now, in the early twenty-first century, we are witnessing the birth of a fourth wave, emerging from youth around the world.

The first wave of feminism took place in the late nineteenth and early twentieth centuries, and its major goal was to open up opportunities for women, with a focus on suffrage. The wave formally began in 1848 with Elizabeth Cady Stanton's "Seneca Fall Declaration" when three hundred men and women rallied to the cause of equality for women.

In its early stages, feminism was interrelated with the temperance and abolitionist movements. Victorian America saw women acting in very "un-ladylike" ways (public speaking, demonstrating, stints in jail). Discussions about the vote and women's participation in politics led to an examination of the perceived differences between men and women. Some claimed that women were morally superior to men, and so their presence in the civic sphere would improve public behavior and the political process.

The second wave began in the 1960s and continued into the 90s. This wave unfolded in the context of the anti-Vietnam War and civil rights movements and the growing self-awareness of a variety of minority groups. The New Left was on the rise, and the voice of the second wave was increasingly radical. In this phase, sexuality and reproductive rights were dominant issues, and much of the movement's energy was focused on passing the Equal Rights Amendment to the Constitution guaranteeing legal regardless of sex.

This phase began with protests against the Miss America pageant in Atlantic City in 1968 and 1969. Feminists parodied what they held to be a degrading "cattle parade" that reduced women to objects of beauty dominated by a patriarchy that sought to keep them in the home or in dull, low-paying jobs. The radical New York group, Redstockings, staged a counter pageant in which they crowned a sheep as Miss America and threw "oppressive" feminine artifacts such as bras, girdles, high-heels, makeup and false eyelashes into the trashcan.

Feminists formed women-only organizations and "consciousness raising" groups. In publications like "The BITCH

Manifesto" and "Sisterhood is Powerful," feminists advocated for their place in the sun. The second wave was increasingly theoretical, and began to associate the subjugation of women with broader critiques of patriarchy, capitalism, normative heterosexuality, and the woman's role as wife and mother. Sex and gender were differentiated—the former being biological, and the later a social construct that varies culture-to-culture and over time.

Whereas the first wave of feminism was generally propelled by middle class, Western, cisgender, white women, the second phase drew in women of color and developing nations, seeking sisterhood and solidarity, claiming "Women's struggle is class struggle." Feminists spoke of women as a social class and coined phrases such as "the personal is political" and "identity politics" in an effort to demonstrate that race, class, and gender oppression are all related. They initiated a concentrated effort to rid society top-to-bottom of sexism: from children's cartoons to the highest levels of government.

One of the strains of this complex and diverse "wave" was the development of women-only spaces and the notion that women working together create a special dynamic that is not possible in mixed-groups, which would ultimately work for the betterment of the entire planet. Women, due whether to their long "subjugation" or to their biology, were thought by some to be more humane, collaborative, inclusive, peaceful, nurturing, earth-centered, democratic, and holistic in their approach to problem solving than men.

The third wave of feminism began in the mid-90s and was informed by post-colonial and post-modern thinking. In this phase many constructs have been destabilized, including the notions of "universal womanhood," body, gender, sexuality and heteronormativity. An aspect of third wave feminism is the readoption by young feminists of the very lip-stick, high-heels, and cleavage proudly exposed by low cut necklines that the first two phases of the movement identified with male oppression.

The "grrls" of the third wave stepped onto the stage as strong and empowered, eschewing victimization and defining feminine beauty for themselves as subjects, not as objects of a sexist patriarchy. They developed a rhetoric of mimicry, which appropriated derogatory terms like "slut" and "b*tch" in order to subvert sexist culture and deprive it of verbal weapons. The web is an important tool of "girlie feminism." E-zines have provided "cybergrrls" and "netgrrls." At the same time, it permits all users the opportunity to cross gender boundaries, and so the very notion of gender has been unbalanced in a way that encourages experimentation and creative thought.

This is in keeping with the third wave's celebration of ambiguity and refusal to think in terms of "us-them." Most third-wavers refuse to identify as "feminists" and reject the word that they find limiting and exclusionary. Grrl-feminism tends to be global, multi-cultural, and it shuns simple answers or artificial categories of identity, gender, and sexuality. Its transversal politics means that differences such as those of ethnicity, class, sexual orientation, etc. are celebrated and recognized as dynamic, situational, and provisional. The third wave does not acknowledge a collective "movement" and does not define itself as a group with common grievances. Third wave women and men are concerned about equal rights, but tend to think the genders have essentially achieved parity. This wave supports equal rights, but does not have a term like "feminism" to articulate that notion; struggles are more individual: "We don't need feminism anymore."

Society is now poised to ride a fourth wave. A high school girl in Oregon took her mother aside and revealed in a somewhat confessional tone, "I think I'm a feminist!" It was like she was coming out of the closet. Well, perhaps that is the way to view the fourth wave of Feminism. It is emerging because many young women and men realize that the third wave is either overly optimistic or hampered by blinders. Feminism is now moving from the academy and back into the realm of public discourse. Issues that were central to the earliest phases of the women's movement are receiving national and international attention by mainstream press and politicians: problems like sexual abuse, unequal pay, slut-shaming, the pressure on women to conform to a single and unrealistic body-type, and the realization that gains in female representation in politics and business, for example, are very slight.

Some people who wish to ride this new fourth wave have trouble with the word "feminism," not just because of its older connotations of radicalism, but because the word feels like it is underpinned by assumptions of a gender binary and an exclusionary subtext: "for women only." Many fourth wavers who are completely on-board with the movement's tenants find the term "feminism" sticking in their craws and worry that it is hard to get their message out with a label that raises hackles for a broader audience. Yet the word is winning the day. The generation now coming of age sees that the world faces serious problems and they need a strong "in-your-face" word to combat those problems. Feminism no longer just refers to the struggles of women; it is a clarion call for gender equity.

The emerging fourth wavers bring to the discussion important perspectives taught by third wave feminism. They speak in terms of intersectionality whereby women's suppression can only fully be understood in the context of a larger consciousness of oppression, along with racism, ageism, classism, ableism, and sexual orientation. Among the third wave's bequests is the importance of inclusion, an acceptance of the sexualized human body as non-threatening, and the role the internet can play in gender-bending and leveling hierarchies. The beauty of the fourth wave is that there is a place in it for all-together. The academic and theoretical apparatus is extensive and well honed in the academy, ready to support a new broad-based activism in the home, in the workplace, on social media, and in the streets.

Martha Rampton is the director of Pacific University's Center for Gender Equity, and she has published widely on feminist issues.

Rampton is also a professor of history at Pacific; her focus is on women in early medieval Western Europe.

Sexual Reassignment Surgery: History and Controversy
John Galbraith Simmons

Sexual reassignment surgery (SRS) refers to an established set of surgical interventions designed to change a transsexual person's gender identity and sexual function. As it developed over the past half century, SRS has emerged as a controversial therapeutic effort to improve the intensely subjective experience of self which is, however, also inevitably and fundamentally social. In the context of contemporary life in a globalized world, SRS frequently supplants, impinges upon, and challenges ordinary beliefs, local tradition and religious precepts. Consequently, the legal and socio-political implications of SRS, especially in technologically advanced societies with sophisticated means of human interaction, from the most banal to the most intimate, have been especially notable. This chapter provides an introductory glimpse into the history and underlying dynamics of SRS.

Only in the 20th century, with the emergence of plastic surgery as safe for therapeutic and cosmetic purposes, did gender reassignment become plausible. Over the course of several decades, a small number of surgeons developed techniques to treat individuals who suffered from gender dysphoria, as it is now known, whether they were born with primary male or female sexual characteristics (American Psychiatric Association DSM-5 Task Force 2013). Complementary procedures were invented for male-to-female and female-to-male surgeries. A male transitioning to female, for example, would require orchiectomy and penectomy (removal of the testicles and penis) and vaginoplasty (formation of a vagina) among other procedures; there are also breast/chest surgeries and facial feminization procedures. Congruent surgeries came into use for female-to-male transitions. Gender-changing surgery also makes use of hormonal treatments, which affect the secondary sexual characteristics, such as pubic and body hair (Heath 2006).

Although surgeons created the techniques, patients themselves defined SRS in terms of use and purpose. Candidates for surgery comprised a small but discrete class of individuals who desired and sought to change the gender they had been assigned at birth. Sex assignment, it should be noted, for all of human history, had owed to genital appearance alone. But during the 20th century, advances in biology and psychology generated the concept of gender identity as discrete from physical characteristics, while physiology and biochemistry redefined the understanding of sexual development and the complex weave of biology and self-identity. Early examples of SRS embodied these shifts. Thus, as early as 1917, Alan Hart (né Lucille), who was a physician, had his uterus removed in a female-to-male operation; and by 1930 Magnus Hirschfeld, the pioneering German sexologist and reformer, had publicized the male-to-female surgeries of Dora Richter and Lili Elbe (Lothstein 1982). Most notable was New York-born Christine Jorgensen, who in the early 1950s received sex change surgery in Denmark. She eventually wrote a best-selling autobiography and became a high-profile spokesperson for a condition that had started to acquire the status of a biological-based disorder subject to treatment (Jorgensen 1967).

By the 1960s, institutional attention announced a new phase for SRS that would determine its future trajectory. The first textbook for surgeons, *The Transsexual Phenomenon*, was published in 1966 (Benjamin 1966). About the same time, funded by Erickson Educational Foundation, Johns Hopkins Hospital in Baltimore opened the Gender Identity Clinic and undertook an experimental and investigational program that provided SRS to selected transsexuals. Although these surgeries constituted a historic watershed that lent legitimacy to the procedures, they also came to underscore the controversy around them that endures to the present. Hopkins psychiatrist Jon K. Meyer expressed the skepticism that some colleagues shared and others did not: "My personal feeling is that surgery is not a proper treatment for a psychiatric disorder, and it's clear to me that these patients have severe psychological problems that don't go away following surgery" (Brody 1979). The program ended in 1979 when one longitudinal study indicated that patients who received surgery did not show better psychological adaption over time than patients who received only psychotherapy. SRS at Johns Hopkins, although a watershed in the history of the surgery, has never resumed (Meyerowitz 2002).

Conflicting claims about the success and value of SRS, in fact, became a constant feature of its history and evolution beginning in the 1980s. SRS was expensive, challenged various laws regulating gender identification and sexual behavior, and could pit the interests of an individual against dominant values of a society. The ultimate outcome, the subjective experience of gender well-being, is by nature difficult to measure. From a medical standpoint, the depth of the dispute over the value of SRS can be judged by the paucity of data-driven results. Like other surgeries to treat uncommon conditions, such as preemptive neurosurgical procedures for brain aneurysms or arteriovenous malformations, proof of value is difficult if not impossible to achieve (Thompson, Steinberg et al. 1998). For SRS Studies tend to report high rates of success but they must be viewed with caution because numbers are small and a host of variables raise questions of reliability. However, individual anecdotal reports, whether in favor of SRS or expressions of regret, are similarly suspect.

Although performed on a relatively small number of people, SRS has had outsized implications for law, medicine, and society at large. Legal complications became apparent when courts were asked to rule on any number of issues that affect legal status based on gender, from marriage licenses to tax benefits. Advances in the biological sciences complicated traditional gender determination at birth and obviated the simple binary male/female dichotomy. Courts, asked to decide on the gender of a transsexual person, turned to the evolving medical model, which by the 1980s had largely around come to support SRS as a treatment. Although courts eventually tended to support gender designation based on surgery, the medicalization of transsexualism by the use of SRS involved describing it as a disorder. The result, as Susan Keller has described it, was a "crisis of authority" owing to conflicting claims (Keller 1999) that continues to play out in the judiciary, in legislatures, in the court of public opinion, and in the intimate lives of everyone affected.

By the second decade of the 21st century, SRS could be considered a mature set of procedures to treat a condition, transsexualism, which provided most patients an acceptable remedy for gender dysphoria. If it worked as intended, it could also improve patients' lives and provide better social adaptation and integration in a complex urbanized world that has largely rendered obsolete and unworkable such local traditions such as hijras of India and the xanith of Oman (Bailey 2003). However, a comprehensive understanding of transsexualism can today only be considered a distant goal and SRS remains by various measures controversial.

References

American Psychiatric Association and American Psychiatric Association. DSM-5 Task Force. 2013. *Diagnostic and Statistical Manual of Mental Disorders: DSM-5*. Washington, DC: American Psychiatric Association.

Bailey, J. M. 2003. *The Man Who Would Be Queen: The Science of Gender-Bending and Transsexualism*. Washington, DC: Joseph Henry Press.

Benjamin, H. 1966. *The Transsexual Phenomenon*. New York: Julian Press.

Brody, J. 1979. "Benefits of Transsexual Surgery Disputed as Leading Hospital Halts the Procedure." *The New York*

Times. http://www.nytimes.com/1979/10/02/archives/
benefits-of-transsexual-surgery-disputed-as-leading-
hospital-halts.html?_r=0. Accessed on October 20, 2016.

Heath, R. A. 2006. *The Praeger Handbook of Transsexuality:
Changing Gender to Match Mindset.* Westport, CT: Praeger.

Jorgensen, C. 1967. *Christine Jorgensen: A Personal
Autobiography.* New York: P. S. Eriksson.

Keller, S. E. 1999. "Crisis of Authority: Medical Rhetoric
and Transsexual Identity." *Yale Journal of Law & Feminism*
11(1): 51–74.

Lothstein, L. M. 1982. "Sex Reassignment Surgery: Historical,
Bioethical, and Theoretical Issues." *American Journal of
Psychiatry* 139(4): 417–426.

Meyerowitz, J. J. 2002. *How Sex Changed: A History of
Transsexuality in the United States.* Cambridge, MA:
Harvard University Press.

Thompson, R. C., G. K. Steinberg, et al. 1998. "The
Management of Patients with Arteriovenous Malformations
and Associated Intracranial Aneurysms." *Neurosurgery*
43(2): 202–211.

*A medical writer and nonfiction author, John Galbraith Sim-
mons's most recent book, in collaboration with Justin A. Zivin
MD, PhD, is* tPA for Stroke: The Story of a Controversial Drug
(Oxford University Press 2011). His other nonfiction titles include
The Scientific 100 *(Carol 1996) and* Doctors and Discoveries: Lives That Created Today's Medicine *(Houghton Mifflin
2002). He is the author of more than 300 articles and four published novels.*

Gender on a Faceless Internet
Katherine Tutt

When interacting with someone face-to-face, we automatically
make assumptions. These assumptions are based on the other

person's clothes, hair, voice, and other physical aspects. Even the way that a person stands can affect your automatic assumptions. The subtle clues we take from body language and style paint an image of us. We're sorted into stereotypes on which others will base their interactions with us before saying a word to us.

However, the Internet is a relatively faceless means of interaction. While people can provide pictures of themselves or communicate verbally, many users are represented only by their typing styles, profile pictures, and usernames. This means that taking those cues from a person's physical appearance is impossible and leaves a much more unbiased first opinion.

Interacting in this manner can make it very difficult to assume a person's gender. Two people can speak with and befriend each other without even considering the other's gender. Some will even ask for a person's preferred pronouns at some point during the conversation.

My first experience with questioning my gender identity came through role-playing online. We had started informally, so my character, Doc, was based off of myself. There was no planning or descriptions of our characters. As the roleplay got more serious and the characters more developed, I realized that I had never told the other members of the group my character's gender, or my own.

At first it was almost a game to me. I carefully made sure to not use any pronouns while playing Doc, and watched as the other members of the group made their own assumptions when using pronouns. At first I had believed that Doc was female, as that was how I identified as well, but the other members of the group generally used he/him pronouns when referring to Doc. This led to me using he/him pronouns when thinking about Doc, though I still avoided specifying a gender.

During this roleplay, another member was in the same situation; having not made known their own character's gender, they revealed that both they and the character used they/them pronouns. At first I was surprised. I had heard about people using the singular "they" for pronouns, but I hadn't interacted with anyone who did so. Speaking to and roleplaying with this person showed me how to use they/them as pronouns, and I began to do so for Doc.

At this point we moved to a different platform where we could assign "roles" to ourselves in each server. One member of the group suggested that we add pronouns as roles, to avoid misgendering and confusion. I was faced with a dilemma. I had been using they/them pronouns, as it was established by this point that Doc used they/them and I used my character's pronouns.

Until this point, I hadn't felt that I was using the pronouns for myself, but now I was being directly asked for my out-of-character pronouns. Instead of confidently answering "she/her," I wanted to tell them that I preferred to use "they/them." However, I still wasn't entirely comfortable assigning new pronouns and a new gender to myself. I had been female my entire life, and hadn't experienced many problems with it. I worried that I had simply grown accustomed to using Doc's pronouns, and I was playing around with what is an actual gender.

Eventually I answered that I preferred they/them and I have been called by those pronouns ever since within that group. But my dilemma still existed. I use they/them pronouns while on the internet, where no one knows my physical appearance and can't assume that I am female from my physical features, but when interacting face-to-face I use she/her. And I'm comfortable with both.

I still consider myself questioning, but for now I have decided to just leave my gender without a label. Sometimes I am still asked my pronouns while on the internet, and I still get nervous before telling them that I use they/them. I've also found that I use the singular "they" more when talking about people whose genders I don't know.

Overall, gender on the internet can be an interesting experience, depending on how you are communicating with others. Some groups will be more accepting of genders other than male and female than others. It can be easy to find support and information about a multitude of genders, and can lead to you questioning your own. Are you a girl? All of the time? A boy? Neither? Both? Something else entirely?

You don't even have to label your gender. Gender in and of itself is a very confusing topic. It's expressed in many different ways, ways so subtle it can be hard to pick up on. Just because someone enjoys something "girly" doesn't mean that they want to be called a girl. Just because someone enjoys something "boyish" doesn't mean that they want to be called a boy.

Gender may not be something concrete, and that's okay. As long as you are comfortable with it, your gender identity is valid.

Katherine Tutt is a junior in high school in Colorado.

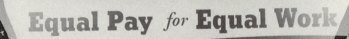

Introduction

Issues of sex and gender, although of considerable academic interest, are first and foremost personal issues. One way to better understand the topic, then, is to review the lives of individuals who have dealt with questions of sex and gender in their own lives. This chapter contains, therefore, a number of biographical sketches of such individuals. The chapter also contains descriptions of a variety of organizations that are interested in specific aspects of the topic, such as intersexuality, transsexualism, women's issues, and LGBT (lesbian, gay, bisexual, and transgender) problems.

Accord Alliance

Accord Alliance is an organization concerned with approaches for enhancing individuals affected by disorders of sex development (DSD) and their families and friends. The organization

---

Sen. Barbara Mikulski (D-MD) (center) speaks in support of the Paycheck Fairness Act during a news conference with Sen. Barbara Boxer (D-CA), Sen. Dianne Feinstein (D-CA), Sen. Al Franken (D-MN), Sen. Debbie Stabenow (D-MI) and Sen. Patty Murray (D-WA) in the Lyndon B. Johnson Room at the U.S. Capitol in Washington, D.C., on May 23, 2012. The senators were joined by representatives of the American Civil Liberties Union, the American Association of University Women, the National Women's Law Center, and the National Partnership for Women and Families. (Chip Somodevilla/Getty Images)

works with patients and their families, health care professionals, clinicians, support groups, and researchers to improve care
of individuals with DSD. Accord Alliance is an offspring of the
Intersex Society of North America (ISNA), founded in 1993
by Cheryl Chase, herself a DSD individual, to help such individuals deal with the shame, secrecy, and unwanted surgical procedures often endured by those with DSD. In 2008,
ISNA acknowledged that some of its policies and practices had
drawn complaints from individuals with DSD, researchers in
the field, and others who would otherwise be clients of ISNA.
The organization decided to work for the formation of a new
organization, Accord Alliance, with a more promising opportunity to provide the kind of support for DSD individuals that
they needed. ISNA transferred all of its assets and support to
the new group. Accord Alliance is a hosted project of the Tides
Center, an organization founded in 1976 for the purpose of
funding young nonprofit organizations in a variety of fields,
such as the environment, health care, labor issues, immigrant
rights, LGBT rights, women's rights, and human rights.

Among the alliance's activities have been:

- Development of a model of care and guidelines for the training and support of interdisciplinary health care teams and
aides for families and DSD individuals
- Cohosting of a conference on DSD Research and Quality
Improvement at the University of Michigan in 2009
- Expanding and improving the organization's website to
provide better information for patients, their families, clinicians, and researchers
- Production of an informational video about the care and
treatment of DSD for use with the general public
- Creation of a teacher's kit for use in college-level courses on
intersex and DSD history and current treatment options

Arguably the most important products of ISNA's and the alliance's work have been two publications, *Clinical Guidelines for*

the Management of Disorders of Sex Development in Childhood and *Handbook for Parents.* The former publication is designed to provide the best available scientific information currently available on the diagnosis and treatment of child with DSD. It includes information on the recommended makeup of inter-disciplinary teams for dealing with DSD, treatment protocols for babies born with the condition and for older children di-agnosed with DSD, information about possible surgical pro-cedures, suggestions for counseling with parents and children, ways of reducing emotional stress and stigma associated with DSD, and extended print and electronic references on the topic.

The *Handbook for Parents* is directed at the families of DSD individuals, covering topics such as background information on the condition, ways of talking with children about DSD at various ages and stages of development, involvement of family and friends, answers to common questions about DSD, and a variety of resources that provide additional information about the condition.

American Association of University Women

The American Association of University Women (AAUW) traces its origins to a meeting held in Boston on November 28, 1881, led by Marion Talbot and Ellen Richards and involv-ing 15 alumnae from eight other colleges. The purpose of the meeting was to discuss educational needs and opportunities for women in institutions of higher education in the United States. That meeting led two months later to the formation of the Association of Collegiate Alumnae, predecessor of today's AAUW. The organization's stated purpose was to work toward "practical education work, for collection and publication of statistical and other information concerning education, and in general, for the maintenance of high standards of education."

AAUW currently claims a membership of more than 150,000 members in 1,500 communities nationwide. Its activities are organized largely around nine major programs: research, campus leadership, STEM (science, technology, engineering, and math) education, public policy, case support, educational funding, global connections, member leadership, and salary negotiation. The public policy program, for example, uses lobbying and grassroots efforts to work for educational and economic equity for women in programs of higher education. The salary negotiation program makes use of two workshops, AAUW Start Smart and AAUW Work Smart, to provide women with the skills needed to gain fair and equitable salary and benefit agreements during employment and negotiations and to retain those benefits during their work career.

AAUW also organizes much of its work around seven themes: advocacy, campus, career and workplace, community, education, leadership, and economic justice. Some of the organization's activities in the field of advocacy, for example, center on education and information about the current national election cycle, reviews of settings in which equal pay battles were successful and unsuccessful, tracking the status of issues of interest to women at the state level, and a review of Native Women Equal Pay Day efforts. The career and workplace campaign includes discussions of and information about work–family related issues faced by women, issues of sexism on college campuses, the work of salary negotiators, proper procedures in writing résumés and cover letters, and gender bias in film making.

On its web page, AAUW offers a dozen ways of becoming involved in the organization's activities and the battle for women's rights: taking action online, sharing issues on Facebook, making a donation, "getting the fact," telling your school to join the AAUW community, joining a student organization, hosting an event, supporting AAUW, joining the AAUW national community, joining the Younger Women's Task Force, connecting with a local branch of AAUW, and collaborating with the national organization.

In addition to a mission statement, vision statement, and value promise, AAUW has announced a diversity statement that says that the "AAUW values and seeks a diverse membership. There shall be no barriers to full participation in this organization on the basis of gender, race, creed, age, sexual orientation, national origin, disability, or class."

Harry Benjamin (1885–1986)

Benjamin was a German-born endocrinologist and sexologist who is often regarded as the first person to recognize transsexualism as a legitimate medical problem. He was also the first person to differentiate transsexualism from homosexuality and transvestism, two other phenomena with which transsexualism is often confused. He is said to have been introduced to the issue of transsexualism by the famous sex researcher Alfred Kinsey in 1948. During his studies on human sexuality, Kinsey had come into contact with a male child who expressed a desire to become a female. The boy had apparently felt that he was actually a girl since his earliest days of consciousness and was eager to take whatever steps were needed to make the transition. Instead of rejecting the boy's expressed feelings, as would many of his colleagues at the time have done, Benjamin began treating the boy with estrogen, in the hopes of inducing a greater sense of confidence in the child. He eventually arranged for the boy to travel to Germany for the purpose of having reconstructive surgery to achieve his wishes.

This initial experience had a profound effect on Benjamin's research outlook, convincing him that the condition he had seen in the young boy was neither unique nor necessarily pathological. Instead, it was a phenomenon that probably occurred more commonly among humans than had previously been recognized, and he decided to commit his research to a better understanding of the characteristics of transsexualism and of ways in which the condition can be handled by medical professionals.

As a result of his studies, Benjamin produced a number of important research papers and books that ultimately revolutionized the study and treatment of transsexuality. Among these works were articles such as "Transsexualism and Transvestism as Psychosomatic and Somatopsychic Syndrome" (1954), "Nature and Management of Transsexualism, with a Report on Thirty-one Operated Cases" (1964), "Clinical Aspects of Transsexualism in the Male and Female" (1964), "Transsexualism, Its Nature and Therapy" (1964), and "Transsexualism" (with C. L. Ihlenfeld; 197), and the books *The Transsexual Phenomenon; a Scientific Report on Transsexualism and Sex Conversion in the Human Male and Female* (1966) and *The Transsexual Phenomenon* (1967).

Harry Benjamin was born in Berlin, Germany, on January 12, 1885. His father, Julius, was a prosperous stockbroker originally a member of the Jewish faith, who had converted to Lutheranism, a religion in which his son was raised. Harry expressed an interest in becoming a doctor, a passion for helping people deal with their physical problems that was to remain with him throughout his life. Benjamin was enrolled for his secondary education at the Königliches Wilhelm Gymnasium, a school popular with the children of the nobility. However, he left the school at the age of 15 and briefly served as an apprentice to a house physician at one of the Berlin opera houses where, as legend has it, he treated the famous tenor Enrico Caruso for a throat condition and had an opportunity to dance with his idol, Geraldine Farrar.

Benjamin then continued his studies in premedicine at the universities of Berlin and Rostock before completing this training at the University of Tübingen in 1912. His doctoral dissertation there dealt with the problem of tuberculosis. Benjamin later commented on his brief introduction to sexual issues by Magnus Hirschfeld, but spent essentially no time thinking about or working on that field during the early years of his career.

Benjamin's career took a critical turn in 1913 when he set off for the United States to work with a doctor who had claimed to have found a cure for tuberculosis, Benjamin's special field of interest at the time. On his return trip to Europe from the United States, his ocean liner was stopped in the middle of the Atlantic by British ships, and he was given the choice of being transported to England as an enemy or alien or returning to the United States. He chose the latter option and remained in the United States for the rest of his life, albeit making a number of visits to Germany during his lifetime. For the rest of his working life, Benjamin spent his summers at an office in San Francisco and the rest of the year at his office in New York City.

Benjamin's greatest contribution to the study of transsexualism is probably expressed in *The Transsexual Phenomenon*. In that book, he took the position that the traditional approach to gender dysphoria, psychotherapy, was wrong. Based on his then-extensive experiences, he claimed that therapy almost never solved the inner conflict felt by those who believed their biological sex and gender were incongruent. He argued, instead, for the use of hormonal treatments to help people develop into the sex with which they feel comfortable and, for those who were good candidates for the procedures involved, surgery to continue the process of transition.

In 1978, Benjamin was one of the founding members of the Harry Benjamin International Gender Dysphoria Association, an organization created to promote communication and discourse among professionals involved in the field of transgender health. One of the organization's first and most important accomplishments was publication of its "Standard of Care" for individuals dealing with gender issues. That document has been updated periodically ever since that time. In 2007, the organization changed its name to the World Professional Association for Transgender Health.

Mary Calderone (1904–1998)

In her obituary in the *New York Times*, medical writer Jane E. Brody wrote about Calderone: "Dr. Calderone did more than any other individual to convince both the medical profession and the public that human sexuality goes far beyond the sex act." Calderone took the liberated (at the time) view that sexual activity among humans was not a "dirty" subject that should be kept from polite (or any other type of) conversation. It was a healthy, positive topic that should be recognized as a normal part of every human life. One of her great accomplishments came when she convinced the American Medical Association in 1964 to change its policy on the release of contraception information by doctors to their patients. She is perhaps best known for her commitment to the provision of sex education classes for students at all levels of education, a philosophy she was to carry out most effectively through the Sex Education and Information Council of the United States (SEICUS), which she founded in 1964.

Born Mary Steichen in Paris on July 1, 1904, Calderone was the daughter of the noted photographer Edward Steichen and Clara Smith Steichen, and the niece of poet Carl Sandburg. Her biographers have suggested that such notable family members and her upbringing as a Quaker may have contributed to her lifelong commitment to a liberal lifestyle and open-minded approach to human problems. The Steinchen family returned to the United States annually so that Edward could exhibit and sell his photographs, and in 1914, the threat posed by the start of World War I prompted the family to remain in this country. Mary was enrolled at the Brearley School in New York City, where she had been sent to live by her parents. One of the important contacts she made in New York was physician Leopold Stieglitz, who often took Mary with him as he conducted his daily visits to patients. This experience proved to be a spark that was later to be expressed in Mary's own decision to pursue medicine as a career.

At first, however, she had other plans. After earning her degree in chemistry from Vassar College in 1925, she decided to enroll at the American Laboratory Theater, with hopes of becoming a professional actor. By 1933, she had given up hope of making a success in the theater and, at the same time, began divorce proceedings from her husband, W. Lon Martin, whom she had married in 1926. She decided to turn to her second love, medicine, enrolling at the University of Rochester School of Medicine, from which she received her MD in 1939. She then continued her studies at Columbia University, from which she received her master's in public health in 1942. During her time at Columbia, Mary met Dr Frank Calderone, then a district health officer for the city of New York. The two were married in 1941 and later had two children. Frank later served as chief administrative officer of the World Health Organization.

In 1953, Mary Calderone took a position as medical director of Planned Parenthood Federation of America (PPFA), a nonprofit organization that offers a wide variety of reproductive health services throughout the United States. Originally established by Margaret Sanger, her sister Ethel Byrne, and Fania Mindell, PPFA was intended as a source of information about birth control for poor women in New York City. During her tenure at the organization, however, Calderone came to realize from questions she was asked that women of all classes were poorly informed about the nature of human sexuality in general, and that the organization faced a much broader challenge than simply providing birth control information and apparatus.

To better meet these needs, Calderone left PPFA in 1964 to establish SEICUS. She conceived of the new organization as a mechanism by which many groups of individuals, including school teachers and administrators, sex educators, physicians, social activists, and parents, could band together to better understand and develop the materials needed to provide young people in particular about the nature of human sexuality and, as its mission statement said, "to establish man's sexuality as a health entity." Calderone served as president and executive director of SEICUS from the organization's founding until 1969, when she resigned as president but remained as executive director. She finally retired from leadership positions in the organization in 1982. She continued to write and speak about issues of sexuality in a variety of settings, however, almost until her death on October 24, 1998, in Kennett Square, Pennsylvania.

Calderone was the author of a number of books on sexuality, including *Abortion in the United States*, *Release from Sexual Tensions*, *Manual of Family Planning and Contraceptive Practices*, *Sexual Health and Family Planning*, *Sexuality and Human Values*, *Questions and Answers about Love and Sex*, *The Family Book about Sexuality* (with Eric Johnson), and *Talking with Your Child about Sex*.

Roberta Cowell (1918–2011)

For anyone interested in the history of transgender persons, an interesting question is who the first person to undergo transition from one sex to another was. The answer to that question can be very difficult to answer, however, as it is not easy to decide precisely what type of transition in which one is interested. Certainly, however, one name that would appear on that list is Roberta Cowell, who died in abject poverty and essentially unknown to the world at the age of 93 on October 11, 2011, in public housing in London.

Roberta Cowell was born as Robert Marshall Cowell in London on April 8, 1918. He was one of three children born to Major General Sir Ernest Marshall Cowell, KBE, CB, and Dorothy Elizabeth Miller. Sir Ernest was a surgeon in the Royal Army Medical Corps in both World War I and World War II and knighted for his services to the country by King George VI in 1944. As a child, Robert was especially interested in mechanical devices, and, at the Whitgift School in Croydon that he attended, he belonged to a club where young boys were allowed to drive cars and motorcycles on school grounds. He left school at the age of 16 to take a job as an apprentice at General Aircraft Limited. He left soon after to join the Royal Air Force (RAF), a decision that proved to be misguided when his instructors discovered how easily he became airsick. He was discharged from the service and chose to enroll at University

College London, where he majored in engineering. It was there that he met his future wife Diana, who was also studying engineering.

While still a student, Cowell became increasingly interested in motor car racing, often sneaking into an event and volunteering to work as a member of a race crew. He also began driving in races, culminating in his participation in the 1936 Antwerp Grand Prix.

With the outbreak of World War II, Cowell joined the Royal Army Service Corps with the rank of second lieutenant. Six months later, he married Diana. Cowell once again applied to serve in the RAF, and this time he was accepted. He served with honor during the war prior to being shot down over Germany and captured by enemy troops. He remained a prisoner for five months before being liberated by advancing Russian troops. He was returned to Great Britain in April 1945.

After the war, Cowell returned to motor car racing and participated in events such as the Brighton Speed Trials and the Grand Prix at Rouen-Les-Essarts. However, he began experiencing serious emotional problems associated with his war experiences, problems that eventually led to his divorce from Diana. His divorce was the result at least partly because of Diana's objections to his wearing her clothes. He also began counseling sessions with a psychiatrist about his subconscious feelings that he was, in reality, a woman in a man's body. He later wrote in his autobiography that "The feminine side of my nature, which all my life I had known of and severely repressed, was very much more fundamental and deep-rooted than I had supposed."

By 1950, Cowell had begun to take estrogen to initiate the process of transitioning to a woman. He had read about the process involved in a 1946 book by physician Michael Dillon, *Self: A Study in Ethics and Endocrinology.* Cowell decided to meet with Dillon who, at that meeting, revealed that he himself had transitioned, from a woman to a man. As a medical student, Dillon agreed to initiate the surgical procedures required to bring about Cowell's own transition, an orchidectomy. In 1951, Cowell completed the transition process when British surgeon Sir Harold Gillies performed a vaginoplasty, the first such successful operation in British history. Cowell then took the name of Roberta Elizabeth Marshall Cowell, a name change that was duly recorded on her birth certificate, another first in British history.

In her new role as a woman, Cowell continued to own and fly an airplane and to own and drive race cars, sometimes competing in formal events. The business she had operated as a man had failed, however, and her only major source of income was payment for articles about her life and transition, and royalties from her autobiography, *Roberta Cowell's Story*. As she grew older, she continued to own her own automobiles, but was less able to drive or care for them. She also developed a number of medical problems that made it difficult for her to care for herself. For the last few years of her life, she lived in subsidized housing with few friends. She died in London on October 11, 2011, with no public notice of her life or death. Only six people attended her funeral.

Simone de Beauvoir (1908–1986)

Simone de Beauvoir is generally regarded as one of the leading feminist writers of the 20th century, and one of the founders of the second wave of feminism. She is best known for her monumental work, *The Second Sex*, published in 1949. That book consists of two volumes of 978 pages in three and four parts consisting of three, five, and three chapters, and of four, six, four, and one chapter, respectively. Those chapters deal with topics such as biological data, the psychoanalytical point of view, ancient history, religious views, "the everlasting disappointment of women," literary views of women, childhood, the girl, mothers, social life, women's situation and character, the women in love, and mystical aspects of womanhood. The book was translated into English in 1953, but was poorly received as being an inadequate expression of de Beauvoir's thoughtful prose. A second English translation published in 2009 was better received and recognized as a historic contribution to feminist thought.

Reviews of *The Second Sex* ranged from the offhanded rejection of scholars like Alfred Kinsey (who said that the book was "interesting," but that it contained no new data about human sexuality) to glowing from others like Camille Paglia (who praised the book as "the supreme work of modern feminism"). Some critics have argued that de Beauvoir's work was to a significant extent the primary motivation for other great works of the second wave of feminism, including Betty Friedan's *The Feminine Mystique*, Kate Millett's *Sexual Politics*, Germaine Greer's *The Female Eunuch*, and Paglia's own *Sexual Personae*. The Vatican was less enthusiastic about the book, placing it on its list of prohibited books, where it remains today.

De Beauvoir was the lifelong companion of French philosopher Jean-Paul Sartre, with whom she maintained both a romantic and an intellectual relationship for more than 50 years. Although she never thought of herself as a philosopher, she played a critical role in describing, explaining, and promoting Sartre's ideas. Today, her writings on his works are regarded as significant philosophical contributions in their own right. In addition to *The Second Sex*, de Beauvoir wrote more than two dozen novels, short-story collections, and four autobiographical books such as *L'Invitée* (*She Came to Stay*), *Le Sang des autres* (*The Blood of Others*), *Tous les hommes sont mortels* (*All Men Are Mortal*), *Les Mandarins* (*The Mandarins*), *Les Belles Images* (*The Beautiful Pictures*), and *Le Femme Rompue* (*The Woman Destroyed*).

De Beauvoir was also very much interested in and involved with a variety of political issues, some of which were inspired by her experiences when living in occupied France during the early years of World War II. Those experiences prompted her to begin thinking and writing about the social and moral consequences of various political positions, Communism in particular. In 1945, she, Sartre, and their friends created the political journal *Les Temps Modernes*, which she edited and to which she contributed articles such as "Moral Idealism and Political Realism," "Existentialism and Popular Wisdom," and "Eye for an Eye."

Simone-Ernestine-Lucie-Marie Bertrand de Beauvoir was born in Paris on January 9, 1908, to Georges Bertrand de Beauvoir and Françoise de Beauvoir (née Brasseur). Her father was a legal secretary who once had had ambitions as an actor, and his mother was the daughter of a wealthy French banker. As a child, Simone was strongly influenced by the religious view of her devoutly Catholic mother. But she had a "crisis of faith" at the age of 14 and decided to become an atheist, a position that she held for the rest of her life. Beauvoir attended a private Catholic school for girls, the Institut Adeline Désir, where she passed the baccalauréat exams in mathematics and philosophy in 1925. She then continued her studies in mathematics at the Institut Catholique, and in literature at the Institut Sainte-Marie. In 1926, she sat for and passed the examinations for the certificate in higher studies in French literature and Latin.

In 1927, de Beauvoir matriculated at the Sorbonne, where she majored in philosophy. At the Sorbonne, she also passed the examinations for certificates in history of philosophy, general philosophy, Greek, logic ethics, sociology, and psychology. In 1929, she sat for the prestigious philosophy agrégation examination, where she finished second to Sartre. It was during this period that she came to know and became close friends with the man who was eventually to be her lifelong companion.

Upon completion of her academic studies, de Beauvoir accepted an appointment to teach at the Lycée Montgrand in Marseilles, where she remained for a year. She then took a position teaching literature and philosophy at the Lycée Jeanne d'Arc in Rouen. It was at Rouen that she encountered one of her first experiences with official concerns about her ideas when she was officially reprimanded for her feminist views as well as her outspoken pacifist views. In 1936, de Beauvoir left Rouen to take a position at the Lycée Molière in Paris, where she taught until discharged by Germany army officials after the fall of Paris. She was able to find another teaching job, however, but was discharged once more on the complaint of "lewd sexual behavior" by a parent of one of her students. De Beauvoir always rejected the legitimacy of that charge, claiming the parent was unhappy with her political views. But she never again returned to teaching.

As they grew older, de Beauvoir and Sartre withdrew from most social and political activities and worked and lived with a small group of personal friends. After Sartre died in 1980, she wrote of her life with the great philosopher in her book *La Cérémonie des Adieux* (*Adieux: A Farewell to Sartre*). De Beauvoir herself died in Paris on April 14, 1986.

dsdfamilies

dsdfamilies (expressed in all lower case format) is an online service operated by a small group of families of individuals with DSD, which they define as "Differences/Disorders of Sex Development." The service is not a membership organization, but an activity designed to provide information and discussion about the condition. Specifically, the website's objective is to provide "access to easy-to-understand medical information, and provide a regular flow of first-hand experience." Founders of the organization say that they chose the name they did because they wanted to focus on issues involving the whole family of an individual with DSD, not just that specific person. The organization attempts to achieve this objective by providing information from as well as conversations with clinicians concerning "the medical care we like, dislike, need and would like to see improved."

dsdfamilies first began operation in July 2011 and is advised by an editorial board of experts in the field of DSD from the

United Kingdom, the United States, Belgium, and Australia. Among its most useful and interesting publications are guest editorials on topics such as "Becoming a DSD Dad," "Here's to a Happy Engagement," "Growing Up and then Adding DSD to the Mix," "The Real Difference," and "What We Wish Our Parents Knew."

In addition to educational and interaction components on its website, dsdfamilies also provides access to a variety of brochures, books, blogs, and other print and electronic resources, as well as listings of meetings, conferences, and other events at which DSD is a major topic of discussion. Links to other organizations are also available on the web page.

Elagabalus (203/204–222)

Elagabalus ruled as emperor of Rome from 218 to 222. He is probably best known today for his exotic sexual behaviors as well as his almost totally ineffectual years as a ruler of the world's then greatest empire. During the first 14 years of his lifetime, Elagabalus was known by his birth name of Varius Avitus Bassianus. Then, upon elevation to the title of emperor, he took the name of Marcus Aurelius Antoninus Augustus. It was only after his death in 222 that he was more commonly referred to as the Emperor Elagabalus.

The story of Elagabalus's life is as convoluted and uncertain as that of many other prominent Romans of the day. He is thought to have been born in 203 or 204 in the city of Emesa in modern-day Syria. He was the son of Sextus Varius Marcellus, who had served as a Roman senator during the reign of the emperor Caracalla, and Julia Soaemias, widow of the consul Julius Avitus. It was through his mother's connections that Elagabalus was to achieve rapid promotion through the Roman hierarchy to become emperor, a post that he held, however, for only four years.

At the time of Elagabalus's birth, Rome was ruled by Emperor Caracalla, who had ruled since 198. By 217, however, the emperor had begun to lose favor among the general citizenry as well and, more importantly, among the legions. This loss of favor resulted in his assassination by members of his troops in 2017, and the accession of one of his subordinates, Macrinus.

It was at this point that Elagabalus's family became involved in the question of succession to the Roman throne. His grandmother, Julia Maesa, held Macrinus responsible for her sister's death and began to plot to place her grandson on the throne. She put out word that Elagabalus was the bastard son of Caracalla and, therefore, rightful ruler of the empire. Maesa's plot came to fulfillment on the night of May 15, 218, when a rogue troop of legionnaires declared Elagabalus to be the rightful ruler of Rome and led a march against Macrinus. Two weeks later, the revolution was complete, Macrinus was executed, and Elagabalus was installed as emperor.

Rome soon found itself uncomfortable with the lifestyle of the new emperor. Elagabalus brought with him the religious traditions and observances of his native region, much to the discomfort and disapproval of Rome's citizens. His personal behavior also raised questions about his suitability to serve as emperor. He is said to have explored the possibility of changing his sex and becoming a woman. He had the hair on his body removed and frequently appeared in public in women's clothing and wearing women's makeup. He is also said to have posed as a prostitute, appearing in a window waving a curtain, a common practice among such women, as well as exposing himself naked in public settings. Although he was married at least five times to a woman, he obviously much preferred the company of men and declared at least four of his palace attendants as his husbands. Overall, his public behavior was so problematic that at least one of his modern biographers refers to the emperor throughout his biography as "she" and "her," based on the assumption that Elagabalus was at the very least a transvestite and, more likely, a transsexual.

The emperor's reign came to an end on March 11, 222, when a group of soldiers apparently decided they could no longer accept the outrageous behaviors—sexually, religiously, and culturally—of the emperor and killed him and his mother. They then beheaded the two victims and dragged their naked bodies through the streets of Rome. A number of his male lovers and supporters suffered similar fates.

Gender Spectrum

Gender Spectrum is a nonprofit agency based in the San Francisco Bay area whose purpose it is to create a "gender-inclusive" world for all children and youth. It works toward that goal by providing educational and counseling services to help people understand a broad and more comprehensive sense of the meaning of gender among human beings.

Founder and chair of the board of directors of Gender Spectrum is Stephanie Brill who has been engaged in LGBT issues for many years. In 1993, she founded MAIA, an agency for assisting LGBT individuals with problems of pregnancy, parenthood, and family issues. She is the author of *The Queer Parent's Primer: A Lesbian and Gay Families' Guide to Navigating the Straight World* (2001), *The Essential Guide to Lesbian Conception, Pregnancy, and Birth* (with Kim Toevs; 2002), *The New Essential Guide to Lesbian Conception, Pregnancy, and Birth* (2006), *The Transgender Child: A Handbook for Families and Professionals* (2008), and *The Transgender Teen* (with Lisa Kenney; 2016). She founded Gender Spectrum in 2007.

Gender Spectrum deals with a complete range of topics and issues of interest to transgender children, adolescents, and their families. The primary topics treated on its website are parenting and family, teens, education, medical issues, mental health, legal questions, social services, and faith and its relationship to transgenderism. The website provides extensive and detailed discussions of each of these topics. In the case of parenting and family, for example, it presents information and views on ways in which individuals can better understand the concept of gender; general parenting considerations; the characteristics

of affirming and unaffirming parenting practices; ways of recognizing when transgender concerns are and are not "passing phases" in a child's life; ways in which a parent can deal
with his or her own personal feelings about a child's struggle
with transgenderism; considerations for other family members
and children who may not be dealing with transgender issues
themselves; involving members of the extended family; privacy
and safety considerations; steps in the process of transitioning; dealing with school, church, sport, camp, and related issues; and medical, mental health, and legal factors involved in
transitioning.

Some of the mechanisms Gender Spectrum provides to
those who seek its help include:

- Training sessions for organizations and institutions seeking
  guidance for ways of understanding and helping their members and clients with transgender issues

- A monthly national call-in support group for individuals
  not located in the Bay Area, where problems, ideas, concerns, and opinions about transgender issues can be shared
  with other individuals

- The Child and Adolescent Gender Center, a collaboration
  between the University of California at San Francisco's Be-
  nioff Children's Hospital and a number of local community agents working to improve the health and well-being of
  transgender and gender-expansive children

- The Lounge, a setting in which transgender and questioning
  children and adolescents can meet and share experiences,
  information, and questions with each other and with professionals in the field

- Spanish Language Support Group, designed for trans individuals whose primary language may not be English, through
  which many of the organization's efforts can be channeled

- Bay Area Parent/Caregiver Support Group, which provides an opportunity for such individuals to get together

and offer help and support to each other on issues of common concern

- A research component, in which the center attempts to match researchers in the field of transgenderism with individuals who may be willing and interested in participating in such research projects

The Gender Spectrum website is also an excellent source of articles on all aspects of transgenderism such as "What Is Gender?," "Transgender and Gender Non-Conforming Students: Your Rights at School," "FAQ for Transgender and Gender-Nonconforming Youth," "Changing Names State-by-State Guide," "Understanding the New Passport Gender Change Policy," "TLC's Guide to Changing California & Federal Identity Documents to Match Your Gender Identity," "Prohibition of Gender Bullying in Schools," "Title IX Gender Protections," and "LGBTQ Legal Issues in Schools: An Overview." The website also maintains a number of blogs on transgender issues and a site for listing one's personal stories about transgenderism.

GLBTQ Legal Advocates & Defenders

GLBTQ Legal Advocates & Defenders (GLAD) was founded in 1978 by attorney John Ward in response to a series of "sting" operations by the Boston police department against men purportedly carrying out "lewd and illegal" behaviors at the Boston Library. Ward filed a suit against the city on behalf of a man apprehended in one such sting who was later found not guilty of the crime for which he was arrested. The organization's original name was Gay & Lesbian Advocates & Defenders, by which it was known until it adopted its current name in February 2016 to better reflect its broader range of legal concerns that include both transgender individuals and those questioning their sexual orientation.

Over its 40 plus years of operation, GLAD has won an impressive number and variety of court victories, such as winning the right of Rhode Island high school senior Aaron Fricke to bring his male companion to the school's senior prom in 1980, successfully defending the constitutionality of Massachusetts's gay rights bill in 1983, filing a suit against a dentist for refusing to treat a man with AIDS in 1985, winning the first honorable discharge for a gay service member in 1986, coauthoring the Massachusetts domestic partnership bill in 1992, winning a censorship battle against a local school district that tried to prevent photo exhibit on gay and lesbian families in 1996, successfully defending an eighth-grade transgender girl's right to wear female attire at her school, obtaining legislative approval for the nation's first same-sex marriage act in 2003, winning protection for transgender antidiscrimination policies in Vermont in 2004, gaining a victory for transgender individuals in the U.S. Tax Court in 2010, winning a case in New Hampshire against cyberbullying of gay and lesbian students in 2012, achieving success in a four-year court battle against the U.S. Defense of Marriage Act (DOMA) in 2013, gaining approval for the asylum admission of Ugandan gay rights activist John Abdallah Wambere in 2014, fighting denial of same-sex spouse benefits by Walmart in 2014, and leading the battle for approval of same-sex marriage at the U.S. Supreme Court in 2015. (For a complete history of GLAD cases, see http://www .glad.org/about/history.)

GLAD's work is currently divided into four major categories, AIDS, civil rights, transgender rights, and youth rights. In addition to its litigation work, the organization advocates before legislative and administrative agencies on behalf of gay men, lesbians, bisexuals, transgender individuals, and people questioning their sexual orientation. It also includes a public education component in its work. The GLAD website is a rich source of resources on all aspects of the rights of LGBTQ individuals, including a collection of books, brochures, pamphlets, and online resources on topics such as anti-LGBT discrimination, criminal justice system and prisons, DOMA, employment, hate crimes and violence, health care, HIV/AIDS, immigration, marriage, parents and kids, relationships, trans-gender rights, and youth.

Magnus Hirschfeld (1868–1935)

Hirschfeld was a German Jewish physician and sexologist who became one of the first individuals to treat sexual issues as a legitimate topic of scientific research. Much, although by no means all, of his research was directed at issues of same-sex rela-tionships. He himself was a gay man, and much of his writing, lectures, and organizational activities were directed at a better understanding and treatment of men and women who were attracted to the same sex. As a consequence of his research, he posited the existence of a "third sex" in addition to male and female that might include hermaphrodites, cross-dressers, and gay men and lesbians. In 1899, he published the first annual edition of the *Yearbook of Intermediate Sexual Types*, contain-ing research and opinion on the characteristics of "third sex" individuals. The book was published annually until 1923. In 1910, he also published one of the first scholarly papers on transvestism, *The Transvestites* (for a selection from this paper, see http://visuality.org/queer_sensibilities/wmst420_readings/magnus_hirschfeld.pdf).

In some respects, Hirschfeld's most important contribu-tion was the creation of the Institut für Sexualwissenschaft (IfS; Institute of Sexology or the Institute of Sex Research) in Berlin in 1919. The institute was designed to carry out origi-nal research on human sexuality. In addition, it maintained a very large library and archive and provided counseling on sexual and marriage issues. One of its main divisions was the Wissenschaftlich-humanitäres Komitee (WhK; Scientific-Humanitarian Committee), founded more than two decades earlier by Hirschfeld, publisher Max Spohr, lawyer Eduard Oberg, and writer Franz Joseph von Bülow. WhK was created to promote a more better understanding and more humane treatment of gay men, lesbians, and other sexual minorities.

It is generally regarded as the first gay rights organization in the world. The IfS, WhK, and other organizations created by Hirschfeld were eventually destroyed by the German Nazi Party in the 1920s because of its strong objection to any form of nontraditional sexuality.

Magnus Hirschfeld was born on May 14, 1868, in Kolberg, Prussia, now Kotobrzeg, Poland, to Hermann and Frederika (Mann) Hirschfeld. The Hirschfelds were Ashkenazi Jews who had long resided in the region and were highly respected as patriots and scholars. Hermann Hirschfeld had studied under the eminent German virologist Rudolf Virchow, and had served as a physician in the first Schleswig War of 1848–1851 before settling in Kolberg.

Magnus developed a particular interest in issues of human sexuality as a young boy, eventually adopting the view that sexuality was a healthy and normal topic that could and should be studied and discussed along with other topics of scholarly interest. This view, however, stood in stark opposition to general cultural views of the time, reflecting a long Judaeo-Christian history, that sexual matters were not an appropriate topic of discussion in polite society, and certainly not a topic of interest for young children. Hirschfeld's position as an outsider in this regard was to persist through most of his life.

After completing his high school years in Kolberg in 1887, Hirschfeld matriculated at the University of Breslau, where he majored in the study of languages. After two years at Breslau, he transferred to the University of Strasbourg, where he enrolled in the pre-med program. In 1892, he was awarded his medical degree by the university, after which he traveled to the United States for an eight-month vacation that included a visit to the World's Columbian Exhibition in Chicago. At the end of that time, he returned to Germany, where he established an office of naturopathic medicine in Magdeburg, before finally setting up a permanent traditional practice in Berlin in 1896.

For the next 30 years, Hirschfeld divided his time between his medical practice and his organization, and social and political efforts on behalf of issues of sexuality. During this time, his work was constantly in conflict with generally accepted social, cultural, and political views of the German state, explicitly expressed in Paragraph 175 of the German Penal Code. Paragraph 175, first adopted in 1871, established severe penalties for many forms of nontraditional sexual behavior, including same-sex acts, prostitution, and bestiality. By some estimates, more than 140,000 individuals were convicted under this law until it was revoked in 1994.

Hirschfeld's status in Germany became increasingly precarious with the rise of National Socialism in the later 1920s and early 1930s. He was regularly attacked verbally and physically, and, by 1932, he no longer felt it was safe for him to remain in his homeland. On an international speaking tour in 1932, he decided not to return to Germany and went instead to Switzerland, where he settled in Zurich. Two years later he moved to Paris, hoping to recreate in France institutions similar to those he had lost in Germany. The IfS came to an inglorious end at about the same time, when members of the Nazi Party attacked and destroyed its buildings in Berlin and burnt essentially all of the institute's books and archival materials.

Hirschfeld's efforts to recreate his work in Paris never came to fruition, and, in 1934, he moved to Nice with plans to continue his efforts to do so there. He survived in his new home for less than two years, however, dying of a heart attack on May 14, 1935, his 67th birthday. The Magnus Hirschfeld Society, founded in 1982, was created to memorialize his work and that of the IfS, as well as to promote and conduct research on the history of sexology (http://magnus-hirschfeld.de/).

Joan of Arc (1412–1431)

Joan of Arc (Jeanne d'Arc) was a 15th-century woman who came to the aid of the French nation at a time in its history when its very survival was in peril. In 1429, she led an army that ended a year-long siege of the city of Orléans by English troops that marked a turning point in the war between the two countries. After achieving other military successes, she was captured by the English and handed over to the Roman Catholic Inquisition, which eventually found her guilty of heresy, based on her practice of wearing men's clothing.

Jeanne d'Arc was born on January 6, 1412, to a peasant family in at Domrémy in northeastern France. At the time, Domrémy was an isolated village in a portion of the country that had largely fallen under the control of English troops who had slowly built up a stranglehold around an ever-diminishing stretch of French-held territory. At the age of 13, she begin reporting having visitations in her father's garden from three saints, Catherine, Margaret, and Michael. At first, the saints only provided instructions in ways in which she could live a good and holy life. But eventually, they began telling her that it was her destiny to take command of a French army, drive the English out of her native land, and restore the French crown to the dauphin as Charles VII.

When she told her father of her visions, he warned Joan to ignore the saints' proscriptions as such acts would be far too dangerous for a young girl. Joan rejected her father's advice, however, and set out for Chinon, where the dauphin was in residence. Having been told in advance of Joan's mission, the dauphin disguised himself as a commoner upon her arrival to test her authenticity. She was able to pick him out of the crowd of observers, confirming in the dauphin's mind the legitimacy of her mission. After consultations between the two, the dauphin provided Joan with a battalion of fighters and sent her to Orléans to overcome the year-long siege of the city established by the English. In preparation for this mission, Joan cut her hair short and began wearing male (i.e., military) attire. Much discussion has occurred as to the reasons for her taking this action, one of which was almost certainly her efforts to avoid sexual molestation by her soldiers. In any case, she continued to present herself in male clothing throughout her brief career in the military. Her success in freeing Orléans from siege on

May 7, 1429, eventually earned her the sobriquet by which she is often known, the Maid of Orléans.

Over the next few months, Joan was involved in a series of military actions that were extraordinarily successful in driving the English from many regions they had previously occupied. This success made possible the coronation of the dauphin as King Charles VII in Reims on July 17, 1429, an event at which Joan was present. Rather than continuing their battle against the English, at this point, the French decided to sign a truce with the enemy, bringing armed conflict to an end for at least a few months. When the truce collapsed in May 1430, Joan once again went on the offensive against the English. On this occasion, however, she was less successful, and, in a battle outside the town of Compiègne, she was ambushed and captured.

Instead of simply holding Joan as a prisoner of war, the English turned her over to Pierre Cauchon, the bishop of Beauvais, a town that Joan had liberated from English rule some time earlier. Cauchon, in turn, decided to turn Joan over to the Inquisition for investigation of a charge of heresy. The charge was based on Joan's repeated use of men's clothing, even after she had been directed to appear before the court only in women's clothing. (Cauchon believed that obtaining a guilty verdict in this trial would invalidate Charles's claim to the French throne.) Joan was found guilty of heresy on May 30, 1431, and was burned at the stake on the same day.

Doubts about the legitimacy of the decision in Joan's trial began to arise almost as soon as she was executed. Those doubts rose to the level of formal indignation only a decade later when Joan's mother and Inquisitor-General Jean Bréhal asked Pope Callixtus III to convene a new trial for Joan. The pope initiated an investigation of this request in 1452, a process that led three years later to a formal appeal of the original verdict. An appellate court formed to consider the case eventually found Joan innocent of all charges against her on July 7, 1456, and indicted Cauchon for heresy in the case.

Joan's reputation continued to improve over the centuries until she was beatified by in 1909 by Pope Pius X and finally canonized as a saint by Pope Benedict XV in 1920.

Franklin Kameny (1925–2011)

Kameny has been described by a historian of gay and lesbian rights as "[o]ne of the most significant figures" in the American gay rights movement. Trained as an astronomer, Kameny became active in the gay and lesbian rights movement when he was fired from his job with the Army Map Service (now the Defense Mapping Agency) in January 1958 for being gay. He then spent the rest of his life working for gay and lesbian rights, largely in response to this action. Throughout his career, Kameny took a strong, confrontational approach in an effort to obtain equal rights for gay men and lesbians. In 1965, for example, he and Jack Nichols organized the first picket line around the White House in pushing for gay and lesbian rights. He is also credited with having created the slogan "Gay is good" in 1968. In 1971, Kameny became the first openly gay man to run for national public office when he ran for the post of nonvoting delegate to the U.S. House of Representatives from the District of Columbia.

Kameny was born in New York City on May 21, 1925. His parents were Polish and Austro-Hungarian Jews. He taught himself to read by the age of 4, and two years later had decided that he wanted to become an astronomer. He entered Queens College at the age of 15, but his education was interrupted by World War II. At the war's conclusion, he returned to Queens and earned his BS in physics in 1948. He then continued his education at Harvard College, from which he received his master's degree in astronomy in 1949 and his PhD in astronomy in 1956. After a year of teaching at Georgetown University, Kameny took a position with the Army Map Service. He served in that position for only a brief period of time before being fired for being gay. Not given to yielding on matters of principle,

Kameny then began a long series of court battles to regain his job. His fundamental premise throughout this fight was that his employer (the U.S. government) had no right to inquire into his personal life unless it interfered with his work, a claim the government never made. No organization, including the American Civil Liberties Union, was willing to support Kameny's position, and when his case finally reached the Supreme Court, he had to write his own brief. The Court declined in March 1961 to hear Kameny's case, and he decided that his life thenceforward would have a new direction: he was going to become a gay activist.

One of his first acts was to organize (with Nichols) a Washington chapter of New York City's Mattachine Society. Kameny began to put into practice his attitudes about the gay rights issue. It was necessary not for gays to change and adapt to an oppressive society, he argued, but to help educate the nongay world and help them to recognize the legitimacy of the gay rights cause. He outlined his position in an article he wrote for *The Ladder* in 1965 when he said

> We ARE right; those who oppose us are both morally and factually wrong. . . . We must DEMAND our rights boldly, not beg cringingly for mere privileges, and not be satisfied with the crumbs tossed to us.

Kameny died at his home in Washington D.C., on October 11, 2011. In 2002, the Harvard Gay and Lesbian Caucus gave its lifetime Achievement Award to Kameny for his contributions to the gay and lesbian rights movement. Kameny has also been honored by the naming of a minor planet, Frankkameny, and dedication of a memorial headstone at the Washington Congressional Cemetery that contains the phrase "Gay is good."

Alfred Kinsey (1894–1956)

In 1948, Kinsey and his colleagues, Wardell Pomery and Clyde E. Martin, published one of the most significant books in the history of sexuality, *Sexual Behavior in the Human Male*. Five years later, he, Pomeroy, Martin, and Paul H. Gebhard followed up with a companion volume on *Sexual Behavior in the Human Female*. Both books had a profound influence on the way in which Americans and others throughout the world viewed and understood human sexual behavior. Kinsey's research has also been the subject of scathing criticisms, not only because of the subject matter with which the books deal, but also about methodological issues involving the conduct of the research on which the books are based.

Alfred Charles Kinsey was born on June 23, 1894, in Hoboken, New Jersey. His mother was Sarah Ann (née Charles) Kinsey, a homemaker, and his father, Alfred Seguine Kinsey, an instructor of shop practice at Stevens Institute of Technology in Hoboken. One of Kinsey's biographers has called his father a "domestic autocrat" and a devout Methodist who required his family to attend church three times on every Sunday. He was also a committed prohibitionist. Young Alfred was a sickly child who suffered from rickets, rheumatic fever, and typhoid fever, none of which were adequately treated because of the family's limited financial resources.

The Kinsey family moved to Orange, New Jersey, where, in spite of his poor health, he became active in a variety of outdoor activities, eventually earning an Eagle Scout ranking with the Boy Scouts in 1913, one of the first young men to receive that title in the Scout organization. He attended Columbia High School, in Maplewood, New Jersey, where he developed a special interest in biology, botany, and zoology, In fact, Kinsey later mentioned his high school biology teacher, Natalie Roeth, as being a strong influence on his eventual decision to pursue a career in the biological sciences.

With high school graduation looming, Kinsey's father insisted that he set aside his plans to study biology and enroll instead at Stevens to study engineering. Kinsey followed his father's wishes but, after two years, found that engineering held no interest for him. He transferred to Bowdoin College in

Maine, where he was finally able to begin courses in the field
that had captured his heart, biology. That decision caused a rift
between father and son that apparently never healed; the senior
Kinsey, in fact, refused even to attend his son's graduation from
Bowdoin in 1916.

Kinsey then decided to continue his studies at Harvard University, where he chose the study of gall wasps for his doctoral
thesis. His extensive and intensive research on this organism
eventually earned him his doctor of science degree from Harvard
in 1919 and something of a reputation as an expert on this very
limited subject. It is reported that, by the end of the 20th century, about a quarter of all the insect specimens in the American
Museum of Natural History are gall wasps collected by Kinsey.

Upon completion of his doctoral program at Harvard,
Kinsey accepted an offer to join the biology faculty at Indiana
University in Bloomington. Over the next two decades, he
devoted his attention to teaching responsibilities in that department and to researching and writing about gall wasps. In
1938, an event occurred that was to change his life. A group
of women from the university's Association of Women petitioned university president Herman B. Wells for a course on
marriage for students who were already married or who anticipated being married in the near future. Wells approved of the
proposal, but imposed some severe restrictions on its conduct.
He said that only married students could attend the course, it
could enroll seniors only, and there would be no advance publicity. Kinsey, as was his wont, ignored all of these restrictions,
and the course turned out to be very popular. In the first year,
98 students—70 women and 28 men—enrolled for the noncredit class. The course consisted of 12 lectures on basic aspects
of human sexuality, 4 of which Kinsey himself taught. The
other lectures were handled by other members of the faculty.

As Kinsey prepared for the course, he made the somewhat
amazing (to him) discovery that very little scientific information was available on the most fundamental aspects of sexuality,
such as the frequency of masturbation or same-sex behaviors

among men or women. He decided to begin a research program of his own on the topic as a way of solving this problem. By 1940, then, his work on gall wasps had been set aside for research on and teaching about human sexuality. At that point, Wells gave him the option of continuing with one or the other, but not both, programs. Kinsey chose research.

That research was eventually made possible by a grant from the Rockefeller Foundation in 1941 in the amount of $1,600, a minuscule sum in today's world, but enough to get Kinsey's research under way. Six years later, Rockefeller and the National Research Council's Committee for Research on the Problems of Sex provided additional funding for the establishment of a separate institute at Indiana on sex research, the Institute for Sex Research, now known as the Kinsey Institute. That institute continues to function today, working on a host of problems related to issues of human sexuality.

Kinsey continued to conduct the interviews on which his sex research was based almost to the day of his death, on August 25, 1956. By that time, he had conducted 7,985 of the more than 18,000 detailed interviews that staff members had completed. Kinsey and his work continue to be the focus of discussion and debate more than half a century after his death. Most recently, his story has been told in a motion picture, *Kinsey* (2004); a novel, *The Inner Circle* (2004); a PBS documentary film, *Kinsey* (2005); and a BBC radio play, *Dr. Sex* (2005).

Phyllis Lyon (1924–)

Lyon's name is inextricably linked with that of Del Martin, her domestic partner of 56 years. Lyon and Martin founded the Daughters of Bilitis in 1955, the first political and social organization in the United States designed specifically for lesbians. Throughout their lives, Lyon and Martin were involved in a number of gay, lesbian, and feminist organizations, including the Council of Religion and Homosexuality, whose goal was to encourage religious leaders to include gay men and lesbians in church activities, and the Alice B. Toklas Memorial Democratic Club, the first gay and lesbian political organization in San Francisco, and still one of the most influential such groups in the city.

Phyllis Lyon was born in Tulsa, Oklahoma, on November 10, 1924. She grew up in Seattle, southern California, and San Francisco, graduating from Sacramento High School in 1943. She then attended the University of California at Berkeley, from which she received her BA in journalism in 1946. Like many women of her day, Lyon felt that her life would eventually have to center on a man. As she told historian John D'Emilio, "If you were a woman, you had to have a man. There was no other way." By the 1950s, however, she learned otherwise. After a stint as a general reporter for the *Chico Enterprise-Record*, Lyon moved to Seattle to work on a trade magazine. There she met Del Martin and fell in love. In 2004, they were the first same-sex couple to be married in San Francisco after Mayor Gavin Newsom had issued an order permitting same-sex marriage licenses in the city. Four years later, after the California Supreme Court ruled that same-sex marriages were legal in the state, the couple were married a second time.

In 1972, Lyon and Martin coauthored *Lesbian/Woman*, a book that discussed lesbian lives in a strongly positive tone, an approach that was virtually unknown at the time. *Publishers Weekly* called the book one of the 20 most important women's book of its generation. In the last three decades, Lyon has been especially interested in the topic of human sexuality in general and, in 1970s, cofounded the Institute for Advanced Study of Human Sexuality in San Francisco, from which she received her EdD in 1976. She also served on the San Francisco Human Rights Commission for more than a decade, acting as chairperson for two of those years.

Del Martin (1921–2008)

With her long-time domestic partner, Phyllis Lyon, Martin was deeply involved in the gay and lesbian political rights movement for more than half a century. In 1955, Martin and Lyon founded the Daughters of Bilitis, the first organization created to push for political rights of lesbians in the United States. A year later, they also founded and edited the nation's first lesbian periodical, *The Ladder*. The two women were also involved in creating the Council on Religion and the Homosexual in 1964 and San Francisco's Alice B. Toklas Memorial Democratic Club in 1972.

Martin was born Dorothy L. Taliaferro in San Francisco on May 5, 1921. Early in life, she became better known as Del. She attended George Washington High School in San Francisco before matriculating at the University of California at Berkeley. She later transferred to San Francisco State College (now San Francisco State University), where she met her future husband, James Martin. She then left San Francisco State, gave birth to a daughter, Kendra, and moved with her family to the suburbs. Before long, she realized that her longstanding attraction to women made her marriage impossible, and she was divorced from Martin (although she did keep her husband's surname).

In 1950, Martin moved to Seattle to take a job with a publisher of construction trade information. There she met Lyon, who was working with the same company. They made a commitment to each other in 1952 and, in 1955, moved to San Francisco. There they bought a house where they continued to live for more than 50 years.

In addition to her political activities, Martin wrote two important books, *Lesbian/Woman* (with Lyon) and *Battered Wives*, a book that became critical in the development of a national movement against domestic violence. Martin and Lyon were married twice, the first time in 2004, and again in 2008. Martin died in San Francisco on August 27, 2008, as the result of complications arising from a broken arm that exacerbated her already poor health.

National Center for Transgender Equality

The National Center for Transgender Equality (NCTE) was founded in 2003 by a group of transgender individuals who were aware of a range of issues with which they had to deal in their daily lives and felt that a formal organization was needed to attack these problems. One of the founders of the group was Mara Keisling, who continues to serve as executive director today. NCTE calls itself "the nation's leading social justice advocacy organization winning life-saving change for transgender people."

The primary goals of the organization are as follows:

- Advancing federal policy: working to improve access to health care; updating gender designations on passports and Social Security records; reducing assaults in federal prisons; and working for nondiscrimination in employment, housing, and education.
- Educating policy makers: providing information about transgender for members of Congress, federal agencies, corporations, and other organizations.
- Passing federal legislation: working to add transgender to a variety of nondiscrimination acts and bills, such as the Matthew Shepard and James Byrd, Jr. Hate Crimes Prevention Acts.
- Supporting state and local trans activists.
- Continuing the 2011 National Transgender Discrimination Survey.
- Establishing and maintaining the Trans Legal Services Network to provide advice and support for transgender individuals.

The specific areas in which NCTE is currently operating are aging; antiviolence; employment; families; health and HIV; housing and homelessness; identity documents and privacy; immigration; international; military and veterans; National Transgender Discrimination Survey; nondiscrimination laws; police, jails, and prisons; racial and economic justice; research and data needs; travel; voting rights; and youth and students.

The organization's website is a valuable source of information about basic questions concerning transgenderism, as well as providing information for transgender individuals about problems they may face. It also contains a blog with information and opinion on a variety of transgender issues.

National Eating Disorders Association

The National Eating Disorders Association (NEDA) was formed in 2001 with the merger of Eating Disorders Awareness & Prevention and the American Anorexia Bulimia Association, at the time said to be the two oldest and largest eating disorder organizations in the world. Eight years later, NEDA also absorbed Anorexia Nervosa and Related Eating Disorders, Inc., resulting in what has become the primary agency in the United States for dealing with anorexia nervosa, bulimia, and other types of eating disorders. The organization currently maintains a national NEDA Network of other state and local eating disorder associations with similar goals and objectives, a network that includes groups such as American Anorexia/Bulimia Association of Philadelphia; Community Outreach for the Prevention of Eating Disorders, Florida; Diana Jodel Foundation, Georgia; The Eating Disorder Foundation, Colorado; Eating Disorder Network of Maryland; The Elisa Project, Texas; Michigan Eating Disorders Alliance; Missouri Eating Disorders Association of St. Louis; Multi-Service Eating Disorders Association, Inc. of Massachusetts; National Association for Males with Eating Disorders; Ophelia's Place, New York; Project Heal; Renewed Eating Disorders Support, Tennessee; Realize Your Beauty; and Walden Center for Education & Research. According to its mission statement, NEDA "supports individuals and families affected by eating disorders, and serves as a catalyst for prevention, cures and access to quality care."

NEDA provides a variety of services for individuals with eating disorders, including an extensive section on its website explaining the phenomenon of eating disorders. The website includes sections on contributing factors and prevention, treatment, recovery, diversity, and special issues, as well as notes for family and friends and educators and coaches, and a list of print and electronic resources. The website also provides a variety of resources for dealing with the condition, such as a toll-free number to call for emergencies; tool kits for parents, educators, and coaches and athletic trainers; a list of insurance resources; and loss support and recovery networks. Almost any type of assistance that one could ask for in the field of eating disorders can be found on the NEDA website.

NEDA acknowledges body image, especially as being portrayed in advertising campaigns, as a possible source of eating disorder problems and provides reprints on a number of articles dealing with this connection.

National Organization for Women

The post–World War II period in the United States saw a disappointing retreat in the effort to bring women into the nation's political, economic, and social mainstream. Having been largely successful during the mid-20th century in achieving the goals of the first wave of feminism, especially gaining the right to vote, women in the 1950s began to realize that they still lacked many of the basic rights available to men in the society, especially rights in the workplace.

At a conference held in Washington, D.C., on June 28–30, 1966, on "Targets for Action," the frustration and anger felt by many women in attendance boiled over. It had become obvious that the new Equal Employment Opportunity Commission (EEOC), created a year earlier, was not inclined to carry out the legislative mandate of Title VII of the Civil Rights Act of 1964, namely to guarantee equal rights in the job market for women. Midway through the conference, this concern resulted in concrete action by a handful of delegates who decided it was time for the creation of a new organization with the specific mission of speaking out and working for the equal rights of women both in employment and in other fields of American society. And thus was born the National Organization for Women (NOW).

Formal creation of the organization took place at a sparsely attended (28 women) conference in Washington on October 29–30, 1966. The primary achievement of that conference was the adoption of a formal structure for the organization that included a ringing statement of purpose that read "The purpose of NOW is to take action to bring women into full participation in the mainstream of American society now, exercising all privileges and responsibilities thereof in truly equal partnership with men . . ." The conference also established a corporate structure consisting of 35 board members and 5 officers to meet every three months on a regular basis (a structure that remains largely in place today). The women also decided to begin taking action on the EEOC's failure to act on Title VII issues immediately, and discussed the formation of a number of task forces to deal with a variety of other issues of interest to women.

NOW currently claims to be the largest feminist organization in the United States, with more than 500,000 contributing members in 500 local and campus chapters in all 50 states and the District of Columbia. The organization has an annual budget of about $3 million. Two associated entities are the NOW Political Action Committee (NOW/PAC), which endorses candidates in federal elections, and the NOW Equality PAC (NEP), which supports candidates at the state, county, and local levels. Some NOW chapters also maintain their own political action committees to work on the behalf of candidates in their own districts. The NOW Foundation was established in 1986 as the tax-deductible arm of the organization, working on issues of litigation, education, and advocacy for women's issues.

The six issues in which NOW is primarily interested today are reproductive rights and justice, economic justice, ending violence against women, racial justice, LGBTQ rights, and constitutional equality. The last of these topics focuses on ongoing efforts for the adoption of an amendment to the U.S. Constitution, guaranteeing equal rights to all citizens of the United States, regardless of sex. That amendment was first proposed to the U.S. Congress in 1923, after which it was reintroduced in every session of Congress—but not approved by the Congress—until 1970. The amendment was finally approved by the House of Representatives in 1971 and by the Senate a year later. The amendment failed of ratification by two-thirds of the states, however, and died. It has since been reintroduced in every session of the Congress, largely as the result of efforts by NOW to keep the issue alive in the country.

Virginia Prince (1912–2009)

Virginia Prince was an American biological male who lived as a transvestite for most of her life (Prince preferred the use of female pronouns) and was an outspoken advocate for the right of primarily heterosexual men to dress in women's clothing and behave in feminine roles in society.

Prince was born Arnold Lowman to a socially prominent and economically well-to-do family in Los Angeles in November 23, 1912. He began cross-dressing in his teenage years, often sneaking out of his house and appearing in public as a female. He wrote in his autobiography that the experience of wearing high heels and wearing women's garments provided a sexual "charge" for him that he could not resist. A turning point occurred in his life when he attended a Halloween party at the age of 18 dressed as a girl, an event at which he won first prize. It was the first time that he had acknowledged being a cross-dressing male.

In an attempt to understand her desire to cross-dress, Prince consulted a series of psychiatrists, the first of whom explained that she suffered from an Oedipal complex that was responsible for her "aberrant behavior." Eventually she found a therapist who suggested that she recognized that her feelings were normal and natural and that her goal in counseling should really be to learn self-acceptance of the lifestyle she had chosen.

After completing high school in 1931, Prince enrolled at Pomona College in Los Angeles, from which she received her BA degree in chemistry with honors. She then continued her studies at the University of California at San Francisco (UCSF), where she earned her PhD in pharmacology. While still a student at UCSF, Prince met Dorothy Shepherd, a secretary at the university, whom she married in 1941. The couple was later to have one son. Prince had by then decided to abjure his interest in cross-dressing and burned all his women's clothing the day before the wedding.

That act was destined for failure, however, as Prince soon began cross-dressing again. During this period, he was working at UCSF as a research assistant and lecturer in pharmacology. He had the opportunity to use the university library to learn more about transvestism and to come into contact with a number of other men with similar proclivities. Slowly, it occurred to Prince that it might be helpful to form an organization of likeminded individuals, along with the publication of a journal for such individuals. Those events eventually took place in 1960 with the first issue of *Transvestia: The Journal of the American Society for Equality in Dress* and in 1962 with the founding of the Foundation for Personality Expression.

Meanwhile, Dorothy's discovery of her husband's interest in cross-dressing convinced the couple that their marriage could not be saved, and they were divorced in 1948. By that time, Prince had already begun to use her new assumed name by combining her father's first name, Charles, with the name of the street on which she lived, Prince Street. She later added "Virginia" to her name and was generally referred to for most of the rest of her life as "Virginia Prince."

It was at UCSF that Prince also met the psychiatrist who was to change her own view of her fascination with cross-dressing. As Prince later wrote in his autobiography, the psychiatrist, Karl Bowman, told her to "stop fighting, it [cross-dressing] is not so terrible. There are thousands of others like you and always have been. Medical science hasn't been able to do much for them, so the best thing to do is to relax and learn to accept yourself."

Partially at the urging of his mother, Prince was married a second time, this time to Doreen Skinner, an Englishwoman whom he referred to as "dowdy" and "old-fashioned" when they were first married. Largely with his guidance, however, she eventually learned more about feminine makeup and attire and became a more attractive woman. Doreen was originally skeptical about Prince's cross-dressing, but eventually accepted its place in her life. The two became close partners both personally and in business, where they created a company for the manufacture and sale of beauty products for humans and their pets.

Prince continued to write and speak out as an advocate for transvestism for the rest of her life. She was especially interested in pointing out the difference between cross-dressing and transsexuality and homosexuality, both of which were—and still are—often conflated with transvestism. Prince wrote three books, *The Transvestite and His Wife* (1967), *Understanding Cross-Dressing* (1976), and *How to Be a Woman though Male* (1987); along with a number of articles and chapters in books, including "My Accidental Career" in Bonnie Bullough, et al., eds., *How I Got into Sex* (1997); "Seventy Years in the Trenches of the Gender Wars," in Vern Bullough, et al., eds., *Gender Bending*, 1997; "Homosexuality, Transvestism and Transsexualism," *American Journal of Psychotherapy* (1957); "The Expression of Femininity in the Male," *Journal of Sex Research* (1967); and "Survey of 504 Cases of Transvestism," *Psychological Reports* (1972). Prince died in Los Angeles on May 2, 2009, at the age of 96.

Sexuality Information and Education Council of the United States

SEICUS was founded in 1964 by Dr. Mary Calderone, Wallace Fulton, Reverend William Genne, Lester Kirkendall, Dr. Harold Lief, and Clark Vincent for the purpose of more complete and more accurate information about human sexuality for adults, children, and teenagers in the United States. Seed money for the new organization was provided by Hugh Hefner, publisher of *Playboy* magazine, who believed in the goals for which SEICUS had been formed. Over the decades, the organization had taken a number of steps to achieve its basic objectives, such as publication of the popular *SEICUS Reports*, a newsletter that provides information about all aspects of human sexuality including current developments in the field; cosponsorship of the advocacy and educational group Gay Men's Health Crisis during the rise of the HIV/AIDS crisis in the mid-1980s as well as publication of the first book for the general public about the disease, *How to Talk to Your Children about AIDS*; an increased interest in advocacy and lobbying of the U.S. Congress and other legislative groups about needed programs in the area of human sexuality in the 1990s; the creation of an international arm of the organization at about the same time; and the creation of the group's website in 1996.

Current issues in which SEICUS is most interested are comprehensive sex education in the United States, evaluation of abstinence-only until marriage sex education programs, adolescent sexuality, teenage pregnancy, sexually transmitted diseases, sexual orientation, and sexual and reproductive health. For each of these areas of concern, the organization provides a variety of fact sheets, resources for educators, policy resources, information on research, community action updates, and external links. The SEICUS website is a particularly valuable source of information on topics within these areas, such as fact sheets on the Healthy Youth Act; President Obama's President's Teen Pregnancy Prevention Initiative; status of the recently adopted Personal Responsibility Education Program; public opinion about the status of sex education programs in the United States; status reviews of sex education programs in all 50 states; reviews of state legislation on sex education; and country profiles, policy updates, and other information on sex education in other nations of the world.

Other books, articles, and other resources available from the center include *Guidelines for Comprehensive Sexuality Education: Kindergarten–12th Grade*; a handbook, *Developing Guidelines for Comprehensive Sexuality Education*; a teacher's manual, *Filling the Gaps: Hard-to-Teach Topics in Sexuality Education*; a guide for youth-serving organizations, *On the Right Track?*; a framework for child care centers, *Right from the Start: Guidelines for Sexuality Issues, Birth to Five Years*; a book for young people, *Talk about Sex?*; and two specialized bibliographies, *Sexuality and Disabilities Bibliography* and *Sexuality in Mid- and Later Life Bibliography*.

Shi Pei Pu (1938–2009)

A person's decision to dress in the clothing and to assume the gender role of someone of the opposite sex is generally a personal decision, one that may affect one's own life, that of his or her family, and perhaps a somewhat wider community. Seldom does transvestism become an issue of wider interest and concern. Such was the case with Shi Pei Pu, a Chinese opera singer, born as a man, who spent much of his life living as a woman.

Shi Pei Pu was born in Shandong, China, on December 21, 1938, the youngest of three children and the only son of a university professor and school teacher. He claimed to have attended the University of Kunming and received his degree in literature from that institution. His primary career, however, was as a singer in Chinese opera, where he had already achieved some success by the age of 17.

In 1964, Shi met French embassy clerk Bernard Boursicot at a party and struck up a conversation with the 20-year-old diplomat. Shi presented a glowing account of his early life and his success on the stage, and the two soon struck up a romantic relationship. That relationship was somewhat out of the ordinary since Boursicot was very inexperienced in sexual matters, Shi was presenting himself as a female, and Boursicot was apparently unable to realize that such was not the case. Specifically, Shi told Boursicot that he was in reality a female who had been forced to assume the role of a man by his parents. And, since Shi managed to limit their relationship to brief encounters that occurred only under conditions he carefully controlled, the relationship continued for an extended period of time.

(The story told by Shi was, in fact, drawn from one of the roles he, himself, had played in a traditional Chinese opera, namely, *The Story of Butterfly*. In that opera, a young girl assumes the role of a male by dressing in her brother's clothing so that she is able to attend school, something she would not be able to do as a female.)

Most of Shi's encounters with Boursicot occurred at the former's lodgings in Beijing. During one of these meetings, Boursicot was introduced to two Chinese men to whom he boasted of his access to sensitive documents at the French embassy. Over a period of more than 10 years, he passed a number of these documents to the Chinese agents, although it is not clear that any of the documents was of particular value to them.

Early in their relationship, Shi also told Boursicot that she had become pregnant and borne a son, whom she called Shi Du Du. She provided pictures of the boy to Boursicot, but did not introduce him to the purported father until about 1977. At that point, the romantic relationship between Shi and Boursicot had come to an end, but the Frenchman continued to travel to Beijing to see "his son."

During a trip by Shi to Paris in 1983, French officials discovered the relationship between the now widely popular Chinese singer and Boursicot. They determined that Shi, in spite of his protests to the contrary, was indeed a man, and not a woman. They also discovered, again contrary to Shi's protestations, of Boursicot's transmittal of sensitive embassy documents to Chinese representatives over an extended period of time. After their trial in 1986, both Shi and Boursicot were sentenced to six years in prison, although neither served the full period of that sentence.

Shi Pei Pu died in Paris on June 30, 2009, at the age of 70. He had lived most of his life as a woman, even after the French government had definitely determined his sex to be male more than 20 years earlier. The story of Shi and Boursicot was retold in a play written in 1988 by David Henry Hwang, *M. Butterfly*, which was later made into a popular motion picture of the same name in 1993.

Society for the Scientific Study of Sex

The Society for the Scientific Study of Sex (SSSS) was founded in 1957 largely through the efforts of American psychologist Albert Ellis, who was long considered one of the world's leading sexologists. In addition to his work in the creation of SSSS, Ellis founded the Albert Ellis Institute in New York City in 1959. The purpose of the institute has been to "promote emotional well-being through the research and application of effective, short-term therapy with long-term results." His goal in establishing SSSS focused more specifically on the role of sex and a happy and satisfying human life. Ellis also served as president of SSSS from its founding until 1960. Other founding members of the organization included Hugo G. Beigel, Harry Benjamin, Henry Guze, Hans Lehfeldt, and Robert V. Sherwin.

Today, SSSS claims to have more than 700 members from a wide array of professions, including anthropology, biology, education, history, nursing, medicine, psychology, sociology, theology, psychotherapy, psychiatry, and many other disciplines. The major event of the year for SSSS is its annual convention, held in 2016 in Phoenix, Arizona; and scheduled to be held in 2017, in San Juan, Puerto Rico; and in 2018, in Montreal.

In addition to the annual convention, the most important feature of SSSS's work is an impressive array of publications dealing with most aspects of human sexual behavior. Its three major publications are the *Annual Review of Sex Research*, which reports on important progress in a scientific understanding of human sexual behavior; *The Journal of Sex Research*, a scholarly, peer-reviewed publication that appears eight times a year and contains reports of original research, as well as news and commentaries about progress in sex research; and *Sexual Science Newsletter*, an online publication with updates from SSSS committees and society leaders; and information on conferences, training opportunities, job announcements, lab news, and accomplishments; as well as information from laboratory and field research being conducted by members. All publications are available to members of the association only.

A resource of particular significance to the general public, however, is a collection of articles on specialized topics in the field of human sexuality available on the website under the rubric of "What Sexual Scientists Know." Some of the topics covered in this section are compulsive sexual behavior, correct condom use, HIV-AIDS, love, rape, pornography, sexual satisfaction in committed relationships, transgender identity and sexuality, and gender differences and similarities in sexuality.

SSSS claims to have a special commitment to the younger generation of sex researchers, offering a variety of ways in which to encourage their own growth and development. For example, the organization offers a mentoring program in which young researchers are paired with established workers in the field in order to gain experience and additional training in their work. It also offers an Ambassador Program in which students and young professionals are provided with an opportunity to take leadership roles at the SSSS annual convention. SSSS also provides a variety of ongoing educational opportunities for students and young researchers, such as information about and connections with certification programs; undergraduate programs; individual courses and undergraduate minors; doctoral programs; lectures and workshops; masters programs; and graduate certificates, internships, and minor programs.

Tri-Ess

Tri-Ess is an organization for male cross-dressers, founded in 1976 by the joining of two existing transvestite organizations, the Foundation for Free Personality Expression (FPE) and Mamselle. FPE had been formed originally in 1961 as the Hose and Heels Club by Virginia Prince, a transvestite activist in San Francisco. Prince soon found a somewhat more sophisticated name for the group, which it retained until it merged with Mamselle. The latter group had been created in 1971 by Carol Beecroft, herself a former member and chapter chair of FPE. Upon merger of the two groups, the new organization took the name of the Society for the Second Self, or Tri-Ess. The "three-S" designation has also been translated into the three major goals of the organization: support, serenity, and service. Tri-Ess currently has 14 chapters in nine regions, located in Atlanta; upstate New York; Austin, TX; Minneapolis/St. Paul; Omaha, NE; Salt Lake City; Tucson; Cedar Rapids, IA; Denver; East Derry, NH; Champaign, IL; Houston (two chapters); and Trenton, NJ.

Tri-Ess expresses its overall mission in the acronym FIBER, which comes from the following statement of purpose:

F: Full personality expression in both its masculine and its feminine aspects. We do not wish to destroy our masculinity, but to soften its harsher aspects, and be all we can be.

I: Integration of masculinity and femininity to create a happier whole person.

B: Balance between masculinity and femininity.

E: Education or crossdressers and their families toward self-acceptance; education of society toward accepting crossdressing people.

R: Relationship-building in the context of crossdressing.

Some of the organization's regular activities include publication of the quarterly magazine, *The Femme Mirror*, a quarterly newsletter for wives, *Sweetheart Connection*, and a variety of special brochures and pamphlets on cross-dressing; an annual get-together called "Holiday en Femme" that includes seminars and social events; an annual Spouses' and Partners' International Conference, designed exclusively for spouses; outreach to professional groups such as the National Association of Social Workers at their annual conventions; and an international outreach called "Sisters across the Sea Program" intended to reach cross-dressers outside of the United States.

Sojourner Truth (ca. 1797–1883)

Sojourner Truth was born Isabella (Bell) Baumfree in about 1797 in Swartekill, New York, as a slave in the household of Colonel Johannes Hardenbergh. Hardenbergh was a Dutch landowner who operated a grist mill on a small plot of land maintained by seven slaves, of whom Bell's parents, James (also called Bomefree) and Betsey (also known as Mau Mau Bett) were two. As was the case with nearly all slaves at the time, Bell was not taught to read or write, and she spoke only in the low Dutch language used on Hardenbergh's property. In about 1815, Isabella was married to another slave named Thomas. She had five children over the next 10 years, the first of whom died in childbirth and the last of whom, Sophia, was born in 1826. Over these years, she was sold to various men on four occasions.

By the mid-1820s, the state of New York had begun to discuss the abolition of slave-holding and decided to take that action by 1827. Isabella's owner at the time, one John Dumont, had promised her her freedom prior to that time, provided she continued to work diligently for him. When he then changed his mind and announced that he would keep her at work for him, Isabella decided to escape with her daughter Sophia. She was taken in by Isaac and Maria Van Wagenen, who eventually paid Dumont $20 as a purchase price for Isabella, who stayed with the family for a year before the state's emancipation act took effect in 1827.

Now legally free, Isabella's life became more complicated when she learned that Dumont had illegally sold her five-year-old son Peter to a new owner in Alabama prior to emancipation. She decided to go to court to have Peter returned to her, an action virtually unheard of in New York or any place else in the country at the time. After a battle that lasted more than a year, she won her court case, had Peter returned to her, and moved with her two children to New York City.

After arriving in New York, Isabella found work as a housekeeper to a successful businessman named Elijah Pierson, who also claimed to be a prophet of the word of God. Pierson later fell under the influence of one Robert Matthews, who also called himself Jesus Matthias, Matthias the Prophet, and Joshua the Jewish Minister. Isabella, Pierson, and Matthews became active in preaching and proselytizing among the very poor citizens of the city. When Pierson died suddenly from food poisoning in 1834, Matthews and Isabella were charged with his murder, a case in which they were both found innocent.

A turning point in Isabella's life came in 1843 when she claimed to have had a calling from God to begin preaching the gospel and speaking out for the abolition of slavery. She decided to change her name to Sojourner Truth and began traveling around the country speaking at camp meetings, religious conventions, and other group settings. Along the way, she also began dictating her memoirs a friend, Olive Gilbert, a project that resulted in the publication of her book, *The Narrative of Sojourner Truth: A Northern Slave* (reprinted by Vintage Books in 1993).

The speech for which Truth is perhaps best known is an extemporaneous addressed presented in May 1851 at the Ohio Women's Rights Convention in Akron. In that speech, she called for equal rights not only for all African Americans, but also for all women. In her speech, she pointed out that

> I have as much muscle as any man, and can do as much work as any man. I have plowed and reaped and husked and chopped and mowed, and can any man do more than that? I have heard much about the sexes being equal. I can

carry as much as any man, and can eat as much too, if I can get it. I am as strong as any man that is now. As for intellect, all I can say is, if a woman have a pint, and a man a quart—why can't she have her little pint full?

Over the next three decades, Truth continued to speak out on the issues of women's rights and the rights of people of color, as well as a variety of other social issues, such as prison reform, elimination of the death penalty, abolition, and the rights of freed slaves. She died in Battle Creek, Michigan, at the age of 86, still battling for the causes in which she believed, but also exhausted from her long battles for those causes. Among the many honors that have come to her are the inclusion of her picture on the U.S. 10 dollar bill (sometime before 2020); the naming of a number of schools for her in California, Minnesota, New Jersey, New York, and Oregon, and of Sojourner-Douglass College in Baltimore; statues and busts made in her honor at a variety of locations, including the U.S. Capitol; the naming of an asteroid and a NASA robotic rover to Mars in her honor; and the naming of a section of interstate highway 94 near Battle Creek in her honor.

Ella Flagg Young (1845–1918)

Young was appointed superintendent of schools in Chicago in 1909, the first woman to assume that post in a major American city. In 1913, Young recommended to the city board of education that students in all 21 of the city's high schools be taught a course in "sex hygiene." Her suggestion came about as the result of extraordinarily high rates of prostitution and sexual disease among school-age children in the cities. She recommended a series of three lectures, to be taught by "specialists in sex hygiene who lecture in simple, yet scientifically correct language." The three lectures were to cover "personal sexual hygiene," "problems of sex instinct," and "a few of the hygienic and social facts regarding venereal disease."

Unsurprisingly, Young encountered strong opposition from the board to her suggestion; most members were uncomfortable with introducing such a potentially controversial subject into the public school curriculum. But she eventually won over a majority of the board, and more than 20,000 students received such lectures (renamed as lectures in "personal purity") in the school year 1913–1914.

Reaction from students was generally positive, with many noting that they had never received information of the type presented in the classes even in their own homes. They understood its value in their own adolescent lives. One study found that more than 90 percent of students who took the course found it to be "helpful and worth continuing in the future." Perhaps more significantly, only 8 percent of parents exercised their option to remove their children from the lectures.

However, the board of education's concerns about the controversial nature of the course soon proved to be justified when the general public—led by the leaders of the Roman Catholic Church in the city—produced an outcry against the change. Indeed, reaction to Young's program (as well as support for it) became a topic for critics across the Midwest and throughout the nation. Eventually the pressure became too great, and Young was dismissed as superintendent of schools in 1915.

Ella Flagg was born in Buffalo, New York, on January 15, 1841, to Theodore, a skilled mechanic, and his wife, Jane (Reed) Flagg. Ella was said to have a "delicate" nature as a child, so was kept from contact with other children. Not being able to attend school, she taught herself how to read and write and was prepared, therefore, when she was able to enroll in the local grammar school at the age of 11. In 1858, with deteriorating economic conditions in Buffalo, Ella's parents decided to move to Chicago, where work opportunities were more encouraging.

Once in Chicago, Flagg enrolled at the Brown School, an upper grammar school, in preparation for high school. She was soon bored with the Brown curriculum and dropped out after a few months there. She did not resume her schooling until

1860, when she took an examination for teacher certification. She passed that exam and began her studies at the Chicago Normal School, from which she received her teaching certificate in 1862.

Flagg's first teaching assignment was at the Foster primary school in one of Chicago's most notorious ghettos. There she was assigned a class informally known to other teachers as the "cowboy class" because of the rowdy character of its students. She was successful in this first assignment, and soon began to work her way up through the system: to teaching assistant at the Brown school, supervisor of student teachers, and principal of other city elementary schools. As might perhaps be expected, she also became involved in educational controversies with supervisors and colleagues because of her firmly held beliefs about the way education for young people should be conducted.

In 1868, Flagg married William Young, with whom she lived for only four years, until his death in 1872.

In the fall of 1895, Young enrolled in a seminar with the eminent philosopher and educator John Dewey at the University of Chicago. She found that graduate studies agreed with her, and she enrolled in a doctoral program at the university. Five years later, she was awarded her PhD in education. By that time she had also been appointed associate professor of pedagogy at the university and, upon receiving her doctorate, was promoted to full professor.

In 1905, Young left the University of Chicago to become principal (head) of her alma mater, the Chicago Normal School. She held that post until 1909, when she was appointed superintendent of schools in Chicago. The uproar over her "personal purity" classes, along with other controversies over her philosophy of education, led to her resignation in 1915. She lived only three years more, dying on October 26, 1918, during the great flu epidemic of that year. In 1910, the University of Illinois had conferred on Young the honorary Doctor of Laws degree. In 1924, the Chicago school system named an elementary school in the Austin neighborhood of the city in her honor.

Introduction

This chapter provides two types of research resources for the reader. The first is a set of data tables that contain statistics on one or another of the topics discussed in the book, such as pay wage inequity and steroid use by American teenagers. The second is a set of excerpts from important documents dealing with various aspects of sex and gender, such as laws and court cases dealing with transgender, same-sex, sex discrimination, and related issues. These data and documents are provided not only because of their potential interest to the reader, but also as hints as to additional research that one might wish to pursue on some aspect of the general topic.

Data

Table 5.1   Partial List of Gender Options Available on Facebook UK

Agender

Androgyne

Asexual

Bigender

(continued)

A student holds a sticker for a new gender-neutral bathroom as members of the cheer squad applaud behind during a ceremonial opening for the restroom at Nathan Hale High School in Seattle on May 17, 2016. (AP Photo/Elaine Thompson)

Table 5.1 *(continued)*

Cis female

Cis male

Female to male

Gender fluid

Gender neutral

Gender nonconforming

Gender questioning

Gender variant

Genderqueer

Hermaphrodite

Intersex

Male to female

Man

Neither

Neutrois

Non-binary

Pangender

Polygender

Transfemale

Transmale

Transperson

Transexual man

Transexual person

Transexual woman

Two spirit

Woman

Source: Williams, Rhiannon. 2016. "Facebook's 71 Gender Options Come to UK Users." *The Telegraph*. http://www.telegraph.co.uk/technology/facebook/10930654/Facebooks-71-gender-options-come-to-UK-users.html. Accessed on August 30, 2016.

Table 5.2 Median Usual Weekly Earnings of Full-Time Wage and Salary Workers, by Selected Characteristics, 2014

Characteristic	Total		Women		Men		
	Number of Workers[1]	Weekly Wage ($)	Number of Workers[1]	Weekly Wage ($)	Number of Workers[1]	Weekly Wage ($)	Women as Percentage of Men
Age							
16 to 19	1,144	378	443	357	701	392	91.1
20 to 24	8,439	491	3,647	468	4,792	507 3	92.3
25 to 34	25,722	726	11,083	679	14,639	755	89.9
35 to 44	24,589	881	10,633	781	13,957	964	81.0
45 to 54	25,359	899	11,558	780	13,801	1,011	77.2
55 to 64	17,607	911	8,062	780	9,545	1,021	76.4
65 and older	3,665	824	1,650	740	2,016	942	78.6
Race/Ethnicity							
White	84,177	816	36,119	734	48,058	897	81.8
African American	12,910	639	6,781	611	6,129	680	89.9
Asian	6,273	953	2,784	841	3,488	1,080	77.9
Hispanic or Latino	17,475	594	6,721	548	10,754	616	89.0

(continued)

Table 5.2 (continued)

Characteristic	Total		Women		Men		Women as Percentage of Men
Age	Number of Workers[1]	Weekly Wage ($)	Number of Workers[1]	Weekly Wage ($)	Number of Workers[1]	Weekly Wage ($)	
Marital Status							
Never married	29,840	624	12,974	607	16,866	648	93.7
Married, spouse present	59,297	908	24,218	787	35,079	1,001	78.6
Divorced	11,701	800	6,688	740	5,013	894	82.8
Separated	4,029	659	1,960	598	2,069	730	81.9
Widowed	1,659	729	1,237	682	422	883	77.2
Union Affiliation							
Members of unions	13,132	970	5,671	904	7,461	1,015	89.1
Represented by unions	14,491	965	6,324	899	8,167	1,013	88.7
Not represented by a union	92,035	763	40,752	687	51,283	840	81.8

Educational Attainment

Educational Attainment						
25 years and older	96,943	839	42,986	752	53,957	922	81.6
Less than a high school diploma	6,927	488	2,107	409	4,819	517	79.1
High school graduates, no college	25,529	668	10,093	578	15,437	751	77.0
Some college or associate degree	26,408	761	12,462	661	13,946	872	75.8
Bachelor's degree and higher	38,080	1,193	18,324	1,049	19,756	1,385	75.7

[1] in thousands.

Source: "Highlights of Women's Earnings in 2014." 2015. U.S. Bureau of Labor Statistics, table 1, p. 9. http://www.bls.gov/opub/reports/womens-earnings/archive/highlights-of-womens-earnings-in-2014.pdf. Accessed on September 1, 2016.

Table 5.3   Sex-Based Charges Filed under Title VII of the Civil Rights Act of 1964, FY1997–FY2015

	1997	1998	1999	2000	2001	2002	2003	2004	2005	2006
Receipts	24,728	24,454	23,907	25,194	25,140	25,536	24,362	24,249	23,094	23,247
Resolutions	32,836	31,818	30,643	29,631	28,602	29,088	27,146	26,598	23,743	23,364
Resolutions by Type										
Settlements	1,355	1,460	1,988	2,644	2,404	2,720	2,877	3,008	2,601	2,828
Withdrawals w/Benefits	1,205	1,148	1,269	1,332	1,321	1,304	1,329	1,347	1,418	1,460
Administrative closures	11,127	10,056	8,747	6,897	6,391	5,819	5,484	5,052	4,188	4,409
No reasonable cause	17,832	17,493	16,689	15,980	15,654	16,752	15,506	15,481	13,853	13,191
Reasonable cause	1,317	1,661	1,950	2,778	2,832	2,493	1,950	1,710	1,683	1,476
Successful conciliation	332	454	535	707	739	686	520	491	454	437
Unsuccessful conciliation	985	1,207	1,415	2,071	2,093	1,807	1,430	1,219	1,229	1,039
Merit resolutions	3,877	4,269	5,207	6,754	6,557	6,517	6,156	6,065	5,702	5,764
Monetary benefits (millions of dollars)	72.5	58.7	81.7	109.0	94.4	94.7	98.4	100.8	91.3	99.1

	2007	2008	2009	2010	2011	2012	2013	2014	2015
Receipts	24,826	28,372	28,028	29,029	28,534	30,356	27,687	26,027	26,396
Resolutions	21,982	24,018	26,618	30,914	32,789	32,149	28,605	26,002	27,045
Resolutions by Type									
Settlements	2,900	2,842	2,748	3,138	3,200	3,073	2,696	2,342	2,458
Withdrawal w/Benefits	1,443	1,646	1,701	1,774	1,780	1,768	1,708	1,672	1,773
Administrative closures	4,304	4,563	5,701	5,727	5,728	5,433	5,124	4,805	5,015
No reasonable cause	12,036	13,670	15,139	18,709	20,660	20,454	17,936	16,280	16,790
Reasonable cause	1,299	1,297	1,329	1,566	1,421	1,421	1,141	903	1,009
Successful conciliation	439	382	407	475	510	500	459	351	373
Unsuccessful conciliation	860	915	922	1,091	911	921	682	552	636
Merit resolutions	5,642	5,785	5,778	6,478	6,401	6,262	5,545	4,917	5,240
Monetary benefits (millions of dollars)	135.4	109.3	121.5	129.3	145.7	138.7	126.8	106.5	130.9

For definitions of terms, see https://www.eeoc.gov/eeoc/statistics/enforcement/definitions.cfm.

Source: Sex-Based Charges. FY 1997–FY 2015. 2016. U.S. Equal Employment Opportunity Commission. https://www.eeoc.gov/eeoc/statistics/enforcement/sex.cfm. Accessed on September 1, 2016.

Table 5.4 Prevalence of 30-day Steroid Use by American Youth, 1991–2015 (percentage of respondents)

Age Group	1991	1992	1993	1994	1995	1996	1997	1998	1999	2000	2001	2002
Grade 8	0.4	0.5	0.5	0.5	0.6	0.4	0.5	0.5	0.7	0.8	0.7	0.8
Grade 10	0.6	0.6	0.5	0.6	0.6	0.5	0.7	0.6	0.9	1.0	0.9	1.0
Grade 12	0.8	0.6	0.7	0.9	0.7	0.7	1.0	1.1	0.9	0.8	1.3	1.4

Age Group	2003	2004	2005	2006	2007	2008	2009	2010	2011	2012	2013	2014	2015
Grade 8	0.7	0.5	0.5	0.5	0.4	0.5	0.4	0.3	0.4	0.3	0.3	0.2	0.3
Grade 10	0.8	0.8	0.6	0.6	0.5	0.5	0.5	0.5	0.5	0.4	0.4	0.4	0.4
Grade 12	1.3	1.6	0.9	1.1	1.0	1.0	1.0	1.1	0.7	0.9	1.0	0.9	1.0

Source: Johnston, Lloyd D., et al. 2016. "Monitoring the Future: 2015 Overview," table 7, p. 77. http://www.monitoringthefuture.org/pubs/monographs/mtf-overview2015.pdf. Accessed on September 2, 2016.

Table 5.5 Disapproval of Steroid Use by 12th Graders, American Youth, 1990–2015 (percentage of respondents)[1]

1990	1991	1992	1993	1994	1995	1996	1997	1998	1999	2000	2001	2002
90.8	90.5	92.1	92.1	91.9	91.0	91.7	91.4	90.8	88.9	88.8	86.4	86.8

2003	2004	2005	2006	2007	2008	2009	2010	2011	2012	2013	2014	2015
86.0	87.9	88.8	89.4	89.2	90.9	90.3	89.8	89.7	90.4	88.2	87.5	87.8

[1] Percentage of respondents who disapprove or strongly disapprove of steroid use. This question was asked of 8th and 10th graders only from 1991 through 1994.

Source: Johnston, Lloyd D., et al. 2016. "Monitoring the Future: 2015 Overview," table 14, pp. 92–93. http://www.monitoringthefuture.org/pubs/monographs/mtf-overview2015.pdf. Accessed on September 2, 2016.

Documents

Civil Rights Act (1964)

The fundamental document that provides protection for individuals in employment on the basis of their sex is the Civil Rights Act of 1964. That protection is enshrined specifically in Title VII of that act, the core portion of which is quoted here.

Discrimination because of Race, Color, Religion, Sex, or National Origin

SEC. 703. (a) It shall be an unlawful employment practice for an employer—

(1) to fail or refuse to hire or to discharge any individual, or otherwise to discriminate against any individual with respect to his compensation, terms, conditions, or privileges of employment, because of such individual's race, color, religion, sex, or national origin; or

(2) to limit, segregate, or classify his employees in any way which would deprive or tend to deprive any individual of employment opportunities or otherwise adversely affect his status as an employee, because of such individual's race, color, religion, sex, or national origin.

(b) It shall be an unlawful employment practice for an employment agency to fail or refuse to refer for employment, or otherwise to discriminate against, any individual because of his race, color, religion, sex, or national origin, or to classify or refer for employment any individual on the basis of his race, color, religion, sex, or national origin.

(c) It shall be an unlawful employment practice for a labor organization—

(1) to exclude or to expel from its membership, or otherwise to discriminate against, any individual because of his race, color, religion, sex, or national origin;

(2) to limit, segregate, or classify its membership, or to classify or fail or refuse to refer for employment any individual,

in any way which would deprive or tend to deprive any individual of employment opportunities, or would limit such employment opportunities or otherwise adversely affect his status as an employee or as an applicant for employment, because of such individual's race, color, religion, sex, or national origin; or

(3) to cause or attempt to cause an employer to discriminate against an individual in violation of this section.

(d) It shall be an unlawful employment practice for any employer, labor organization, or joint labor-management committee controlling apprenticeship or other training or retraining, including on-the-job training programs to discriminate against any individual because of his race, color, religion, sex, or national origin in admission to, or employment in, any program established to provide apprenticeship or other training.

Source: Civil Rights Act of 1964. Public Law 88-352. *U.S. Statutes at Large*, 78 (1964): 241.

Federal Regulations for Equal Participation in Sports (1972)

In 1972, the U.S. Congress passed a bill called the Education Amendments of 1972 (20 U.S.C. 1681, et seq.). Title IX of that act prohibits discrimination on the basis of sex in educational programs receiving federal financial assistance. The obligations of an institution in meeting the conditions of this act fall into one of three basic areas: student interests and abilities, athletic benefits and opportunities, and financial assistance. The primary requirements in each of these areas are described here.

Student Interests and Abilities

The athletic interests and abilities of male and female students must be equally and effectively accommodated. Compliance with this factor is assessed by examining a school's: (a) determination of the athletic interests and abilities of its students;

(b) selection of the sports that are offered; and (c) levels of competition, including opportunity for team competition.

Measuring Athletic Interests

Colleges and universities have discretion in selecting the methods for determining the athletic interests and abilities of their students, as long as those methods are nondiscriminatory. The only requirements imposed are that institutions used methods that:

- take into account the nationally increasing level of women's interests and abilities;
- do not disadvantage the underrepresented sex (i.e., that sex whose participation rate in athletics is substantially below its enrollment rate);
- respond to the expressed interests of students capable of intercollegiate competition who belong to the underrepresented sex.

Selection of Sports

A college or university is not required to offer particular sports or the same sports for each sex. Also, an institution is not required to offer an equal number of sports for each sex. However, an institution must accommodate to the same degree the athletic interests and abilities of each sex in the selection of sports.

A college or university may sponsor separate teams for men and women where selection is based on competitive skill or when the activity is a contact sport. Contact sports under the Title IX regulation include boxing, wrestling, rugby, ice hockey, football, basketball and other sports in which the purpose or major activity involves bodily contact.

Equally effective accommodation also requires a college or university that sponsors a team for only one sex to do so for members of the other sex under certain circumstances. This applies to contact and non-contact sports. For example, a separate team may be required if there is sufficient interest and ability among members of the excluded sex to sustain a team and a reasonable expectation of competition for that team. Also, where an institution sponsors a team in a particular non-contact sport for members of one sex, it must allow athletes of the other sex to try-out for the team if, historically, there have been limited athletic opportunities for members of the other sex.

Levels of Competition

Colleges and universities must provide opportunity for intercollegiate competition as well as team schedules which equally reflect the competitive abilities of male and female athletes. An institution's compliance in this area may be assessed in any one of the following ways:

- the numbers of men and women participating in intercollegiate athletics are substantially proportionate to their overall enrollment; or
- where members of one sex are underrepresented in the athletics program, whether the institution can show a continuing practice of program expansion responsive to the developing interests and abilities of that sex; or
- the present program accommodates the interests and abilities of the underrepresented sex.

In considering equivalent opportunities for levels of competition, compliance will be assessed by examining whether:

- male and female athletes, in proportion to their participation in athletic programs, are provided equivalently advanced competitive opportunities; or
- the institution has a history and continuing practice of upgrading the competitive opportunities available to the historically disadvantaged sex as warranted by the developing abilities among the athletes of that sex.

Colleges and universities are not required to develop or up-grade an intercollegiate team if there is no reasonable expectation that competition will be available for that team within the institution's normal competitive region. However, an institution may be required to encourage development of such competition when overall athletic opportunities within that region have been historically limited for the members of one sex.

Discriminatory rules established by a governing athletic organization, or league do not relieve recipients of their Title IX responsibilities. For example, a college or university may not limit the eligibility or participation of women based on policies or requirements imposed by an intercollegiate athletic body.

Athletic Benefits and Opportunities

In determining whether equal opportunities in athletics are available, the Title IX regulation specifies the following factors which must be considered

- accommodation of athletic interests and abilities (which is addressed separately in the section above);
- equipment and supplies;
- scheduling of games and practice time;
- travel and per diem allowances;
- opportunity for coaching and academic tutoring;
- assignment and compensation of coaches and tutors;
- locker rooms and other facilities;
- medical and training services;
- housing and dining services; and
- publicity.

The Title IX regulation also permits OCR to consider other factors in determining whether there is equal opportunity. Accordingly, the Policy Interpretation added recruitment of student athletes and provision of support services, since these factors can affect the overall provision of equal opportunity to male and female athletes.

The Policy Interpretation clarifies that institutions must provide equivalent treatment, services, and benefits regarding these factors. The overall equivalence standard allows institutions to achieve their own program goals within the framework of providing equal athletic opportunities. To determine equivalency for men's and women's athletic programs, each of the factors is assessed by comparing the following:

- availability;
- quality;
- kind of benefits;
- kind of opportunities; and
- kind of treatment.

Under this equivalency standard, identical benefits, opportunities, or treatment are not required. For example, locker facilities for a women's team do not have to be the same as for a men's team, as long as the effect of any differences in the overall athletic program are negligible.

If a comparison of program components indicates that benefits, opportunities, or treatment are not equivalent in quality, availability, or kind, the institution may still be in compliance with the law if the differences are shown to be the result of nondiscriminatory factors. Generally, these differences will be the result of unique aspects of particular sports or athletic activities, such as the nature/replacement of equipment and maintenance of facilities required for competition. Some disparities may be related to special circumstances of a temporary nature. For example, large disparities in recruitment activity for any particular year may be the result of annual fluctuations in team needs for first-year athletes. Difficulty in compliance will exist only if disparities are of a substantial and unjustified nature in a school's overall athletic program; or if disparities in individual program areas are substantial enough in and of themselves to deny equality of athletic opportunity. This equivalency approach allows institutions great flexibility in conducting their athletic programs and maintaining compliance without compromising the diversity of athletic programs among institutions.

Financial Assistance

To the extent that a college or university provided athletic scholarships, it is required to provide reasonable opportunities for such awards to members of each sex in proportion to the participation rate of each sex in intercollegiate athletics. This does not require the same number of scholarships for men and women or individual scholarships of equal value.

However, the total amount of assistance awarded to men and women must be substantially proportionate to their participation rates in athletic programs. In other words, if 60 percent of an institution's intercollegiate athletes are male, the total amount of aid going to male athletes should be approximately 60 percent of the financial aid dollars the institution awards.

Disparities in awarding financial assistance may be justified by legitimate, nondiscriminatory (sex-neutral) factors. For example, at some institutions the higher costs of tuition for out-of-state residents may cause an uneven distribution between scholarship aid to men's and women's programs. These differences are nondiscriminatory if they are not the result of limitations on the availability of out-of-state scholarships to either men or women. Differences also may be explained by professional decisions college and university officials make about program development. An institution beginning a new program, for example, may spread scholarships over a full generation (four years) of student athletes, thereby, awarding fewer scholarships during the first few years than would be necessary to create proportionality between male and female athletes.

Source: Requirements under Title IX of the Education Amendments of 1972. 2015. U.S. Department of Education. http://www2.ed.gov/about/offices/list/ocr/docs/interath.html.

City of Chicago v. Wilson (1978)

Municipal laws prohibiting cross-dressing began to appear in the United States in the second half of the 19th century, at least partially in an attempt to stem the number of women dressing as men in order to fight in the Civil War. The first such ordinance was passed in Columbus, Ohio, in 1848 prohibiting a person from appearing in public "in a dress not belonging to his or her sex." That law was overturned in 1974. The excerpt below from City of Chicago *is typical of the response by courts when such laws are challenged by individuals convicted of violating them.*

Defendants were arrested on February 18, 1974, minutes after they emerged from a restaurant where they had had breakfast. Defendant Wilson was wearing a black, knee-length dress, a fur coat, nylon stockings and a black wig. Defendant Kimberley had a bouffant hair style and was wearing a pants suit, high-heeled shoes and cosmetic makeup. Defendants were taken to the police station and were required to pose for pictures in various stages of undress. Both defendants were wearing brassieres and garter belts; both had male genitals.

. . .

Section 192-8 of the [City of Chicago] Code provides:

"Any person who shall appear in a public place * * * in a dress not belonging to his or her sex, with intent to conceal his or her sex, * * * shall be fined not less than twenty dollars nor more than five hundred dollars for each offense."

Defendants contend that section 192-8 is unconstitutionally vague, overly broad, and denies them equal protection under the law on account of sex. They argue that the section is overly broad, both on its face and as applied to them, in that it denies them freedom of expression protected by the first amendment and personal liberties protected by the ninth and fourteenth amendments of the United States Constitution.

The city asserts that section 192-8 is neither vague nor overly broad and that the section does not deny defendants equal protection under the law.

We find that the above-cited section, as applied to defendants here, is unconstitutional . . .

. . .

Inasmuch as the city has offered no evidence to substantiate its reasons for infringing on the defendants' choice of dress under the circumstances of this case, we do not find the ordinance invalid on its face; however, we do find that section 192-8 as applied to the defendants is an unconstitutional infringement of their liberty interest.

Source: 75 Ill.2d 525 (1978). 389 N.E.2d 522. *City of Chicago v. Wilson.* No. 49229.

Ledbetter v. Goodyear Tire & Rubber Co.
550 U.S. 618 (2007)

Lilly Ledbetter was employed at the Goodyear Tire & Rubber company plant in Gadsden, Alabama, from 1979 to 1998. When she started working at the company, her wages were the same as male workers doing the same job. By the time she retired, she was earning at least $3,727 per month less than some employees, and as much as $4,286 per month. Convinced that her wages were less because of discrimination based on her sex, she filed suit to regain lost wages. Her case worked its way up through the judicial system until, on May 29, 2007, the U.S. Supreme Court denied her claim, saying that she had waited too long to file her suit. The essence of the Court's judgment was as follows. Omitted references are indicated by asterisks.

The Court's decision in this case prompted the U.S. Congress to pass new legislation that would allow cases such as Ledbetter's to go forward in the courts. See the next entry for this act.

Held: Because the later effects of past discrimination do not restart the clock for filing an EEOC charge, Ledbetter's claim is untimely. ***

(a) An individual wishing to bring a Title VII lawsuit must first file an EEOC charge within, as relevant here, 180 days "after the alleged unlawful employment practice occurred." *** In addressing the issue of an EEOC charge's timeliness, this Court has stressed the need to identify with care the specific employment practice at issue. Ledbetter's arguments—that the paychecks that she received during the charging period and the 1998 raise denial each violated Title VII and triggered a new EEOC charging period—fail because they would require the Court in effect to jettison the defining element of the disparate-treatment claim on which her Title VII recovery was based, discriminatory intent. *United Air Lines, Inc. v. Evans*, 431 U.S. 553, *Delaware State College v. Ricks*, 449 U.S. 250, *Lorance v. AT&T Technologies, Inc.*, 490 U.S. 900, and *National Railroad Passenger Corporation v. Morgan*, 536 U.S. 101, clearly instruct that the EEOC charging period is triggered when a discrete unlawful practice takes place. A new violation does not occur, and a new charging period does not commence, upon the occurrence of subsequent nondiscriminatory acts that entail adverse effects resulting from the past discrimination. But if an employer engages in a series of separately actionable intentionally discriminatory acts, then a fresh violation takes place when each act is committed. Ledbetter makes no claim that intentionally discriminatory conduct occurred during the charging period or that discriminatory decisions occurring before that period were not communicated to her. She argues simply that Goodyear's nondiscriminatory conduct during the charging period gave present effect to discriminatory conduct outside of that period. But current effects alone cannot breathe life into prior, uncharged discrimination. Ledbetter should have filed an EEOC charge within 180 days after each allegedly discriminatory employment decision was made and communicated to her. Her attempt to shift forward the intent associated with prior discriminatory acts to the 1998 pay decision is unsound, for it would shift intent away from the act that consummated the discriminatory employment practice to a later act not performed with bias or discriminatory motive, imposing liability in the absence of the requisite intent.

Source: *Ledbetter v. Goodyear Tire and Rubber Co., Inc.* No. 05-1074. 2007.

Lilly Ledbetter Fair Pay Act (2009)

In response to the Supreme Court's decision in Ledbetter v. Goodyear Tire & Rubber Company *(previous entry), the U.S. Congress passed the Lilly Ledbetter Fair Pay Act, whose major provisions are as follows:*

Sec. 2. Findings

Congress finds the following:

(1) The Supreme Court in *Ledbetter v. Goodyear Tire & Rubber Co.*, 550 U.S. 618 (2007), significantly impairs statutory protections against discrimination in compensation that Congress established and that have been bedrock principles of American law for decades. The Ledbetter decision undermines those statutory protections by unduly restricting the time period in which victims of discrimination can challenge and recover for discriminatory compensation decisions or other practices, contrary to the intent of Congress.

(2) The limitation imposed by the Court on the filing of discriminatory compensation claims ignores the reality of wage discrimination and is at odds with the robust application of the civil rights laws that Congress intended.

(3) With regard to any charge of discrimination under any law, nothing in this Act is intended to preclude or limit an aggrieved person's right to introduce evidence of an unlawful

employment practice that has occurred outside the time for filing a charge of discrimination.

(4) Nothing in this Act is intended to change current law treatment of when pension distributions are considered paid.

Sec. 3. Discrimination in Compensation Because of Race, Color, Religion, Sex, or National Origin

Section 706(e) of the Civil Rights Act of 1964 (42 U.S.C. 2000e–5(e)) is amended by adding at the end the following:

"(3)(A) For purposes of this section, an unlawful employment practice occurs, with respect to discrimination in compensation in violation of this title, when a discriminatory compensation decision or other practice is adopted, when an individual becomes subject to a discriminatory compensation decision or other practice, or when an individual is affected by application of a discriminatory compensation decision or other practice, including each time wages, benefits, or other compensation is paid, resulting in whole or in part from such a decision or other practice.

"'(B) In addition to any relief authorized by section 1977A of the Revised Statutes (42 U.S.C. 1981a), liability may accrue and an aggrieved person may obtain relief as provided in subsection (g)(1), including recovery of back pay for up to two years preceding the filing of the charge, where the unlawful employment practices that have occurred during the charge filing period are similar or related to unlawful employment practices with regard to discrimination in compensation that occurred outside the time for filing a charge."

Source: Public Law 111-2. 111th Congress. 2009.

Wisconsin Act 219 (2011)

Many people are pleased when state, local, and federal legislators pass laws that guarantee equal treatment for women in employment and other areas. However, such steps are not guaranteed to remain in effect forever, and are sometimes repealed by later legislative action. In 2011, the House and Senate of the state of Wisconsin passed, and Governor Scott Walker signed, a bill to repeal the state's Equal Pay Enforcement Act (EPEA) of 2009. Among the justification for this action, according to state senator Glenn Grothman, was that "money is more important for men [than women]." "[A] huge number of discrimination claims," he went on to say, "are baseless . . . [and] are filed by fired employees." (http://www .businessinsider.com/wisconsin-republican-says-women-are-paid-less-because-money-is-more-important-for-men-2012-4.) The bill repealing EPEA was brief, simple, and to the point. The major section, showing the portion of existing law to be deleted, is cited here.

SECTION 1. 111.39 (4) (d) of the statutes is amended to read:

111.39 **(4)** (d) The department shall serve a certified copy of the findings and order on the respondent, the order to have the same force as other orders of the department and be enforced as provided in s. 103.005. Any person aggrieved by noncompliance with the order may have the order enforced specifically by suit in equity. ~~If the examiner finds that the respondent has not engaged in discrimination, unfair honesty testing, or unfair genetic testing as alleged in the complaint, the department shall serve a certified copy of the examiner's findings on the complainant, together with an order dismissing the complaint. If the examiner finds that the respondent has engaged in discrimination, unfair honesty testing, or unfair genetic testing as alleged in the complaint, the department shall serve a certified copy of the examiner's findings on the complainant, together with a notice advising the complainant that after the completion of all administrative proceedings under this section he or she may bring an action as provided in s. 111.397 (1) (a) to~~

~~recover compensatory and punitive damages as provided in~~
~~s. 111.397 (2) (a) and advising the complainant of the time~~
~~under s. 111.397 (1) (b) within which the action must be com-~~
~~menced or be barred.~~

Source: 2011 Senate Bill 202. 2012. State of Wisconsin. https://
docs.legis.wisconsin.gov/2011/related/acts/219.pdf. For more
details on this issue, see Glazer, Saul C. 2012. "Bill Will Eliminate Compensatory and Punitive Damages under Wisconsin's
Fair Employment Act." Inside Track. State Bar of Wisconsin.
http://www.wisbar.org/newspublications/insidetrack/pages/
article.aspx?Volume=4&Issue=5&ArticleID=7997.

Arcadia Resolution Agreement (2013)

*The practice of dressing in the clothing of a person generally as-
sociated with someone of the opposite biological sex can become
an issue in two quite different circumstances. In one case, cross-
dressing may be practiced by transvestites, who simply enjoy dressing
up in clothing of the opposite sex. As noted in* City of Chicago v.
Wilson, *reviewed above, some cities have adopted ordinances to
prohibit such practices. In the other case, cross-dressing may be
practiced by individuals who are in the process of transitioning,
or have already transitioned, from one gender to the other gender.
Such cases can be particularly problematic when the individuals involved are dysmorphic boys or girls who are still attending
school. The question may then become how, if at all, a school
should respond to a student who dresses in clothing opposite that
of his or her biological sex. A number of court cases have arisen
out of this problem, one of which involved a student in the Arcadia
(CA) school district who had already transitioned from female to
male before returning to middle school. The school required that
he follow special instructions for using a restroom and for changing
clothes for gym class. The student was also subjected to significant
harassment and ridicule about which the school did nothing. The
student eventually brought suit against the school district, which*

eventually agreed to a resolution agreement outlining its respon-sibilities in the future for such cases. The main features of that document are as follows.

Terms of the Agreement

I. Expert Consultant

A. No later than ninety (90) calendar days after execution of this Agreement, the District will engage one or more third-party consultants with expertise in child and adolescent gender identity, including discrimination against transgen-der and gender nonconforming youth, to support and as-sist the District in implementing this Agreement.

B. The consultant(s) will be agreed upon by both the District and the United States.

C. The District will promptly notify the United States if it in-tends to retain additional or alternative consultants during the term of this Agreement for purposes of implementing this Agreement.

D. The District will be responsible for all costs, if any, associ-ated with the retention of expert consultants.

II. Individual Measures

A. For the duration of the Student's enrollment in the Dis-trict, the District will continue to:

1. provide the Student access to sex-specific facilities des-ignated for male students at school consistent with his gender identity; however, the Student may request access to private facilities based on privacy, safety, or other concerns;

2. provide the Student access to sex-specific facilities des-ignated for male students at all District-sponsored ac-tivities, including overnight events and extracurricular activities on and off campus, consistent with his gender

identity; however, the Student may request access to private facilities based on privacy, safety, or other concerns;

3. treat the Student the same as other male students in all respects in the education programs and activities offered by the District; and

4. ensure that any school records containing the Student's birth name or reflecting the Student's assigned sex, if any, are treated as confidential, personally identifiable information; are maintained separately from the Student's records; and are not disclosed to any District employees, students, or others without the express written consent of the Student's parents or, after the Student turns 18 or is emancipated, the Student.

B. The District will notify the Student and his parents that they may, at any point during the Student's enrollment in the District, request that the District establish a support team to ensure the Student has access and opportunity to participate in all programs and activities, and is otherwise protected from gender-based discrimination at school. If the District receives such a request, it will form a support team that will:

[The agreement then lists specific activities the district is responsible for performing with the family.]

III. District-Wide Measures

A. *Policies, Procedures and Regulations*

[The agreement then lists some community-wide activities in which it must engage, such as:]

1. No later than November 30, 2013, the District, in consultation with its consultant(s) and following approval by the United States, will revise all of its policies, procedures, regulations, and related documents and

materials (e.g., complaint forms, handbooks, notices to students and parents, website information) related to discrimination (including harassment) to:

a. specifically include gender-based discrimination as a form of discrimination based on sex, and

b. state that gender-based discrimination includes discrimination based on a student's gender identity, gender expression, gender transition, transgender status, or gender nonconformity.

Source: Resolution Agreement. 2013. https://www.justice .gov/sites/default/files/crt/legacy/2013/07/26/arcadiaagree.pdf.

Treatment of Transgender Employment Discrimination Claims under Title VII of the Civil Rights Act of 1964 (2014)

Increased attention in the United States on transgender issues has raised the question as to whether federal legislation dealing with "sex discrimination" also refers to instances of "gender discrimination." In 2014, Attorney General Eric Holder issued a memorandum in which he attempted to clarify the Department of Justice's current thinking on this issue, which is, essentially, that the latter is covered by all federal rules and regulations that cover the former. Omissions of references are indicated by asterisks.

After considering the text of Title VII *[of the Civil Rights Act of 1964]*, the relevant Supreme Court case law interpreting the statute, and the developing jurisprudence in this area, I have determined that the best reading of Title VII' s prohibition of sex discrimination is that it encompasses discrimination based on gender identity, including transgender status. The most straightforward reading of Title VII is that discrimination "because of . . . sex" includes discrimination because an employee's gender identification is as a member of a particular sex, or because the employee is transitioning, or has transitioned, to another sex. As the Court explained in *Price Waterhouse*, by using "the simple words 'because of,' . . . Congress meant to obligate" a Title VII plaintiff to prove only "that the employer relied upon sex-based considerations in coming to its decision." *** It follows that, as a matter of plain meaning, Title VII' s prohibition against discrimination "because of . . . sex" encompasses discrimination founded on sex-based considerations, including discrimination based on an employee's transitioning to, or identifying as, a different sex altogether. Although Congress may not have had such claims in mind when it enacted Title VII, the Supreme Court has made clear that Title VII must be interpreted according to its plain text, noting that "statutory prohibitions often go beyond the principal evil to cover reasonably comparable evils, and it is ultimately the provisions of our laws rather than the principal concerns of our legislators by which we are governed."

For these reasons, the Department will no longer assert that Title VII's prohibition against discrimination based on sex does not encompass gender identity per se (including transgender discrimination).

Source: Holder, Eric. 2014. "Treatment of Transgender Employment Discrimination Claims under Title VII of the Civil Rights Act of 1964." https://www.justice.gov/sites/default/files/opa/press-releases/attachments/2014/12/18/title_vii_memo.pdf

Truth in Advertising Act (2014)

Legislators at all levels of government have become increasingly aware of and concerned about the deleterious effects of advertising on individuals' body image perceptions and, in some cases, have decided to take actions to deal with the problem. An example on the federal level is the Truth in Advertising Act, first proposed by Representative Ileana Ros-Lehtinen (R-FL) in 2014, and reintroduced two years later. The basis for the bill and its primary instructions are excerpted here.

Sec. 2. Findings

Congress finds the following:

(1) Advertisers regularly alter images used in print and electronic media to materially change the physical characteristics of models' faces and bodies, often altering the models' size, proportions, shape, and skin color, removing signs of ageing, and making other similar changes to models' appearance.

(2) An increasing amount of academic evidence links exposure to such altered images with emotional, mental, and physical health issues, including eating disorders, especially among children and teenagers. There is particular concern about the marketing of such images to children and teenagers through distribution in teen-oriented publications, advertising displayed in public places outside the home, and online media.

(3) Such altered images can create distorted and unrealistic expectations and understandings of appropriate and healthy weight and body image.

(4) The dissemination of unrealistic body standards has been linked to eating disorders among men and women of varying age groups, but it has a particularly destructive health effect on children and teenagers.

(5) Academic evidence has demonstrated a connection between the use of very thin models in advertising and consumer attitudes toward a brand based on such advertising, as well as a material influence of the use of such models on consumer purchase intent, conduct, and reliance.

(6) In 2011, the American Medical Association adopted a policy encouraging advertising associations to work with public and private sector organizations concerned with child

and adolescent health to develop guidelines for advertisements, especially those appearing in teen-oriented publications, that would discourage the altering of photographs in a manner that could promote unrealistic expectations of appropriate body image.

Sec. 3. Report by Federal Trade Commission

(a) In general.—

Not later than 18 months after the date of the enactment of this Act, the Federal Trade Commission shall submit to Congress a report that contains—

(1) a strategy to reduce the use, in advertising and other media for the promotion of commercial products, of images that have been altered to materially change the physical characteristics of the faces and bodies of the individuals depicted; and

(2) recommendations for an appropriate, risk-based regulatory framework with respect to such use.

Source: H.R. 4341 (113th). 2014.

National Legal Services Authority v. Union of India, No. 400 of 2012 (2014)

In 2014, the Supreme Court of India announces its decision on a case brought by the National Legal Services Authority to have hijras in the country declared to be a legal gender, along with male and female, with all consequent legal rights associated with that designation. In a particularly comprehensive review both of Indian law and international laws and policy, the Court voted in favor of the authority. Key portions of its reasoning were as follows:

49. Indian Law, on the whole, only recognizes the paradigm of binary genders of male and female, based on a person's sex assigned by birth, which permits gender system, including the

law relating to marriage, adoption, inheritance, succession and taxation and welfare legislations. We have exhaustively referred to various articles contained in the Universal Declaration of Human Rights, 1948, the International Covenant on Economic, Social and Cultural Rights, 1966, the International Covenant on Civil and Political Rights, 1966 as well as the Yogyakarta principles. Reference was also made to legislations enacted in other countries dealing with rights of persons of transgender community. Unfortunately we have no legislation in this country dealing with the rights of transgender community. Due to the absence of suitable legislation protecting the rights of the members of the transgender community, they are facing discrimination in various areas and hence the necessity to follow the International Conventions to which India is a party and to give due respect to other non-binding International Conventions and principles.

. . .

Hijras/transgender persons have been facing extreme discrimination in all spheres of the society. Non-recognition of the identity of Hijras/transgender persons denies them equal protection of law, thereby leaving them extremely vulnerable to harassment, violence and sexual assault in public spaces, at home and in jail, also by the police. Sexual assault, including molestation, rape, forced anal and oral sex, gang rape and stripping is being committed with impunity and there are reliable statistics and materials to support such activities. Further, non-recognition of identity of Hijras/transgender persons results in them facing extreme discrimination in all spheres of society, especially in the field of employment, education, healthcare etc. Hijras/transgender persons face huge discrimination in access to public spaces like restaurants, cinemas, shops, malls etc.

. . .

70. Self-identified gender can be either male or female or a third gender. Hijras are identified as persons of third gender and are not identified either as male or female. . . .

77. We, therefore, conclude that discrimination on the basis of sexual orientation or gender identity includes any discrimination, exclusion, restriction or preference, which has the effect of nullifying or transposing equality by the law or the equal protection of laws guaranteed under our Constitution, and hence we are inclined to give various directions to safeguard the constitutional rights of the members of the TG community.

Source: "In the Supreme Court of India. Civil Original Jurisdiction Writ Petition (Civil) No.400 of 2012. National Legal Services Authority versus Union of India and Others." http://supremecourtofindia.nic.in/outtoday/wc40012.pdf.

Interim Arbitral Award (2015)

The most recent criterion used for determining the eligibility of women to participate in international sports and the Olympic Games is a test to determine the concentration of androgens in a woman's body. Individuals with blood concentrations greater than a certain level (currently 10 nmol/L [nanomoles per liter]) are said to have a condition known as hyperandrogenism, that is, an excess of male hormones in their body. Such individuals are assumed to have an advantage in sports because of the additional speed, strength, and agility thought to be associated with male hormones. In September 2014, Indian sprinter Dutee Chand was found to display hyperandrogenism in blood tests to which she submitted, and she was banned from participating in international sports and the Olympic Games. Her supporters filed suit on her behalf with the Court of Arbitration for Sports (CAS) claiming that there was no specific evidence that excess levels of androgens actually improved performance in sports. In a July 2015 ruling, the CAS agreed with that claim, gave the International Association of Athletics Federations (IAAF) two years to provide such evidence, and said that Chand could not be banned from competition over that period of time. The core of the CAS ruling was as follows.

F. Conclusion and Next Steps

For the reasons explained above, the Panel concludes that the IAAF has not discharged its onus of establishing that the Hyperandrogenism Regulations are necessary and proportionate to the pursuit of organising competitive female athletics to ensure fairness in athletic competition. Specifically, the IAAF has not provided sufficient scientific evidence about the quantitative relationship between enhanced testosterone levels and improved athletic performance in hyperandrogenic athletes. In the absence of such evidence, the Panel is unable to conclude that hyperandrogenic female athletes may enjoy such a significant performance advantage that it is necessary to exclude them from competing in the female category.

In these circumstances, the Panel is unable to uphold the validity of the Regulations. The Panel therefore suspends the Hyperandrogenism Regulations for a period of two years, subject to the following provisos. At any time during that two-year period, the IAAF may submit further written evidence to the CAS concerning the magnitude of the performance advantage that hyperandrogenic females enjoy over other females as a result of their abnormality of high androgen levels. In the event that the IAAF submits such evidence, the Panel will issue further directions enabling the athlete to respond to that evidence and listing the matter for a further hearing for the Panel to consider whether that evidence is sufficient to establish the validity of the regulation. In the event that the IAAF does not file any evidence within that two-year window (or if it notifies the CAS in writing that it does not intend to file such an evidence) then the Hyperandrogenism Regulations shall be declared void.

Source: Interim Arbitral Award Delivered by the Court of Arbitration for Sport. 2015. http://www.tas-cas.org/fileadmin/user_upload/award_internet.pdf. Used by permission of the Court of Arbitration for Sport.

North Carolina House Bill 2 (2016)

Arguably one of the most controversial state laws passed in recent years in the United States is House Bill 2 (HB2), adopted by a special session of the North Carolina legislature in March 2016. The primary purpose of the bill was to establish state policy on the use of public rest rooms, changing facilities, and similar sites, particularly in light of the federal government's efforts to make such facilities more consistent with the needs of transgender people. The primary feature of the bill was to require individuals to use such facilities that correspond with the sex with which they were born (their "biological sex"), not the sex with which they currently espouse, if that differs from their biological sex. A secondary feature of the bill was a provision that made state law superior to local law in all matters of conflict between the two, an action that some observers took as an effort to invalidate local LGBT rights nondiscrimination legislation. Underlined sections of the bill represent amendments to existing legislation on these topics.

§ 115C-521.2. Single-sex multiple occupancy bathroom and changing facilities.

(a) Definitions.—The following definitions apply in this section:

(1) Biological sex.—The physical condition of being male or female, which is stated on a person's birth certificate.

. . .

(b) Single-Sex Multiple Occupancy Bathroom and Changing Facilities.—Local boards of education shall require every multiple occupancy bathroom or changing facility that is designated for student use to be designated for and used only by students based on their biological sex.

. . .

§ 143-760. Single-sex multiple occupancy bathroom and changing facilities.

(a) Definitions.—The following definitions apply in this section:

   (1) Biological sex.—The physical condition of being male or female, which is stated on a person's birth certificate.

   . . .

(b) Single-Sex Multiple Occupancy Bathroom and Changing Facilities.—Public agencies shall require every multiple occupancy bathroom or changing facility to be designated for and only used by persons based on their biological sex.

   . . .

Part II. Statewide Consistency in Laws Related to Employment and Contracting

SECTION 2.1. G.S. 95-25.1 reads as rewritten:

"§ 95-25.1. Short title and legislative ~~purpose.~~ *purpose; local governments preempted.*

(a) This Article shall be known and may be cited as the "Wage and Hour Act."

(b) The public policy of this State is declared as follows: The wage levels of employees, hours of labor, payment of earned wages, and the well-being of minors are subjects of concern requiring legislation to promote the general welfare of the people of the State without jeopardizing the competitive position of North Carolina business and industry. The General Assembly declares that the general welfare of the State requires the enactment of this law under the police power of the State.

(c) The provisions of this Article supersede and preempt any ordinance, regulation, resolution, or policy adopted or imposed by a unit of local government or other political subdivision of the State that regulates or imposes any requirement upon an employer pertaining to compensation of employees, such as the wage levels of employees, hours of labor, payment of earned wages, benefits, leave, or well-being of minors in the workforce.

Source: General Assembly of North Carolina. Second Extra Session 2016. House Bill 2. 2016. http://www.ncleg.net/Sessions/2015E2/Bills/House/PDF/H2v1.pdf.

State of Texas, et al. v. United States of America, et al. (2016)

In May 2016, the U.S. Department of Education (DOE) issued a letter to all public schools in the United States on the topic of bathrooms, locker rooms, and similar facilities for transgender students, an action that eventually drew a response from a number of state attorneys general who objected to that rule (see Chapter 1). A decision on the case was issued on August 21, 2016, by the Federal District Court for the Northern District of Texas. The court ruled in favor of the plaintiffs (the attorneys general), finding two errors in the DOE's action: that it did not provide an opportunity for notice and comment on its ruling and it confused the issues of transgender students' sex and gender. The core of the court's ruling was as follows (asterisks indicate the omission of footnotes and other references).

The APA [Administrative Procedures Act of 1946] requires agency rules to be published in the Federal Register and that the public be given an opportunity to comment on them. *** This is referred to as the notice and comment requirement. The purpose is to permit the agency to understand and perhaps adjust its rules based on the comments of affected individuals. . . .

Here, the Court finds that Defendants rules are legislative and substantive. Although Defendants have characterized the Guidelines as interpretive, post-guidance events and their actual legal effect prove that they are "compulsory in nature." ***

Defendants confirmed at the hearing that schools not acting in conformity with Defendants' Guidelines are not in compliance with Title IX. *** Further, post-Guidelines events, where Defendants have moved to enforce the Guidelines as binding, buttress this conclusion. *** The information before the Court demonstrates Defendants have "drawn a line in the sand" in that they have concluded Plaintiffs must abide by the Guidelines, without exception, or they are in breach of their Title IX obligations. Thus, it would follow that the "actual legal effect" of the Guidelines is to force Plaintiffs to risk the consequences of noncompliance. . . .

The Guidelines are, in practice, legislative rules—not just interpretations or policy statements because they set clear legal standards. *** As such, Defendants should have complied with the APA's notice and comment requirement. *** Permitting the definition of sex to be defined in this way would allow Defendants to "create de facto new regulation" by agency action without complying with the proper procedures. *** This is not permitted.

[With regard to the issue of "sex" versus "gender" in the DOE's ruling, the court noted that]

Based on the foregoing authority, the Court concludes § 106.33 is not ambiguous. *[Section 106.33 is a section of the U.S. Code that outlines the obligations schools have in providing equality between the sexes in their facilities.]* It cannot be disputed that the plain meaning of the term sex as used in § 106.33 when it was enacted by DOE following passage of Title IX meant the biological and anatomical differences between male and female students as determined at their birth. *** determined at the time the regulations are promulgated). It appears Defendants at least tacitly agree this distinction was the intent of the drafter. ***

Additionally, it cannot reasonably be disputed that DOE complied with Congressional intent when drawing the distinctions in § 106.33 based on the biological differences between male and female students. *** As the support identified by

Plaintiffs shows, this was the common understanding of the term when Title IX was enacted, and remained the understanding during the regulatory process that led to the promulgation of § 106.33. This undoubtedly was permitted because the areas identified by the regulations are places where male and female students may have to expose their "nude or partially nude body, genitalia, and other private parts," and separation from members of the opposite sex, those whose bodies possessed a different anatomical structure, was needed to ensure personal privacy. *** This conclusion is also supported by the text and structure of the regulations. Section

106.33 specifically permits educational institutions to provide separate toilets, locker rooms, and showers based on sex, provided that the separate facilities are comparable. The sections immediately preceding and following § 106.33 likewise permit educational institutions to separate students on the basis of sex. . . .

Based on the foregoing, the Court concludes § 106.33 is not ambiguous. . . . Defendants' interpretation is entitled to respect, but only to the extent it has the power to persuade. *** . . . Accordingly, the Court concludes Defendants' interpretation is insufficient to overcome the regulation's plain language and for the reasons stated above is contrary to law.

Source: *State of Texas, et al. v. United States of America, et al.* 2016. Civil Action No. 7:16-cv-00054-O. https://www.tex asattorneygeneral.gov/files/epress/Texas_et_al_v._U.S._et_al_-_ Nationwide_PI_(08-21-16).pdf.

Protecting Freedom of Conscience from Government Discrimination Act (Mississippi) (2016)

The U.S. Supreme Court decision in Obergefell v. Hodges *in 2015 led to a variety of responses by individual states that wished to retain some measure of control over marriage law and policy in their own jurisdiction. One of the most controversial of those*

actions was taken by the state of Mississippi in early 2016, when the state legislature passed House Bill 1523, making it illegal for the state to prosecute companies and individual citizens who declined to participate in some activity related to same-sex marriage. Seven sections of the bill listed areas in which the state was not allowed to take action against such activities. Some of those sections are listed here.

SECTION 3. (1) The state government shall not take any discriminatory action against a religious organization wholly or partially on the basis that such organization:

(a) Solemnizes or declines to solemnize any marriage, or provides or declines to provide services, accommodations, facilities, goods or privileges for a purpose related to the solemnization, formation, celebration or recognition of any marriage, based upon or in a manner consistent with a sincerely held religious belief or moral conviction described in Section 2 of this act;

(b) Makes any employment-related decision including, but not limited to, the decision whether or not to hire, terminate or discipline an individual whose conduct or religious beliefs are inconsistent with those of the religious organization, based upon or in a manner consistent with a sincerely held religious belief or moral conviction described in Section 2 of this act; or

(c) Makes any decision concerning the sale, rental, occupancy of, or terms and conditions of occupying a dwelling or other housing under its control, based upon or in a manner consistent with a sincerely held religious belief or moral conviction described in Section 2 of this act.

(2) The state government shall not take any discriminatory action against a religious organization that advertises, provides or facilitates adoption or foster care, wholly or partially on the basis that such organization has provided or declined to

provide any adoption or foster care service, or related service, based upon or in a manner consistent with a sincerely held religious belief or moral conviction described in Section 2 of this act.

[The bill then provides similar prohibitions against "a person" in sections 3 through 7 and adds one more provision, as follows.]

(8) (a) Any person employed or acting on behalf of the state government who has authority to authorize or license marriages, including, but not limited to, clerks, registers of deeds or their deputies, may seek recusal from authorizing or licensing lawful marriages based upon or in a manner consistent with a sincerely held religious belief or moral conviction described in Section 2 of this act.

[The manner in which such recusal is to occur is then described.]

[Section 2, referred to in these passages, reads as follows.]

SECTION 2. The sincerely held religious beliefs or moral convictions protected by this act are the belief or conviction that:

(a) Marriage is or should be recognized as the union of one man and one woman;

(b) Sexual relations are properly reserved to such a marriage; and

(c) Male (man) or female (woman) refer to an individual's immutable biological sex as objectively determined by anatomy and genetics at time of birth.

Source: House Bill No. 1523. 2016. Mississippi Legislature. http://billstatus.ls.state.ms.us/documents/2016/pdf/HB/1500-1599/HB1523SG.pdf.

Select Task Force on the Study of Harassment in the Workplace (2016)

In June 2016, the Select Task Force on the Study of Harassment in the Workplace of the U.S. Equal Employment Opportunity Commission presented a report summarizing the current status of this

issue in the United States. The report covered all forms of harass-
ment in the workplace, the most common of which was sexual
harassment. The major findings of the report in this area are re-
printed here. (Footnotes have been removed.)

Sex-Based Harassment

Based on testimony to the Select Task Force and various academic articles, we learned that anywhere from 25% to 85%
of women report having experienced sexual harassment in the
workplace. Given these widely divergent percentages, we dug
deeper to understand what these numbers could tell us about
the scope of harassment based on sex.

We found that when employees were asked, in surveys using a
randomly representative sample (called a "probability sample"),
if they had experienced "sexual harassment," without that term
being defined in the survey, approximately one in four women
(25%) reported experiencing "sexual harassment" in the workplace. This percentage was remarkably consistent across probability surveys. When employees were asked the same question
in surveys using convenience samples (in lay terms, a convenience sample is not randomly representative because it uses
respondents that are convenient to the researcher (e.g., student
volunteers or respondents from one organization)), with sexual
harassment not being defined, the rate rose to 50% of women
reporting they had been sexually harassed.

We then found that when employees were asked, in surveys
using probability samples, whether they have experienced one
or more specific sexually-based behaviors, such as unwanted
sexual attention or sexual coercion, the rate of reported harassment rose to approximately 40% of women. When respondents were asked in surveys using convenience samples about
such behaviors, the incidence rate rose to 75%. Based on this
consistent result, researchers have concluded that many individuals do not label certain forms of unwelcome sexually
based behaviors—even if they view them as problematic or
offensive—as "sexual harassment."

The most widely used survey of harassment of women at work, the Sexual Experiences Questionnaire (SEQ), not only asks respondents whether they have experienced unwanted sexual attention or sexual coercion, but also asks whether they have experienced sexist or crude/offensive behavior. Termed "gender harassment" in the SEQ, these are hostile behaviors that are devoid of sexual interest. Gender harassment can include sexually crude terminology or displays (for example, calling a female colleague a "c*nt" or posting pornography) and sexist comments (such as telling anti-female jokes or making comments that women do not belong in management.) These behaviors differ from unwanted sexual attention in that they aim to insult and reject women, rather than pull them into a sexual relationship. As one researcher described it, the difference between these behaviors is analogous to the difference between a "come on" and a "put down."

When sex-based harassment at work is measured by asking about this form of gender harassment, almost 60% of women report having experienced harassment in surveys using probability samples. Indeed, when researchers disaggregate harassment into the various subtypes (unwanted sexual attention, sexual coercion, and gender harassment), they find that gender harassment is the most common form of harassment.

Whether or not women label their unwanted experiences as sexual harassment appears to have little influence on the negative consequences of these experiences. As one group of researchers pointed out, data from three organizations "demonstrate that whether or not a woman considers her experience to constitute sexual harassment, she experiences similar negative psychological, work, and health consequences."

Most of the surveys of sex-based harassment at work have focused on harassment experienced by women. One exception has been the surveys conducted by the Merit Systems Protection Board of federal employees in 1980, 1987, and 1994. When respondents were asked whether they had experienced unwanted sexual attention or sexual coercion, 42% of women and 15% of men responded in the affirmative in 1981; as did 42% of women and 14% of men in 1988; and 44% of women and 19% of men in 1994.

Source: "Select Task Force on the Study of Harassment in the Workplace." 2016. U.S. Equal Employment Opportunity Commission. https://www.eeoc.gov/eeoc/task_force/harassment/report.cfm#_Toc453686297.

State Nondiscrimination Laws Based on Sexual Orientation

No federal law currently exists prohibiting discrimination in housing, employment, accommodation, credit services, and other areas on the basis of sexual orientation. As a consequence, such protection is available only in the 26 states and District of Columbia that have passed legislation of this kind. An example of state nondiscrimination laws is the Connecticut statute reproduced here.

Sec. 46a-81b. Sexual orientation discrimination: Associations of licensed persons. (a) It shall be a discriminatory practice in violation of this section for any association, board or other organization the principal purpose of which is the furtherance of the professional or occupational interests of its members, whose profession, trade or occupation requires a state license, to refuse to accept a person as a member of such association, board or organization because of such person's sexual orientation.

Sec. 46a-81c. Sexual orientation discrimination: Employment. It shall be a discriminatory practice in violation of this section: (1) For an employer, by himself or his agent, except in the case of a bona fide occupational qualification or need, to refuse to hire or employ or to bar or to discharge from employment any individual or to discriminate against him in compensation or in terms, conditions or privileges of employment because of the individual's sexual orientation or civil union status, (2) for any employment agency, except in the case of a bona fide occupational qualification or need, to fail or refuse to classify properly or refer for employment or otherwise to discriminate against any individual because of the individual's sexual orientation or civil union status, (3) for a labor organization, because of the sexual orientation or civil union status of any individual to exclude from full membership rights or to expel from its membership such individual or to discriminate in any way against any of its members or against any employer or any individual employed by an employer, unless such action is based on a bona fide occupational qualification, or (4) for any person, employer, employment agency or labor organization, except in the case of a bona fide occupational qualification or need, to advertise employment opportunities in such a manner as to restrict such employment so as to discriminate against individuals because of their sexual orientation or civil union status.

Sec. 46a-81d. Sexual orientation discrimination: Public accommodations. (a) It shall be a discriminatory practice in violation of this section: (1) To deny any person within the jurisdiction of this state full and equal accommodations in any place of public accommodation, resort or amusement because of such person's sexual orientation or civil union status, subject only to the conditions and limitations established by law and applicable alike to all persons; or (2) to discriminate, segregate or separate on account of sexual orientation or civil union status.

Sec. 46a-81e. Sexual orientation discrimination: Housing. (a) It shall be a discriminatory practice in violation of this section:

(1) To refuse to sell or rent after the making of a bona fide offer, or to refuse to negotiate for the sale or rental of, or otherwise make unavailable or deny, a dwelling to any person because of sexual orientation or civil union status.

(2) To discriminate against any person in the terms, conditions, or privileges of sale or rental of a dwelling, or in the provision of services or facilities in connection therewith, because of sexual orientation or civil union status.

(3) To make, print or publish, or cause to be made, printed or published any notice, statement, or advertisement, with respect to the sale or rental of a dwelling that indicates any preference, limitation, or discrimination based on sexual orientation or civil union status, or an intention to make any such preference, limitation or discrimination.

(4) (A) To represent to any person because of sexual orientation or civil union status, that any dwelling is not available for inspection, sale or rental when such dwelling is in fact so available. (B) It shall be a violation of this subdivision for any person to restrict or attempt to restrict the choices of any buyer or renter to purchase or rent a dwelling (i) to an area which is substantially populated, even if less than a majority, by persons of the same sexual orientation or civil union status as the buyer or renter, (ii) while such person is authorized to offer for sale or rent another dwelling which meets the housing criteria as expressed by the buyer or renter to such person and (iii) such other dwelling is in an area which is not substantially populated by persons of the same sexual orientation or civil union status as the buyer or renter. As used in this subdivision, "area" means municipality, neighborhood or other geographic subdivision which may include an apartment or condominium complex.

(5) For profit, to induce or attempt to induce any person to sell or rent any dwelling by representations regarding the entry or prospective entry into the neighborhood of a person or persons of a particular sexual orientation or civil union status.

(6) For any person or other entity engaging in residential-real-estate-related transactions to discriminate against any person in making available such a transaction, or in the terms or conditions of such a transaction, because of sexual orientation or civil union status.

(7) To deny any person access to or membership or participation in any multiple-listing service, real estate brokers'

organization or other service, organization, or facility relating to the business of selling or renting dwellings, or to discriminate against him in the terms or conditions of such access, membership or participation, on account of sexual orientation or civil union status.

[Part (8) lists additional provisions to those noted here.]

Sec. 46a-81f. Sexual orientation discrimination: Credit practices. (a) It shall be a discriminatory practice in violation of this section for any creditor to discriminate on the basis of sexual orientation or civil union status, against any person eighteen years of age or over in any credit transaction.

Source: Chapter 814c*. Human Rights and Opportunities. 2015. General Statutes of Connecticut. https://www.cga.ct.gov/current/pub/chap_814c.htm#sec_46a-81a.

Introduction

Sex and gender are topics of major interest to both professionals in the field and to everyday individuals. Untold numbers of books, articles, book chapters, reports, and web pages have been devoted to a discussion of one or more aspects of these topics. This bibliography provides only a sampling of some of the most recent of these items, as well as some publications of historical interest. In some cases, an item has appeared both in print and on the Internet, in which case it is so designated in the print listing.

Books

Abrams, Mike. 2017. *Sexuality and Its Disorders: Development, Cases and Treatment.* Thousand Oaks, CA: SAGE Publications. This book provides a review for the general reader of a number of basic issues relating to human sexuality, such as the history of Western sexuality, basic ideas of sexuality, major figures in sex research and theory, theories of love and attachment, dating and mating, sexual disorders and paraphilias, treatment of sexual problems, and sexuality and the Internet.

Artist Chloe LaCasse poses at Wrong Brain Art Collective where a group exhibit, "This Is What TRANS Feels Like," is on display in Dover, NH, January 25, 2017. (AP Photo/Elise Amendola)

Ball, Carlos A., ed. 2016. *After Marriage Equality: The Future of LGBT Rights*. New York: New York University Press.

Although the U.S. Supreme Court's approval of same-sex marriage was a historic step forward for LGBT (lesbian, gay, bisexual, and transgender) rights, the question remains what other legal issues LGBT people still face. This book consists of a number of papers that attempt to answer that question, which may include issues of aging for LGBT people, adoption questions, protection for other sexual minorities, and interactions of racism and homophobia. The status of LGBT rights in other countries is also considered.

Baudewijntje, P. C. Kreukels, Thomas D. Steensma, and Annelou L. C. De Vries, eds. 2014. *Gender Dysphoria and Disorders of Sex Development: Progress in Care and Knowledge*. New York: Springer.

The papers that make up this anthology provide a review of the current state of the art of care and treatment of individuals with gender dysphoria or DSD. They also cover the history of the condition and future prospects for their care and treatment.

Bevan, Thomas E. 2017. *Being Transgender: What You Should Know*. Santa Barbara, CA: Praeger.

The author provides an introduction to the topic of transgenderism for the general reader with chapters on biology, culture, transgender pathways, coping with transgender issues, and questions and answers about transgenderism.

Biegel, Stuart. 2010. *The Right to Be Out: Sexual Orientation and Gender Identity in America's Public Schools*. Minneapolis, MN: University of Minnesota Press.

The author reviews the history of equal rights for gay men and lesbians in the United States and then focuses on the effect of this history on the rights of students. He argues that all boys and girls in schools have the inherent right to be whoever they are, and that it is the school's job to provide the legal conditions and environment to allow that to happen.

Blakemore, Judith E. Owen, Sheri A. Berenbaum, and Lynn S. Liben. 2014. *Gender Development.* New York: Psychology Press.
This book is divided into four major parts: history and background of gender development, describing differences between the sexes, approaches to explaining gender development, and social and cognitive agents of gender development. Specific chapters deal with topics such as biological foundations of sex and gender; personality and social behaviors; and the family, the peer group, the media, and the school as agents of gender development.

Bradley, Harriet. 2014. *Gender,* 2nd ed. Cambridge, UK; Malden, MA: Polity Press.
This book provides a general introduction to the topic of gender, with chapters on the way the term *gender* is used, along with its various meanings; what it means to be a man in the 21st century; family and employment in women's lives; marriage and reproduction; and the future of gender.

Brannon, Linda. 2017. *Gender: Psychological Perspectives,* 7th ed. New York: Routledge.
The latest edition of this acclaimed text deals with essentially all of the fundamental issues related to gender, including the history of studies on sex differences in psychology, the development of women's studies, gender bias in research, the processes and implications of stereotyping, sexual differentiation in humans, theories of gender development, developing gender identity, gender and the expression of emotion, friendships and love relationships, the study of sexuality, sexuality in schools, gender issues in the workplace, sex and gender differences in mortality, and gender issues in therapy.

Brill, Stephanie, and Lisa Kenney. 2016. *The Transgender Teen.* Jersey City, NJ: Cleis Press.

Based on the authors' own extensive experience in dealing with transgender children and teens, they offer a number of suggestions for dealing with issues relating to the physical and emotional development, social and school pressures, medical considerations, and family communications of adolescents who perceive themselves as transgender.

Brill, Stephanie A., and Rachel Pepper. 2008. *The Transgender Child: A Handbook for Families and Professionals.* San Francisco: Cleis Press.

The authors draw on current research in the field and their own extensive in working with transgender children and adolescents and their families to lay out guidelines for individuals dealing with trans issues. They discuss the process of trans recognition, possible patterns of behaviors and their consequences, legal issues, professional advice on dealing with children's and teen's feelings about transgender, and possible hormonal and surgical treatments.

Butler-Wall, Annika, Kim Cosier, and Rachel L. S. Harper. 2016. *Rethinking Sexism, Gender, and Sexuality.* Milwaukee, WI: A Rethinking Schools Publication.

This book raises the question as to what sex education ought to be like in light of a generally widespread change in the way that society as a whole thinks about sexuality and related themes. Chapters deal with topics such as "Queering Our Schools," "Seneca Falls, Selma, Stonewall: Moving Beyond Equality," "When the Gender Boxes Don't Fit," "In Search of Safe Bathrooms," "A Midsummer's Night Gender Diversity," "Transsexuals Teaching Your Children," "Save the Muslim Girl," and

Framing Identity: Using Photographs to Rethink Sexism, Gender, and Sexuality."

Crompton, Louis. 2003. *Homosexuality & Civilization*. Cambridge, MA: Belknap Press of Harvard University Press.
    This book provides information found in few other popular sources on same-sex relationships from the ancient Greeks and Romans to the beginning of the 19th century.

Davis, Georgiann. 2015. *Contesting Intersex: The Dubious Diagnosis*. New York: New York University Press.
    Having herself once been diagnosed as intersex, Davis raises some fundamental question about the way in which that condition is currently diagnosed today and the way in which such information is (or, often, is not) shared with individuals who receive that diagnosis. She argues that the way in which the medical profession has handled this issue in the past raises questions as to the proper understanding of intersex itself.

D'Emilio, John, and Estelle B. Freedman. 1988. *Intimate Matters: A History of Sexuality in America*. New York: Harper & Row.
    This extraordinary piece of scholarship reviews the way in which sexuality has developed in the United States from its earliest days, with special attention to the ways in which cultural and political factors have influenced these changes.

Erickson-Schroth, Laura, and Laura A. Jacobs. 2017. *You're in the Wrong Bathroom!: And 20 Other Myths and Misconceptions about Transgender and Gender-Nonconforming People*. Boston: Beacon Press.
    As the topic of transgenderism becomes more widely discussed in the everyday media, a number of incorrect statements about the condition have arisen. This book chooses 21 such "myths" for discussion and correction.

Forestell, Nancy M., and Maureen Anne Moynagh, eds. 2012. *Documenting First Wave Feminisms*. Toronto, Canada: University of Toronto Press.

This anthology brings together a large number of documents that appeared during the first wave of the feminist movement in many parts of the world. Included are speeches and written works by individuals such as Mary Wollstonecraft, Lucretia Mott, Soujourner Truth, Carrie Chapman Catt, Alice Kandaleft, Elizabeth Cady Stanton, Kikue Ide, Doris Stevens, and the Six Point Group.

Halberstam, Jack. 2017. *Trans: A Quick and Quirky Account of Gender Variability*. Berkeley: University of California Press.

The author takes note of the rapid change in public knowledge about and perceptions of transgender issues and attempts to describe the forces that have been responsible for the evolution of views on sex and gender. He also lays out a possible future in which "non-gendered, gender optional, or gender-hacked" identifications are more likely to be present.

Hall, Matthew, Sarach Grogan, and Brendan Gough, eds. 2016. *Chemically Modified Bodies: The Use of Diverse Substances for Appearance Enhancement*. London: Palgrave Macmillan.

The 10 chapters in the book review the evidence about the ways in which adolescent boys and girls make use of a variety of legal and illegal substances in the attempt to acquire the body image they seek, often one that is patterned after models presented in advertising, films, television, social media, and other public sources on influence.

Harrington, Lee. 2016. *Traversing Gender: Understanding Transgender Realities*. Anchorage, AK: Mystic Productions.

This book provides a general introduction to the topic of transgender with chapters on topics such as sex, gender, and orientation; the variety of transgender experiences;

social, medical, mental, and sexual health; transgender and the law, and "being a trans ally."

Hewitt, Nancy A. 2010. *No Permanent Waves: Recasting Histories of U.S. Feminism.* New Brunswick, NJ: Rutgers University Press.

Hewitt argues that the generally accepted view of "three waves" of feminism is overly simplistic and diverse range of themes has been intermixed in the efforts of women to achieve equal rights over the past 150 years or so.

Hiort, O., and S. F. Ahmed, eds. 2014. *Understanding Differences and Disorders of Sex Development (DSD).* Basel, Switzerland: Karger.

The papers that make up this book provide an excellent general introduction to the topic of disorders of sex development and related issues.

Howell, Ally Windsor. 2016. *This Is Who We Are: A Guide to Transgenderism and the Laws Affecting Transgender Persons.* Washington, DC: American Bar Association.

This book is written from the perspective of the legal profession for families, friends, colleagues, advocates, and acquaintances, and members of the general public. It outlines the rights that transgender individuals have and the ways in which they can exercise those rights.

Hutson, John M., G. L. Warne, and Sonia R. Grover, eds. 2012. *Disorders of Sex Development: An Integrated Approach to Management.* Heidelberg; New York: Springer-Verlag Berlin Heidelberg.

This collection of papers provides a somewhat technical review of basic issues related to the subject of DSD. Examples of the topics covered are the molecular basis of gonadal development and disorders of sex development, embryology of the human genital tract, hormones regulating sexual development, abnormal embryology in DSD, and nonhormonal DSD. Some specific types of DSD, such as 46, XX and 46, XY are also covered.

Jeydel, Alana S. 2004. *Political Women: The Women's Movement, Political Institutions, the Battle for Women's Suffrage and the ERA.* London; New York: Routledge.

This book provides a good, general overview of the first three waves of the feminist movement, along with an extensive bibliography on the topic.

Kantor, Martin. 2015. *Why a Gay Person Can't Be Made Ungay: The Truth about Reparative Therapies.* Santa Barbara, CA: Praeger.

The author reviews the history of reparative therapy, the claims made by proponents of the procedure, the scientific evidence on its effectiveness, and the political, religious, and other motivations that drive the reparative therapy industry.

Katz, Jonathan. 1976. *Gay American History: Lesbians and Gay Men in the U.S.A.: A Documentary.* New York: Crowell.

This extraordinary documentary history follows in great detail events in the history of non-heterosexual individuals and groups in the United States from precolonial days to the mid-1970s.

Knuttila, Kenneth Murray. 2016. *Paying for Masculinity: Boys, Men and the Patriarchal Dividend.* Halifax, UK; Winnipeg, Canada: Fernwood Publishing.

The author argues that, although the cost of patriarchy for women has been widely discussed, the dominance of men in society also has its price for men and boys.

Lerner, Gerda. 1986. *The Creation of Patriarchy.* New York; Oxford: Oxford University Press.

In one of the most important books on the history of patriarchy ever written, the author argues that patriarchy is neither biologically ordained nor inevitable. She traces the history of the practice from the second millennium BCE to show how its growth and development have taken place in human history.

Lindsey, Linda L. 2015. *Gender Roles: A Sociological Perspective.* London: Routledge.
The author discusses the topic of gender from a sociological standpoint, with special attention to subjects such as gender development; the expression of gender in language; the construction of gender roles in Western history; global perspectives on gender; gender and family relationships; men and masculinity; religion and patriarchy; and power, politics, and the law.

Mantilla, Karla. 2015. *Gendertrolling: How Misogyny Went Viral.* Santa Barbara, CA: Praeger.
The author discusses the relatively new phenomenon known as gendertrolling, in which online participants react especially strongly to women who express political, social, sexual, gender, or other views on the Internet to which some individuals react strongly. "Strongly" may include threats of rape or other forms of violence, including death threats. For an abbreviated overview of this issue, see the author's online article "Understanding the Difference between Generic Harassment and GenderTrolling," at the Women Media Center's Speech Project, http://wmcspeechproject.com/2016/04/15/understanding-the-difference-between-generic-harassment-and-gender trolling/. Accessed on November 7, 2016.

Mogul, Joey L., Andrea J. Ritchie, and Kay Whitlock. 2011. *Queer (In)justice: The Criminalization of LGBT People in the United States.* Boston: Beacon Press.
The authors consider the way in which the legal system treats LGBT people in the United States. After an opening chapter on the history of this theme in colonial America,

they go on to review the treatment of LGBT people in the streets, in the courts, in prisons, and in other parts of the legal system.

Montañola, Sandy, and Aurélie Olivesi, eds. 2016. *Gender Testing in Sport: Ethics, Cases and Controversies.* New York: Routledge.

The essays in this anthology are based primarily on the issues surrounding sex testing of Caster Semenya, and deal with topics such as the myth of the level playing field; the science, law, and ethics of categorizing sex; and questions of apartheid and segregation in sports.

Nally, Claire, and Angela Smith, eds. 2015. *Twenty-First Century Feminism: Forming and Performing Femininity.* Houndmills, Basingstoke, Hampshire; New York: Palgrave Macmillan.

This anthology of papers analyzes some of the factors in the early 21st century that have prompted some new directions in feminist thought, including the news media, pornography, and social media.

Nicolazzo, Z. 2017. *Trans* in College: Transgender Students' Strategies for Navigating Campus Life and the Institutional Politics of Inclusion.* Sterling, VA: Stylus Publishing.

The author, a transperson, suggests that this book is designed both for transindividuals themselves as well as the general community in acknowledging and learning how to deal with the unique problems of transpeople on college campuses.

Novic, Richard J. 2014. *Alice in Genderland: A Crossdresser Comes of Age.* New York: iUniverse.

The author, a medical doctor, documents the details of his long journey as a cross-dresser, from early childhood and adolescence to adulthood. He claims that this book is the first detailed story of a heterosexual man who dresses up as a woman and actually leaves his house in feminine apparel.

Penney, James. 2014. *After Queer Theory: The Limits of Sexual Politics*. London: Pluto Press.

The author explains why he believes that queer theory has "run its course," and that its approach to the analysis of important social problems is no longer relevant. He then goes on to suggest a future direction for such problems from a new and different standpoint.

Pieper, Lindsay Parks. 2016. *Sex Testing: Gender Policing in Women's Sports*. Urbana: University of Illinois Press.

Pieper reviews the history of sex-testing policies for women in sport from the 1930s to the early 2000s.

Revati, A. 2010. *The Truth about Me: A Hijra Life Story*. New Delhi: Penguin Books.

This autobiographical book provides a personal and intimate look at the life of an Indian boy who became and then lived his life as a hijra.

Rudd, Peggy J. 2011. *Crossdressing with Dignity: The Case for Transcending Gender Lines*. Katy, TX: Pm Publishers.

The author, whose husband is a cross-dresser, examines a number of personal, social, and ethical issues related to cross-dressing. The book includes input from more than 600 men and women who are involved in cross-dressing in their households. The author has written three other books on the topic, including *My Husband Wears My Clothes* (2011), *Crossdressers and Those Who Share Their Lives* (1995), and *Who's Really from Venus?* (2003), all from the same publisher.

Ryle, Robyn. 2015. *Questioning Gender: A Sociological Exploration*. Los Angeles: SAGE Publications.

The author looks at gender issues from the somewhat different aspect of sociological theory. She discusses topics such as what she means by the sociology of gender, how a person learns about his or her gender and the gender of others, how gender affects a person's affectional orientation, how one's gender impacts his or her relationships with others, how gender affects the way one thinks about his or her own body, the role of one's gender in the workplace, and the influence of gender on one's choices of media and cultural experiences.

Sandberg, Sheryl. 2013. *Lean In: Women, Work, and the Will to Lead.* New York: Alfred A. Knopf.

Sandberg, chief operating officer of Facebook, takes note that women still lag behind men in leadership positions in business by a considerable margin. She examines the root causes of this fact and offers a number of suggestions as to how women can come to play a more important role in America's business community. The book has led to the formation of an organization called Lead In (http://leanin.org/), designed to help women achieve the objectives that Sandberg outlined in her book.

Shultz, Jackson Wright. 2015. *Trans/portraits: Voices from Transgender Communities.* Hanover, NH: Dartmouth College Press.

The author summarizes interviews with more than 30 Americans from 25 different states who identify as transgender, ranging in age from 15 to 72. They discuss personal issues of love and conflict, along with social and institutional challenges they have encountered.

Turk, Katherine. 2016. *Equality on Trial: Gender and Rights in the Modern American Workplace.* Philadelphia: University of Pennsylvania Press.

The author asks the question: What can explain the strengthening of laws that guarantee equality in employment in today's America, at the same time that social inequality between men and women still seems to be growing? She begins with an analysis of the adoption of Title VII of the 1964 Civil Rights Action and the creation of the Equal Employment Opportunity Commission and the changes that these events produce in the workplace for women, and the changes that have taken place in the following 50 years.

Wiesner-Hanks, Merry E. 2011 *Gender in History: Global Perspectives*, 2nd ed. Malden, MA; Oxford, UK: Wiley-Blackwell. The chapters in this book all follow a common historical trend, from the earliest known date at which the topic appeared to the present day. They deal with the family; economic life; ideas, ideals, norms, and laws; religion and political life; education and culture; and sexuality.

Wilchins, Riki Anne. 2014. *Queer Theory, Gender Theory: An Instant Primer*. New York: Magnus Books. This book offers a good general introduction to the topic of queer theory, a way of analyzing social and personal issues from the standpoint of sexual and gender minorities. It covers topics such as women's rights, gay rights, transgender rights, intersexuality, and gender rights.

Williams, Walter L. 1992. *The Spirit and the Flesh*, 2nd rev. ed. Boston: Beacon Press. Winner of many prestigious book awards, *The Spirit and the Flesh* reviews aspects of two spirit people such as the spiritual basis of the tradition, mystical powers and ceremonial roles, economic and social status, gender role, sexual aspects, the berdache's husband and issues of sexual variance, the Spanish campaign against sodomy, the impact of religion and the decline of the berdache tradition, and the modern berdache tradition in the context of gay culture.

Wisniewski, Amy B., Steven D. Chernauset, and Bradley P. Kropp. 2012. *Disorders of Sex Development: A Guide for Parents and Physicians*. Baltimore: Johns Hopkins University Press. This book is written for professionals in the field, parents, caregivers, and others interested in dealing with issues of DSD. Topics covered include a general introduction to DSD, the type of DSD a child may have, how newborns are evaluated for the condition, gender development among DSD children, treatment options, educating children about DSD, long-term health prospects for individuals with the condition, and challenges and special circumstances.

Wood, Julia T. 2015. *Gendered Lives: Communication, Gender, & Culture*, 11th ed. Stamford, CT: Cengage Learning.
This textbook is designed as a broad, general introduction to the topic of gender. It includes sections on theoretical approaches to gender development, competing images of women, competing images of men, gendered verbal communication, gendered nonverbal communication, becoming gendered: the early years, gendered close relationships, gendered organized communication, gendered media, and gendered power and violence.

Zimmerman, Jonathan. 2015. *Too Hot to Handle: A Global History of Sex Education*. Princeton, NJ: Princeton University Press.
The four chapters in this book cover the periods between 1898 and 1939, 1940 and 1964, 1965 and 1983, and 1984 to 2010.

Articles

Some journals that specialize in articles on sex and gender are the following:

- *Feminist Theory*: print ISSN: 1464-7001; online ISSN: 1741-2773
- *Gender & Development*: print ISSN: 1355-2074; online ISSN: 1364-9221
- *Gender & Society*: print ISSN: 089-12432; online ISSN: 1552-3977

- *International Journal of Transgenderism*: print ISSN: 1553-2739; online ISSN: 1434-4599
- *Journal of Gender Studies*: print ISSN: 0958-9236; online ISSN: 1465-3869
- *Journal of the History of Sexuality*: print ISSN: 1043-4070; online ISSN: 1535-3605
- *Journal of Homosexuality*: ISSN: 0091-8369; online ISSN: 1540-3602
- *Journal of Sex Research*: print ISSN: 0022-4499 online ISSN: 1559-8519
- *Psychology of Men & Masculinity*: print ISSN: 1524-9220; online ISSN: 1939-151X
- *Psychology of Sexual Orientation and Gender Diversity*: print ISSN: 2329-0382; online ISSN: 2329-0390
- *Psychology of Women Quarterly*: print ISSN: 0361-6843; online ISSN: 1471-6402

Amaral, Rita Cassia, et al. 2015. "Quality of Life of Patients with 46, XX and 46, XY Disorders of Sex Development." *Clinical Endocrinology* 82(2): 159–164.

This meta-analysis explores the quality of life (QoL) of individuals with two forms of DSD from both developed and developing nations. Researchers found that QoL varied widely from very poor to better than normal, depending on the type of care that was provided.

Auchus, R. J., and E. H. Quint. 2015. "Adolescents with Disorders of Sex Development (DSD)—Lost in Transition?" *Hormone and Metabolic Research* 47(5): 367–374.

The authors of this article review the health issues with which DSD children and adolescents often have to deal and then provides an overview of the transitioning process with the use of a few conditions as examples to illustrate particular aspects of the condition.

Bailey, J. Michael, et al. 2016. "Sexual Orientation, Controversy, and Science." *Psychological Science in the Public Interest* 17(2): 45–101. Available online at http://psi.sagepub.com/content/17/2/45.full.pdf+html. Accessed on November 3, 2016.

Leading researchers in the field of same-sex orientation examine international political issues relating to homosexual behavior, especially in view of what is known about the origin of such behavior. They comment that "the actual relevance of these issues [the causes of homosexuality] to social, political, and ethical decisions is often poorly justified, however."

Berenbaum, Sheri A., and Adriene M. Beltz. 2016. "How Early Hormones Shape Gender Development." *Current Opinion in Behavioral Sciences* 7: 53–60.

Current research suggests that hormones present in the early development of a baby may influence his or her gender roles in addition to the child's biological sex. This article reviews some of that evidence.

Biason-Lauber, A. 2016. "The Battle of the Sexes: Human Sex Development and Its Disorders." *Results and Problems in Cell Differentiation* 58: 337–382.

The author provides a nice general introduction to the process of sexual development in the human embryo, along with a review of some of the problems that can develop during that process.

Blithe, Sarah Jane, and Jenna N. Hanchey. 2015. "The Discursive Emergence of Gendered Physiological Discrimination in Sex Verification Testing." *Women's Studies in Communication* 38(4): 486–506.

The authors argue that chromosomes, hormones, and other biological factors do not necessarily provide a complete definition as to one's sex and are, therefore, not entirely valid determinants for who it is that qualifies for participation in elite sporting event such as the Olympic Games. They suggest, instead, that psychological factors are of considerable importance and that the bases for deciding who is or is not eligible for such contests has historically reflected elements of sexism, patriarchy, racism, and imperialism and is "a new field of power that primarily discriminates against "non-normative" bodily processes."

Brodsky, J. L., and M. Genel. 2016. "The 2015 Pediatric Endocrine Society Ethics Symposium: Controversies regarding 'Gender Verification' of Elite Female Athletes—Sex Testing to Hyperandrogenism." *Hormone Research in Paediatrics* 85(4): 273–274.
This article provides a summary of the symposium named in the title on the history and current status of testing of female athletes to determine their true sex for the purpose of competitive events.

Costa, Rosalia, et al. 2015. "Psychological Support, Puberty Suppression, and Psychosocial Functioning in Adolescents with Gender Dysphoria." *The Journal of Sexual Medicine* 12(11): 2206–2214.
The authors report on research on the use of psychological support mechanisms and puberty suppression to measure the psychological functioning of adolescents with gender dysphoria. They find that both approaches contribute to an increase in scores on this measure.

Dyble, M., et al. 2015. "Sex Equality Can Explain the Unique Social Structure of Hunter-gatherer Bands." *Science* 348(6236): 796–798.
These anthropologists report on their research on primitive tribes to draw conclusions about the social structure of early humans and find evidence that the most successful

of such cultures were probably those in which there was a high degree of equality between women and men.

Ehrensaft, Diane. 2012. "From Gender Identity Disorder to Gender Identity Creativity: True Gender Self Child Therapy." *Journal of Homosexuality* 59(3): 337–356.
This articles "presents concepts of true gender self, false gender self, and gender creativity as they operationalize in clinical work with children who need therapeutic supports to establish an authentic gender self while developing strategies for negotiating an environment resistant to that self."

Eisenberg, Maria L., Melanie Wall, and Dianne Neumark-Sztainer. 2012. "Muscle-Enhancing Behaviors among Adolescent Girls and Boys." *Pediatrics* 130(6): 1019–1926.
The authors report on a study of 2,793 diverse adolescent boys and girls at 20 urban middle and high schools. They find that muscle-enhancing practices are common within this sample, apparently in an effort to conform more closely to public images as to appropriate body images for males and females in American society.

Fuss, Johannes, Matthias K. Auer, and Peera Briken. 2015. "Gender Dysphoria in Children and Adolescents: A Review of Recent Research." *Current Opinion in Psychiatry* 28(6): 430–434.
The authors' review of existing data suggests that gender dysphoria is far more common than had been thought even a short time ago. They examine studies of the use of puberty suppression cross-sex hormonal treatments for the treatment of the condition and find that the procedure seems to be successful in a number of instances.

Gillam, Lynn H., Jacqueline K. Hewitt, and Garry L. Warne. 2010. "Ethical Principles for the Management of Infants with Disorders of Sex Development." *Hormone Research in Paediatrics* 74(6): 412–418.

This article reports on the Halifax Resolutions, a set of principles adopted at the Fifth World Congress on Family Law and Children's Rights concerning the ethical guidelines for the management of infants and children with disorders of sex development.

Glass, Christy, and Alison Cook. 2016. "Leading at the Top: Understanding Women's Challenges above the Glass Ceiling." *The Leadership Quarterly* 27(1): 51–63.

The authors briefly review the concept of the "glass ceiling," the tendency of corporations to allow women to advance to positions of greater responsibility only to a certain point, "the glass ceiling." They then ask what happens to women who *are* able to earn promotions beyond the glass ceiling. They find that such women are often promoted into high-risk jobs with relatively modest corporate support, explaining the fact that they tend to remain at their superior positions for a shorter period of time than their male counterparts.

Gray, Sarah A. L., et al. 2016. " 'Am I Doing the Right Thing?': Pathways to Parenting a Gender Variant Child." *Family Process* 55(1): 123–138.

This paper reports on the actions of a small sample of parents of DSD children, describing the ways they have dealt with the reality of their child's gender variant feelings.

Guercio, Gabriela, et al. 2015. "Fertility Issues in Disorders of Sex Development." *Endocrinology and Metabolism Clinics of North America* 44(4): 867–881.

The authors consider fertility issues for some specific forms of DSD.

Kon, A. A. 2015. "Ethical Issues in Decision-making for Infants with Disorders of Sex Development." *Hormone and metabolic research* 47(5): 340–343.

This article reviews the history of the use of surgical procedures to determine the sex of a DSD individual and suggests that current opinion offers a different view of this practice. He suggests that surgery should generally be delayed until child herself or himself has an opportunity to participate in the decision-making.

Lee, Peter A., and Christopher P. Houk. 2016. "Changing and Unchanging Perspectives regarding Intersex in the Last Half Century: Topics Presented in the Lawson Wilkins Lecture* at the 2015 Pediatric Endocrine Society Meeting." *Pediatric Endocrinology Reviews* 13(3): 574–584.

This article provides an excellent review of changing (as well as constant) attitudes about the diagnosis and treatment of DSD over the preceding five decades.

Lee, P. A., et al. 2016. "Global Disorders of Sex Development Update since 2006: Perceptions, Approach and Care." *Hormone Research in Paediatrics* 85(3): 158–180.

This review article provides an excellent overview and review of the current status of the diagnosis, analysis, and treatment of disorders of sex development since the Consensus Convention of 2005 held in Chicago.

Leibowitz, Scott, and Annelou L. C. de Vries. 2016. "Gender Dysphoria in Adolescence." *International Review of Psychiatry* 28(1): 21–35.

This paper presents the results of a widely conducted review of reports on methods for dealing adolescents with gender dysphoria. The authors point out that the amount of empirical evidence to guide such treatment programs is still very limited.

Makiyan, Zograb. 2016. "Studies of Gonadal Sex Differentiation." *Organogenesis* 12(1): 42–51.

This technical paper reviews research on the normal process of gonadal sex differentiation in humans and changes that may occur in that process that can result in the development of disorders of sex differentiation.

Martin, Carol Lynn, and Diane N. Ruble. 2010. "Patterns of Gender Development." *Annual Review of Psychology* 61: 353–381. Available online at https://www.ncbi.nlm.nih.gov/pmc/articles/ PMC3747736/. Accessed on November 2, 2016.

This article provides a thorough review of information currently available on the process of gender development, including changes that occur at various stages of an individual's life, how stereotyping develops, how do children exhibit prejudice and discrimination, and how stable gender typing is likely to be.

McGuire, Jenifer K., et al. 2016. "Transfamily Theory: How the Presence of Trans* Family Members Informs Gender Development in Families." *Journal of Family Theory & Review* 8(1): 60–73.

The growth in the number of acknowledged transfamilies has raised some fundamental question about the development of gender roles in such families. This article discusses five issues in particular: non-dimorphic sex, non-binary gender, the biological and social construction of gender, gender identity development, and the ways in which families help define the meaning of transgender identity.

Mouriquanda, Pierre D. E., et al. 2016. "Surgery in Disorders of Sex Development (DSD) with a Gender Issue: If (Why), When, and How?" *Journal of Pediatric Urology* 12(3): 139–149.

The authors take note of the fact that a decade has passed since the meeting on appropriate diagnosis and treatment of disorders of sex development, and most major issues remain largely unresolved, including justifications, timing, and methods of surgeries to be used in dealing with the disorder. They also note that consensus appears to have been reached on at least a few of the most fundamental questions about the treatment of DSD, points that they then review in this article.

Piepere, Lindsay Parks. 2014. "Sex Testing and the Maintenance of Western Femininity in International Sport." *The International Journal of the History of Sport* 31(13): 1557–1576.
The author argues that gender testing in elite sports competition involves more than just questions about one's sexual status. Instead, she says, it is based on a racist, sexist, and "binary notion of sex and privileged white, Western gender norms."

Ristori, Jiska, and Thomas D. Steensma. 2016. "Gender Dysphoria in Childhood." *International Review of Psychiatry* 28(1): 13–20.
The authors note that considerable difference exists among cases in which children express gender dysphoria and that understanding of and treatment for the condition, therefore, may take a variety of forms. This paper summarizes information gained from reports of such programs at a variety of gender identity clinics.

Russo, Francine. 2015. "Transgender Kids." *Scientific American Mind* 27: 26–35.
The author reviews some of the issues arising as a result of a greater number of children and adolescents expressing concerns about their gender identity and some of the ways in which clinicians, parents, and others have attempted to deal with these issues. She suggests that programs that have been developed in the Netherlands may provide a useful model for dealing with some of these challenges.

Sánchez, Francisco J., Mariá José Martínez-Patiño, and Eric Vilain. 2013. "The New Policy on Hyperandrogenism in Elite Female Athletes Is Not about 'Sex Testing.'" *Journal of Sex Research* 50(2): 112–115.
The authors comment on the latest efforts by the International Olympic Committee to devise a way of preventing nonfemale athletes from participating in female events at the Olympic Games. They argue that a decision of this

kind should be made only by those athletes who actually take part in such events, so-called elite athletes.

Telles-Silveira, M., F. Knobloch, and C. E. Kater. 2015. "Management Framework Paradigms for Disorders of Sex Development." *Archives of Endocrinology and Metabolism* 59(5): 383–390.
The authors consider two historical approaches to the treatment of DSD, the so-called money era beginning about 1955 and the "Chicago Consensus" of 2005. They review the effect of both models on current practices and evaluate approaches to the treatment of DSD today and in the future.

Thompson, Helen. 2012. "Performance Enhancement: Superhuman Athletes." *Nature* 487(7407): 287–289.
Thompson provides a succinct overview of the types of performance enhancing substances one can use and the potential effects of those substances. She says that the continued uses of such substances will lead to the "emergence of all kinds of new sports."

Wahogo, Subira, and Ron Roberts. 2012. "Fourth Wave Feminism: Protests and Prospects." *Journal of Critical Psychology Counselling and Psychotherapy* 12(4): 216–220.
The authors describe a new wave of feminism that depends to a considerable extent on the availability of Internet communities and online bloggers. They say that the new wave is "the most inclusive form of the struggle for female emancipation to date" in that it takes as a given that "all forms of systematic oppression are connected."

Zainuddin, Ani Amelia, and Zaleha Abdullah Mahdy. 2016. "The Islamic Perspectives of Gender-Related Issues in the Management of Patients with Disorders of Sex Development." *Archives of Sexual Behavior.* DOI: 10.1007/s10508-016-0754-y.
The article reveals the rather intriguing point that the medical treatment of disorders of sex development has a

strong religious component in at least one of the world's major religions (Islam), a component that is described and discussed in this article.

Zucker, Kenneth J., Anne A. Lawrence, and Baudewijntje P. C. Kreukels. 2016. "Gender Dysphoria in Adults." *Annual Review of Clinical Psychology* 12: 217–247.
The authors summarize current practices in the diagnosis, analysis, and treatment of genetic disorder in adults. They point that increasing attention to the condition among the general public is likely to encourage development of new ways of working with individuals with the condition.

Reports

"About Hate Crime Statistics 2013." 2013. U.S. Department of Justice. Federal Bureau of Investigation. https://ucr.fbi.gov/hate-crime/2013. Accessed on November 7, 2016.
The FBI expanded its definition of hate crime in 2013 to include gender-based crimes. This annual report on crime in the United States provides data on hate crimes against seven classes of individuals, including those based on sexual orientation, gender identity, and gender bias. The report includes extended tables of data.

"Anorexia In-Depth Report." 2008. *New York Times*, from A.D.A.M. http://www.nytimes.com/health/guides/disease/anorexia-nervosa/print.html. Accessed on November 4, 2016.
This report provides detailed data and statistics on all varieties of eating disorders in addition to information on causes, treatments, and related issues for four forms of the disorder.

Greytak, Emily A., et al. 2016. "From Teasing to Torment: School Climate Revisited, a Survey of U.S. Secondary School Students and Teachers." New York: GLSEN.
GLSEN conducts annual surveys on the environment for LGBTQ students in American schools. This title is the

most recent of those reports currently available. After acknowledging that progress has been made over the preceding decade, authors of the report also noted that "Overall, bullying still persists at unacceptable levels, and the gains of the past ten years throw the more intractable aspects of the problem into higher relief. LGBTQ students still face rates of violence much higher relative to their peers. Teachers report that they are less comfortable and less prepared to address the harsh conditions faced by transgender and gender nonconforming students. And amidst progress in reducing the use of most types of biased language in schools, racist language remains as prevalent as it was a decade ago."

Hughes, I. A., et al. 2006. "Consensus Statement on Management of Intersex Disorders." *Archives of Diseases in Childhood* 91(7): 554–563.

This article summarizes the agreements reached at the so-called Consensus Conference in Chicago in 2005 on nomenclature to be used in cases of intersex development among children and adolescents.

"Non-Discrimination Laws." 2016. Movement Advancement Project. http://www.lgbtmap.org/equality-maps/non_discrimination_laws. Accessed on November 3, 2016.

This website provides a summary of state nondiscrimination legislation in the areas of employment, housing, public accommodation, and credit for all 50 states.

Parker, Kim, et al. 2015. "Women and Leadership." Pew Research Center. http://www.pewsocialtrends.org/2015/01/14/women-and-leadership/. Accessed on November 6, 2015.

This report summarizes the results of two public opinion surveys conducted in 2014 on public attitudes about gender and leadership in U.S. politics and business. The specific areas covered include women in positions of political and corporate leadership, what makes a good leader and does gender matter in that regard, and what are the obstacles to female leadership in politics and business. The survey suggests that the general public regard women at least as qualified as men for leadership positions, but that progress does not reflect that fact because women are often held to a double standard that is not used for men.

Schwab, Klaus, et al. 2016. "The Global Gender Gap Report 2016." World Economic Forum. http://www3.weforum.org/docs/GGGR16/WEF_Global_Gender_Gap_Report_2016.pdf. Accessed on November 5, 2016.

The World Economic Forum has published this report annually since 2006. It provides a nation-by-nation summary of the status of women in four general areas: economic participation and opportunity, educational attainment, health and survival, and political empowerment. The 2016 report finds that women are nearly equal to men in the fields of educational attainment and health and survival (95% and 96%, respectively), but fall far behind men in the fields of economic participation and opportunity (59%) and political empowerment (23%).

"The Simple Truth about Gender Pay Gap." Fall 2016 Edition. American Association of University Women. http://www.aauw.org/aauw_check/pdf_download/show_pdf.php?file=The-Simple-Truth. Accessed on November 5, 2016.

This report is updated regularly with the most current statistics from the Bureau of Labor Statistics and the Census Bureau. It provides key facts about the gender pay gap in the United States. Topics covered in the report include a definition of the pay gap; a history of the pay gap in the United States; the size of the pay gap in each state; demographic factors affecting the pay gap, such as age, race, ethnicity, and education; guidance for women facing workplace discrimination; and resources for fair pay advocates.

"Special Reports." 2016. SEICUS. http://www.siecus.org/index .cfm?fuseaction=Page.ViewPage&pageId=484. Accessed on November 4, 2016.

SEICUS regularly publishes a number of special reports on the status of sex education around the nation and worldwide. Some of the reports available in 2016 concern the status of sex education in the states in 2016; sex education in Mississippi; Colorado's abstinence-only-until-marriage sex education programs; HIV/AIDS prevention programs in Zambia; sex education and abstinence-only programs in Florida; and examples of the ways in which federally funded programs discriminate against LGBT youth and families.

"State Policies on Sex Education in Schools." 2016. National Conference of State Legislatures. http://www.ncsl.org/re search/health/state-policies-on-sex-education-in-schools.aspx. Accessed on November 2, 2016.

National Conference of State Legislatures is a reliable source of data and information on a vast number of topics, one of which is the status of sex education in the United States. This website provides details of state laws in all 50 states on sex education requirements and recommendations.

"The Status of Women in the States: Resources." 2016. Institute for Women's Policy Institute. http://www.iwpr.org/initia tives/states/the-status-of-women-in-the-states-state-reports. Accessed on August 5, 2016.

The institute regularly publishes reports on the status of women and girls in the 50 states and the District of Columbia, as well as national reports of the same kind. All reports are available on the organization's website.

Stotsky, Janet Gale, et al. 2016. "Trends in Gender Equality and Women Advancement." Washington, DC: International Monetary Fund. Available online at https://www.imf.org/external/pubs/ft/wp/2016/wp1621.pdf. Accessed on October 31, 2016.

> The authors report on their research on the status of women in a variety of fields worldwide. They conclude that progress is being made in achieving equity for the participation of women in political, economic, social, and other fields, but that more progress is needed.

Thoreson, Ryan. 2016. "Shut Out: Restrictions on Bathroom and Locker Room Access for Transgender Youth in US Schools." New York: Human Rights Watch.

> This report summarizes legal actions that states in the United States have taken to restrict the rights of transgender individuals and explains why such laws are "not only unnecessary, but discriminatory and dangerous."

"United States Global Strategy to Empower Adolescent Girls." 2016. U.S. Department of States. http://www.state.gov/documents/organization/254904.pdf. Accessed on November 5, 2016.

> This report describes the U.S. efforts worldwide to "ensure adolescent girls are educated, healthy, economically and socially empowered, and free from violence and discrimination, thereby promoting global development, security, and prosperity." Efforts developed around this goal include enhancing girls' access to quality education in safe environments, providing economic incentives for girls and their families, empowering girls with the information and skills they need, mobilizing community educational opportunities, and strengthening policy and legal frameworks to achieve these objectives.

Internet

"American Academy of Nursing Position Statement on Reparative Therapy." 2015. *Nursing Outlook* 63(3): 368–369. Also available online at http://www.nursingoutlook.org/article/ S0029-6554(15)00125-6/pdf. Accessed on November 6, 2016.

This position statement on reparative theory cites similar position statements by a number of other professional organizations, such as the American Medical Association, American Psychological Association, American Psychiatric Association, and Pan American Health Organization. It notes that procedures designed to change one's sexual orientation have been "widely discredited by most major health care professional organizations for their lack of scientific justification, failure to achieve intended results, questionable clinical practices, disregard and lack of respect for normal human differences, and inherently harmful effects on mental and physical health of individuals being pressured to change."

"Anti-LGBT Religious Exemption Legislation across the Country." 2016. American Civil Liberties Union. https://www.aclu .org/other/anti-lgbt-religious-exemption-legislation-across-country. Accessed on November 6, 2016.

This web page provides a good summary of so-called religious freedom and LGBT discrimination acts in state legislature around the country. The bills are divided into categories such as religious freedom restoration acts, marriage-related religious exemption laws, First Amendment defense acts, government employees, commercial wedding services, pastor protection acts, other marriage exemption bills, adoption and foster care, college and university student groups, access to health services, and other exemption bills.

Bendery, Jennifer, and Michelangelo Signorile. 2016. "Everything You Need to Know about the Wave of 100+ Anti-LGBT Bills Pending in States." *Huffington Post*. http://www .huffingtonpost.com/entry/lgbt-state-bills-discrimination_ us_570ff4f2e4b0060ccda2a7a9. Accessed on November 3, 2016.

This article lists the types of discriminatory legislation that is currently being passed against LGBT people and the characteristics of each type of legislation. Specific examples of state laws are included for more detailed analysis.

"Body Image." 2016. Raising Children Network. http://raising children.net.au/articles/body_image.html. Accessed on November 4, 2016.

This website provides a good general overview of issues related to body image among children and adolescents. It discusses topics such as risk factors for negative body image, signs of body image problems, ways of developing positive body images, and body image among special needs children.

"Body Image and Self-Esteem." 2016. Teens Health. http:// kidshealth.org/en/teens/body-image.html#. Accessed on November 2, 2016.

This web page provides information for teenagers about body image and self-esteem. It explains why the topic is important to adolescents, what the factors are that affect body image and self-esteem, things a person can do to improve both qualities, and resources that provide more information on the topic.

"The Body Project." 2016. Bradley University. https://bradley .edu/sites/bodyproject/. Accessed on November 2, 2016.

The Body Project was developed by the Women's Studies Program at Bradley University in cooperation with the University's Center for Wellness and Department of Sociology. The purpose of the site is to challenge the way

people think about current standards of beauty and fitness; locate print, visual, and electronic resources that
will help a person to gain acceptance of one's own body;
expand one's understanding of the ways in which political, economic, and cultural forces shape body images; get
information about and assistance with balanced nutrition
and eating disorders; and post one's own ideas about issues of body image and standards of beauty and fitness.

Brayboy, Duane. 2016. "Two Spirits, One Heart, Five Genders." Indian Country. http://indiancountrytodaymedianet
work.com/2016/01/23/two-spirits-one-heart-five-genders.
Accessed on November 7, 2016.
This website provides an excellent general overview of the
nature of two spirit people, their history and culture, and
the travails imposed by the arrival of European colonists
in North America. The controversy raised by responses to
the article is of special interest.

Burkett, Elinor, and Laura Brunell. 2016. "The Third Wave of
Feminism." Encyclopaedia Britannica. https://www.britannica
.com/topic/feminism/The-third-wave-of-feminism. Accessed on
November 3, 2016.
This essay reviews the foundations of the third wave of the
feminist movement, its manifestations, and controversies
surrounding its existence and efforts.

Christ, Carol P. 2013. "Patriarchy as a System of Male Dominance Created at the Intersection of the Control of Women,
Private Property, and War." Feminism and Religion. https://
feminismandreligion.com/2013/02/18/patriarchy-as-an-inte
gral-system-of--male-dominance-created-at-the-intersection-
of-the-control-of-women-private-property-and-war-part-1-by-
carol-p-christ/. Accessed on November 2, 2016.
The author presents a long and detailed analysis of the
way in which patriarchy developed in the world and how
it has and continues to influence virtually every aspect of

life today. The article appears in three parts. See the links at the bottom of the article to parts 2 and 3.

Cochrane, Kira. 2013. "The Fourth Wave of Feminism: Meet the Rebel Women." *The Guardian*. https://www.theguardian .com/world/2013/dec/10/fourth-wave-feminism-rebel-women. Accessed on November 3, 2016.

> The author describes her experiences with women's groups in a number of countries who have begun to push for yet another "wave" of feminist thought and action. She says the new movement is "a consciousness-raising exercise that encourages women to see how inequality affects them, proves these problems aren't individual but collective, and might therefore have political solutions."

Cookson, John. 2015. "Why Women Make Better Politicians." Big Think. http://bigthink.com/women-and-power/ why-women-make-better-politicians. Accessed on October 31, 2016.

> Given the long history of deploring the role of women in the U.S. political system by many observers, this article presents an interesting new take on that issue.

De Melker, Saskia. 2015. "The Case for Starting Sex Education in Kindergarten." PBS. http://www.pbs.org/newshour/ updates/spring-fever/. Accessed on November 2, 2016.

> This article describes a program that initiates teaching about human sexuality in the kindergarten in the Netherlands. It examines the pros and cons of offering this type of instruction at such an early age.

Diamond, Danie, and Eli Erlick. 2016. "Why We Used Trans* and Why We Don't Anymore." Trans Student Educational Resources. http://www.transstudent.org/asterisk. Accessed on October 31, 2016.

> The notation "trans*" has been used in the past—and is still used by some writers—to indicate inclusion of all

types of transindividuals. This essay explains that the writers (and, presumably, other transindividuals) no longer use the notation because of its tendency to be "inaccessible, binarist, and transmisogynist."

"Disorders of Sex Development (DSD) Resources." 2016. University of Michigan Health System. http://www.med.umich .edu/yourchild/topics/dsd.htm. Accessed October 31, 2016.
This website provides some basic information about DSD, along with a very complete list of the specific medical conditions that are included in this diagnosis. Some useful links are also provided.

Drantz, Veronica. 2011. "Intersex People: What You Should Know and Why You Should Care." SlideShare. http://www .slideshare.net/drdrantz/intersex-people. Accessed on July 22, 2016.
This slide presentation for H.E.R. Day at the Center on Halstad in Chicago is a superb general introduction to the topic of intersex, with a detailed explanation of the biological principles involved, along with a review of some issues associated with disorders of sex development.

Dreger, Alice. 2007. "Why "Disorders of Sex Development"? (On Language and Life)." Alice Domurat Dreger. http://alice dreger.com/dsd. Accessed on October 31, 2016.
The author has been very much involved in the selection of terminology to discuss the phenomenon previously known as *intersexuality*. The article provides an excellent introduction to the topic in general as well as links to other related articles on the topic.

"Eating Disorders." 2016. Teens Health. http://kidshealth.org/ en/teens/eat-disorder.html?WT.ac=t-ra. Accessed on November 2, 2016.
This website provides basic information on a variety of topics related to eating disorders, such as anorexia nervosa,

bulimia, binge-eating disorder, and avoidant/restrictive food intake disorder.

"Ex-Gay Consumer Fraud Division." 2014. Truth Wins Out. http://www.truthwinsout.org/ex-gay-consumer-fraud-divi sion/. Accessed on November 6, 2016.
This web page contains an extensive list of publications on the process of gay conversion therapy, including top-ics such as the history of ex-gay ministries, ex-gay scan-dals and defections, research studies on the procedure, and descriptions of specific ex-gay organizations and their work.

"Explaining Disorders of Sex Development & Intersexuality." 2016. Healthy Children.org. https://www.healthychildren .org/English/health-issues/conditions/genitourinary-tract/ Pages/Explaining-Disorders-of-Sex-Development-Intersexuality .aspx. Accessed on October 31, 2016.
This website provides a good overview of the issue of dis-orders of sex development, with an explanation of essen-tial terms and links to additional resources.

"First Wave Feminism and the New Woman." 2009. https:// csivc.csi.cuny.edu/history/files/lavender/389/02-First%20 Wave%20Feminism%20Discovered.pdf. Accessed on Novem-ber 3, 2016.
This PowerPoint presentation highlights some of the main individuals and accomplishments of the first wave of the feminist movement. It also points out the special relation-ship at the time between feminism and abolitionism.

Gaille, Brandon. 2015. "37 Shocking LGBT Discrimination Statistics." Brandon[gaille]. http://brandongaille.com/37-shocking-lgbt-discrimination-statistics/. This blogger assem-bles a collection of more than three dozen specific facts about the ways in which LGBT people are discriminated against in employing, housing, and other settings, and the harm this does to them and to those who commit the discrimination.

"Gay Conversion Therapy." 2016. *The Huffington Post.* http://www.huffingtonpost.com/news/gay-conversion-therapy/. Accessed on November 6, 2016.

Gay conversion therapy (also known as *reparative therapy*) is a process by which counselors attempt to change the sexual orientation of a gay man or lesbian. This website contains links to over 150 online articles about the successes and failures of the procedure and about attempts by a wide variety of individuals and organizations to have it banned from use.

"Gender and Genetics." 2016. Genomic Resource Centre. World Health Organization. http://www.who.int/genomics/gender/en/index1.html. Accessed on July 22, 2016.

This web page is an excellent resource for issues related to the development of biological sex, including problems associated with disorders of sexual development.

"Gender Roles." 2010. Credo. http://search.credoreference.com/content/topic/sex_role. Accessed on October 31, 2016.

This web page is an entry from the *Encyclopedia of Group Processes and Intergroup Relations.* It introduces the topic of gender roles with sections on stereotypes, deviation from gender roles, gender roles and self-concept, origins of gender roles, and the impact of gender roles on individuals and society. A good list of somewhat dated additional references is also provided.

"Gender Testing of Athletes." 2016. hhmi Biointeractive. http://www.hhmi.org/biointeractive/gender-testing-athletes. Accessed on November 4, 2016.

This interactive activity allows the reader to go through many of the steps that are often used in determining the legal sex status of a woman who wishes to compete in an athletic event.

"Genital System." 2016. Human Embryology. Embryology.ch. http://www.embryology.ch/anglais/ugenital/patholgenital01 .html#hermavrai. Accessed on July 20, 2016.
This website is a section of a textbook on embryology that provides an excellent introduction to and explanation of the formation of intersex individuals.

"Glass Ceiling.com." 2016. http://www.glassceiling.com/. Accessed on November 6, 2016.
The purpose of this website is to provide resources for women in the workplace who are seeking to bring through the "glass ceiling" and achieve higher levels of responsibility in their careers. It provides links to online articles such as "Is Women's Work Undervalued?"; "Explore the Gender Pay Gap"; "Gender Bias, STEM, and the Boys Club"; "Study Examines the Difficulty of 'Opting In'"; and "What LeanIn.org and McKinsey Know about Women."

GLSEN. 2016. http://www.glsen.org/. Accessed on November 3, 2016.
GLSEN was founded as the Gay, Lesbian, & Straight Education Network in 1990 as an advocacy group for LGBT students in elementary and high schools. It is arguably the most effective of all agencies working on behalf of those students. The organization currently has 38 chapters in 26 states with more than 4,000 individual gay-straight alliance clubs. The GLSEN website is a good source of information about all school-related issues for LGBTQ youth, including programs such as Ally Week, ThinkB4-YouSpeak, Day of Silence, Safe Space Kit, Changing the Game, and No Name-Calling Week.

"Intersex." 2015. Medline Plus. https://medlineplus.gov/ency/article/001669.htm. Accessed on October 31, 2016.

This website provides a good general introduction to the topic of intersex, much more commonly referred to today as *disorders of sex development*. It lists and describes four major types of intersex conditions, explains how they can be diagnosed, outlines some methods of treatment, and provides links to sources of additional information.

Jagose, Annamarie. 2016. "Queer Theory." New Dictionary of the History of Ideas. Encyclopedia.com. http://www.encyclopedia.com/history/dictionaries-thesauruses-pictures-and-press-releases/queer-theory. Accessed on November 2, 2016.

Queer theory is a school of philosophy and analysis that developed in the 1990s to provide a new way of looking at a number of personal, social, political, and other issues from a non-normative, non-heterosexual, and non-binary sexual perspective. It takes a stance on such issues from the standpoint of gay men, lesbian, transgenders, bisexuals, and other sexual and gender minority individuals and groups. This article provides an excellent general introduction to the topic, along with a list of essential readings in the field.

Kishner, Stephen. 2015. Medscape. http://emedicine.medscape.com/article/128655-overview#showall. Accessed on October 31, 2016.

This somewhat technical article, which is nonetheless readily accessible to the average reader, provides a considerable amount of information on the biological effects and uses of testosterone and other anabolic steroids.

Martin, Carol L. 2014. "Gender: Early Socialization." Encyclopedia on Early Childhood Development. http://www.child-encyclopedia.com/sites/default/files/dossiers-complets/en/gender-early-socialization.pdf. Accessed on November 2, 2016.

This chapter is taken from a UNICEF book on early childhood development. It provides a general overview of the topic, describing the major stages of and forces impacting on development of gender during childhood. The article also contains a review of expert opinion on the subject.

Martin, Nina. 2016. "North Carolina's Terrible Anti-LGBT Law Is Even Worse than We Thought." Mother Jones. http://www.motherjones.com/politics/2016/04/north-carolina%E2%80%99s-terrible-anti-lgbt-law-even-worse-we-thought. Accessed on November 3, 2016.

This lengthy analysis of North Carolina's House Bill 2 shows that it provides for more extensive restrictions on individual actions than merely the use of a specific bathroom.

Mason, Everdeen, Aaron Williams, and Kennedy Elliott. 2016. "The Dramatic Rise in State Efforts to Limit LGBT Rights." *The Washington Post.* https://www.washingtonpost.com/graphics/national/lgbt-legislation/. Accessed on November 3, 2016.

This article reports on the increasing number of new laws passed by states between 2013 and 2016 to discriminate against LGBT people in one way or another.

Munro, Ealasaid. 2016. "Feminism: A Fourth Wave?" Political Studies Association. https://www.psa.ac.uk/insight-plus/feminism-fourth-wave#top. Accessed on November 3, 2016.

The author provides a brief review of the first three waves of feminism. She then explores the conditions existing today—especially the role of social media—that may be responsible for the development of a fourth wave.

"The 1960s–70s American Feminist Movement: Breaking Down Barriers for Women." 2016. Tavaana. https://tavaana.org/en/content/1960s-70s-american-feminist-movement-breaking-down-barriers-women. Accessed on November 3, 2016.

This web page provides a nice general introduction to the second wave of feminism with sections on goals and objectives, leadership, civic environment, message and audience, and outreach activities.

Pound, Pandora. 2016. "What Do Young People Think about Their School-Based Sex and Relationship Education? A Qualitative Synthesis of Young People's Views and Experiences." BMJ Open. e011329 doi:10.1136/bmjopen-2016-011329. http://bmjopen.bmj.com/content/6/9/e011329.full. Accessed on November 2, 2016.

The author conducted a survey of students in 10 countries— Australia, Brazil, Canada, Iran, Ireland, Japan, New Zealand, Sweden, the United Kingdom, and the United States— about their attitudes toward the sex education classes they had experienced. The survey revealed widespread negative feelings about such classes. Those feelings fell into two major categories: teachers did not take into consideration the sensitive nature of the topics and taught the classes in a remote manner similar to one they might take in teaching geography or chemistry, and instructors did not take into consideration the reality that many (most?) students were already sexually active and how that fact would affect the information that was being provided.

Putnam, Jodi, Judith A. Myers-Walls, and Dee Love. 2013. "Gender Development." Provider-Parent Partnership. https://www.extension.purdue.edu/providerparent/child%20growth-development/genderdev.htm. Accessed on November 2, 2016.

This website is sponsored by the Purdue University Extension Service. It provides basic information on the process of gender development at all states of a child's and adolescent's life, along with factors that may influence that process. A good list of additional resources is also provided.

"Q & A: Adding Sexual Orientation & Gender Identity to Discrimination & Harassment Policies in Schools." 2016. American Civil Liberties Union. https://www.aclu.org/other/q-adding-sexual-orientation-gender-identity-discrimination-harassment-policies-schools. Accessed on November 3, 2016.

This article discusses the question as to whether high school students who identify as LGBTQ should be protected from bullying and other forms of discrimination by specific, formal antidiscrimination policies.

rserven. 2013. "A History Lesson on a Cold Evening." Daily Kos. http://www.dailykos.com/story/2013/2/8/1185661/-A-History-Lesson-on-a-Cold-Evening. Accessed on July 30, 2016.
This excellent essay provides detailed information on one of the earliest and most successful of female-to-male sex assignment surgery.

"Sex Education." 2008. Advocates for Youth. http://www.advocatesforyouth.org/sex-education-home. Accessed on November 2, 2016.
This website contains a number of sections on specific aspects of sex education, such as sex education for parents, sex education policy and advocacy, abstinence-only-until-marriage programs, adolescent sexual behavior, publications on sex education, sample sex education advocacy materials, lesson plans, programs that work, what does state law say about teaching sex education, conferences and courses for sex educators, and school health advisory councils.

"Sex and HIV Education." 2016. Guttmacher Institute. https://www.guttmacher.org/state-policy/explore/sex-and-hiv-education. Accessed on November 2, 2016.
The Guttmacher Institute is a research and policy organization "committed to advancing sexual and reproductive health and rights in the United States and globally." This website provides demographic information about the teaching of sex education in the United States. It provides a chart listing sex and HIV teacher requirements in all 50 states as well as the content of sex education courses in the states.

"Sexual Orientation." 2016. Ithaca College. http://www.ithaca
.edu/wise/sexual_orientation/. Accessed on November 3, 2016.
This website lists more than 200 websites dealing with
virtually every aspect of the field of sexual orientation,
such as surveys on the issues faced by LGBTQ students
in schools, formal policy documents on the rights of
LGBTQ students, personal statements on issues faced by
LGBTQ students, and specific events and news reports
on problems faced by LGBTQ students.

"Sexual Orientation and Gender Identity." 2016. American Psychological Association. http://www.apa.org/helpcenter/sexual-
orientation.aspx. Accessed on November 3, 2016.
The American Psychological Association has some useful
publications on various aspects of sexual orientation that
explain topics such as how do people know if they are
gay or lesbian, what causes a person to have a particular
sexual orientation, is homosexuality a mental disorder, at
what age should LGBT individuals "come out," and can
lesbians and gay men be good parents.

Sifferlin, Alexandra. 2016. "Why Schools Can't Teach Sex Ed."
Time. http://time.com/why-schools-cant-teach-sex-ed/. Accessed
on November 2, 2016.
This article discusses issues raised with regard to the teaching of sex education in public schools as a result of the significant changes that have taken place in the modern views
of sexuality that are now currently available in the media.
The article points out that both parents and children are
dissatisfied with sex education classes, although often for
very different reasons. The article also contains some useful
links to other resources that deal with this issue.

Singal, Jesse. 2016. "Should Olympic Athletes Get Sex-Tested
at All?" Science of Us. http://nymag.com/scienceofus/2016/08/
should-olympic-athletes-be-sex-tested-at-all.html. Accessed on
November 4, 2016.

This web page provides a detailed and extensive discussion of the issues involved in sex-testing for female athletes who wish to compete in the Olympics and other major contests.

Sollee, Kristen. 2015. "6 Things to Know about Fourth Wave Feminism." Bustle. https://www.bustle.com/articles/119524-6-things-to-know-about-4th-wave-feminism. Accessed on November 3, 2016.

This brief article lists six things about the fourth wave of feminism, each of which is expanded and discussed in more detail in links to other publications. The characteristics of fourth wave feminism identified by the author are that it is queer, sex-positive, trans inclusive, anti-misandrist, body positive, and digitally driven.

"Three Waves of Feminism: From Suffragettes to Grrls." 2006. http://uk.sagepub.com/sites/default/files/upm-binaries/6236_Chapter_1_Krolokke_2nd_Rev_Final_Pdf.pdf. Accessed on November 3, 2016. (From Charlotte Krøløkke and Ann Scott Sørensen. *Gender Communication Theories & Analyses: From Silence to Performance.* Thousand Oaks, CA: SAGE Publications.

This chapter provides an excellent general overview of the first three waves on the feminist movement.

"What Was the Second Wave Feminist Movement?" 2016. Daily History.org. http://dailyhistory.org/What_was_the_Second_Wave_Feminist_Movement%3F. Accessed on November 3, 2016.

This web page provides a general overview of the events in feminist history that developed in the second half of the 20th century.

"What You Should Know about EEOC and the Enforcement Protections for LGBT Workers." 2016. U.S. Equal

Employment Opportunity Commission. https://www.eeoc
.gov/eeoc/newsroom/wysk/enforcement_protections_lgbt_
workers.cfm. Accessed on November 3, 2016.

Even though the United States has no formal laws banning discrimination against LGBT people in employment, housing, public accommodation, or credit, the
U.S. Equal Employment Opportunity Commission is
still able to offer legal protection under certain specific
provisions of other laws and regulations. This web page
summarizes those forms of protection, along with providing a summary of the number and types of complaints it
received in 2015.

"The Women's Rights Movement, 1848–1920." 2016. History,
Art & Archives. U.S. House of Representatives. http://history.
house.gov/Exhibitions-and-Publications/WIC/Historical-
Essays/No-Lady/Womens-Rights/. Accessed on November 3,
2016.

This extended essay discusses the so-called first wave of
feminism in the United States, in which women began
the battle to take their place in the political scene. The
article provides extensive detail about the women who
participated in the movement as well as the progress they
achieved in their battles.

Zerzan, John. 2010. "Patriarchy, Civilization, and the Origins
of Gender." The Anarchist Library. https://theanarchistlibrary
.org/library/john-zerzan-patriarchy-civilization-and-the-
origins-of-gender. Accessed on November 2, 2016.

The author provides a review of the way patriarchy developed in human history, and the effects it has had on
modern civilization.

Introduction

Humans have been thinking about, writing about, conducting research on, writing laws about, and dealing with issues of sex and gender from the origins of civilization. This chapter provides an introduction to some of the most interesting and/or important events that have taken place over the past 2,000 years or more of that journey.

Ancient Egypt Physicians recommend that one purge about once a week because, they teach, diseases are caused by food.

Third century BCE The first mention of Hermaphroditus, the child of Hermes and Aphrodite, occurs in the works of Theophrastus. The child provides the name by which intersex individuals were later known, hermaphrodites, although that term is no longer considered acceptable.

370 BCE In the first record of bulimic-like behavior, Greek historian Xenophon writes of individuals in the mountains of Asia Minor purging themselves after eating, for reasons that are not known.

Bryan Kimpton, a supporter of the School Success and Opportunity Act (AB1266), waves a flag while celebrating at a rally organized by San Diego LGBTQ rights organizations Canvass for a Cause, SAME Alliance, and Black and Pink after a petition drive to place a proposition on the ballot to repeal the law failed to garner enough signatures on February 24, 2014. (AP Photo/Lenny Ignelzi)

ca. 66 CE   Roman emperor Nero has a young boy named Sporus castrated, after which he marries the young man.

218–222 CE   Reign of the emperor Elagabalus, who is known to have married both women and men, have dressed in women's clothing, and have prostituted himself at the imperial palace.

1380   Saint Catherine of Sienna dies at the age of 33 as a consequence of eating disorders. She, like some other early saints, believed that abstinence from eating and purging were forms of penance for their sins.

1431   The famous French war hero Jeanne d'Arc (Joan of Arc) is burned at the stake for heresy, a charge based to a considerable extent on her cross-dressing in men's clothes for at least the preceding two years.

1597   Italian surgeon Gaspare Tagliacozzi publishes *De Curtorum Chirurgia per Insitionem* (*On the Surgery of Mutilation by Grafting*), generally thought to be the first textbook on plastic surgery.

1654   Queen Christina of Sweden abdicates her throne and assumes a male persona, thenceforth known as Count Dohna.

1689   English physician Richard Morton provides the first clinical descriptions of the eating disorder later to be known as *anorexia nervosa*. (See also **1873**.)

1755   English actress Charlotte Charke writes her autobiography, *Narrative of the Life of Mrs. Charlotte Charke*, in which she writes about her life as a transgender person and her long-term relationships with a "Ms. Brown."

1769   The legal status of women in the American colonies is expressed in legislation adapted from British common law, namely that "[t]he very being and legal existence of the woman is suspended during the marriage, or at least is incorporated into that of her husband under whose wing and protection she performs everything" (Blackstone, William. 1765. *Commentaries on the Laws of England*, volume 1, chapter 29, section 6).

1777   By this date, all of the American colonies have adopted legislation removing any political, economic, social, or other rights of women.

1792   English writer Mary Wollstonecraft publishes her book *A Vindication of the Rights of Woman.* The book is often regarded as the origin of the women's rights movement. Prior to this date, women had essentially few or, at least, very few rights of any kind in the cultures in which they lived.

1839   Mississippi becomes the first state in the union to allow married women to hold property in their own names.

1848   Some 300 individuals, most of them women, attend the Women's Rights Convention, in Seneca Falls, New York, to discuss ways of ending the segregation of women in all aspects of society. About a third of the attendees eventually sign the Declaration of Sentiments, summarizing the results of their deliberations.

1850   The first National Women's Rights Convention is held in Worcester, Massachusetts. Additional meetings were held annually through 1860, after which they were discontinued because of the coming Civil War.

1860   Based on a medical analysis, a French woman known as Herculine Barbin is declared to be male and is forced to live the rest of her life as a man. Although designated as a female at birth, Barbin is found to have a small penis and undescended testicles.

1869   German psychiatrist Carl Westphal is credited with providing the first medical description of transgenderism, which he called "die contraire Sexualempfindung" ("contrary sexual feeling"). Westphal failed, however, to clearly differentiate between transgender individuals, on the one hand, and gay men and lesbians, on the other.

English political theorist John Stuart Mill argues in his essay, "The Subjection of Women," that women deserve the right to vote. His proposal to change the word "man" to "person" in the

Reform Bill of 1867 is defeated by a vote of 196 to 76, and he is laughed out of the House of Commons.

Wyoming becomes the first state to grant women the right to vote.

1870   The first jury containing members of both sexes in the United States is impaneled in Cheyenne, Wyoming.

1873   In the case of *Bradwell v. Illinois*, the U.S. Supreme Court rules that a state has the right to exclude a married woman from practicing law.

Sir William Gull, personal physician to Queen Victoria, supplies the first medical description of the condition known as *anorexia nervosa*. In the same year, the French physician Ernest-Charles Lasègue provides a similar clinical description of the condition. Gull is usually credited with naming the condition to reflect the absence ("αν-"; "an-") of appetite ("-ορξις"; "-orexia") as a nervous condition ("nervosa").

1875   In *Minor v Happersett*, the U.S. Supreme Court decides that a state can prohibit a woman from voting, stating that women constitute a special category of "nonvoting citizens."

1889   British schoolmaster Cecil Reddie is credited with being the first person to offer a sex education class in a school setting at his Abbotsholme School. He based his decision to offer the course on his belief that such a class would "prevent mental illusions due to false ideas from within" and to "prevent false teaching from other fellows."

1896   Women are excluded from participating in the first modern Olympic games. They are also excluded from serving on the International Olympic Committee (IOC), a precedent that survives until 1981.

1898   At its first national convention, the National Congress of Parents and Teachers Association (PTA) includes a session on sex education in which the importance of training in the subject prior to puberty is stressed.

1910 Jewish-German physician and sexologist Magnus Hirschfeld coins the term *Transvestit* (transvestite) to describe individuals who enjoy dressing in the clothes of the opposite sex. He is thought to have been a transvestite himself.

World War I Armenian surgeon Varaztad Kazanjian pioneers a number of maxillofacial surgical techniques on soldiers disfigured during the war, earning him the title of the Father (or one of the fathers) of Modern Plastic Surgery.

1913 Superintendent of Schools Ella Flagg Young introduces the teaching of sex education into the city's schools. The program lasted only a year and was shut down primarily as the result of complaints of local Roman Catholic leaders.

1917 Allan L. Hart becomes the first American to be surgically transitioned from female to male. He goes on to become a well-known physician specializing in radiology and tuberculosis research.

German-born American geneticist Richard Goldschmidt suggests the name *intersex* to describe individuals born with ambiguous genitalia.

1919 Hirschfeld founds the Institute for Sexology in Berlin. The clinic provides services for transgender individuals, as well as conducting research on the phenomenon of transgenderism.

1920 The Nineteenth Amendment to the U.S. Constitution grants women the right to vote.

1922 The U.S. Public Health Service publishes a book, *High Schools and Sex Education*, designed to help students obtain "the proper information and attitudes about the place of sex in the life of a normal adult" as part of the usual high school curriculum of biology, general science, home economics, social studies, and English.

A domestic worker at Hirschfeld's Institute for Sexology (1919), Rudolf Richter, underwent castration, the first stage in the first transsexual surgical procedure in history. Nine years later, Rudolph has his penis removed and an artificial vagina created, becoming a woman who adopts the name of Dora Richter.

1923   Senator Charles Curtis (R-KS) and Representative Daniel R. Anthony, Jr. (R-KS) introduce a constitutional amendment declaring that "Men and women shall have equal rights throughout the United States and in every place subject to its jurisdiction. Congress shall have power to enforce this article by appropriate legislation." The amendment did not receive consideration on the floor of either chamber, and was reintroduced every year through 1970, with no action taken on it in either house.

1924   A small group of men in Chicago led by Henry Gerber form the Society for Human Rights, the first organization in the United States designed to work for equal rights for gay men. The organization is disbanded a few months later when a wife of one member reports the group's activities to the local police.

American surgeon John Davis is named the first professor of plastic surgery in the United States at Johns Hopkins University, where he also establishes the nation's first training program in the field.

1931   German chemist Adolf Butenandt isolates 15 milligrams of the male hormone androsterone from thousands of liters of urine, the first anabolic steroid to have been discovered.

1933   Swedish educator Elise Ottesen-Jensen forms what is thought to be the world's first association for sex education in schools, the National League for Sex Education.

1934   Croatian-Swiss chemist Leopold Ružička synthesizes androstenone, the first anabolic steroid to be produced artificially.

1936   In a 5-to-4 decision in *Morehead v. Tipaldo*, the U.S. Supreme Court rules that New York State's minimum wage law is unconstitutional, and employers may pay women workers whatever wage they choose.

1937   In another 5-to-4 decision in *West Coast Hotel Company v. Parrish*, the U.S. Supreme Court reaches a different decision, upholding Washington State's minimum wage law, saying that "the bare cost of living must be met."

1938   American endocrinologist Henry Turner describes a type of DSD (disorders of sex development), now known by his name, Turner's syndrome, in which a female child is born with a single X chromosome. An estimated 99 percent of Turner pregnancies are thought to end in spontaneous abortion or stillbirth, although prognosis for those who survive is excellent, if marked by a number of physical problems.

The U.S. Congress passes the Fair Labor Standards Act, which requires that a minimum living wage must be established for both sexes.

World War II   Researchers in Nazi Germany are said to test anabolic steroids on soldiers to determine their effectiveness in increasing the men's physical strength, aggressiveness, and endurance.

1940   The U.S. Public Health Service labels sex education in the schools an "urgent need" and begins to promote its inclusion throughout the nation.

1948   American embryologist Harry Benjamin uses hormones to effect the transition of a young boy to a female, the first instance in which hormone therapy was used for such a purpose.

Indiana University researcher Alfred Kinsey publishes *Sexual Behavior in the Human Male*, by far the most comprehensive study of human sexual behavior ever produced. (See also **1953**.)

1950s   American psychologist and sexologist John Money suggests an approach for treating children born with ambiguous genitalia called the optimal gender policy, in which children develop according to the sex with which they are raised rather than their chromosomal or other biological characteristics. This policy eventually became the subject of intense scrutiny and controversy.

1950   The International Association of Athletics Federations (IAAF) initiates testing for gender (European championships in Belgium) as a way of determining which self-identified women can compete in that category in international events. The testing involves visual examination by a team of physicians.

Harry Hay and some friends found the Mattachine Society in Los Angeles, the second (after the Society for Human Rights; **1924**) organization established to work for the civil rights of gay men.

1951   Race car driver and World War II fighter pilot Robert Cowell chooses to have sex reassignment surgery and receives the world's first vaginoplasty.

1952   A research team led by American endocrinologist and rheumatologist Harry Klinefelter first describes a type of DSD in which individuals males have an extra X chromosome (usually XXY), whose most common trait is sterility.

The American Psychiatric Association first lists anorexia nervosa in its *Diagnostic and Statistical Manual of Mental Disorders, First Edition (DSM-I)*.

The unexpected and overwhelming success of the Russian weightlifting contingent at the Olympic Games in Helsinki prompt questions as to whether the competitors have been using testosterone as a performance-enhancing drug. More than 60 years later, a large volume of evidence exists to confirm that the practice was being carried out, if not as early as 1952, certainly within a few years following that date.

1953   Kinsey publishes his companion book, *Sexual Behavior in the Human Female*. (See also **1948**.)

1955   Two lesbians, Del Martin and Phyllis Lyon, create the Daughters of Bilitis, an organization intended to provide lesbians with an opportunity to meet and get to know each other and to work for equal rights for homosexual women.

1958   Dr Judy T. Wu, in Bratsk, Russia, performs the first complete phalloplasty for the purpose of sex reassignment.

The U.S. Food and Drug Administration (FDA) approves the sale of the steroid Dianabol in the United States, the first anabolic steroid to receive such approval. A number of coaches, athletes, trainers, and others affiliated with sports begin to recommend or use the product to improve their athletic performance.

1961 American plastic surgeons Thomas Cronin and Frank Gerow, working with the Dow Corning Corporation, develop the first silicone breast prosthesis. The first use of the implants takes place in 1962.

San Francisco entertainer José Sarria becomes the first gay/transvestite in the United States to run for public office when he enters his name as a candidate for the city's board of supervisors, a race in which he won 6,000 votes, but not the election.

1963 The Equal Pay Act of 1963 requires that equal pay be provided to all employees doing the same job, regardless of race, color, religion, national origin, or sex.

A meeting of the East Coast Homophile Organizations (ECHO) marks the first effort to bring a group of politically active gay and lesbians group together to discuss actions on issues of joint interest and importance.

1964 Physician and public health advocate Mary Calderone and some colleagues form the Sexuality Education and Information Council of the United States to serve as an advocate and source of information for sex education and related issues in the United States.

Title VII of the Civil Rights Act requires that workers not be discriminated against on the basis of race, color, religion, national origin, or sex.

1966 Harry Benjamin publishes *The Transsexual Phenomenon*, in which he describes the process by which one is able to change his or her sex.

The North America Conference of Homophile Organizations organizes to expand on the goals and activities of its short-lived predecessor, ECHO. (See also **1963**.)

1968   The IOC introduces chromosome testing at the Mexico City Games as a way of verifying competitors' sex for Olympic events.

1969   A group of gay men, many of whom are also drag queens, initiate a riot at the Stonewall Inn in New York City. They are responding to harassment by police officers, a common event in the city (and elsewhere) against which they have decided to protest. The riots are generally considered to mark the beginning of the modern gay rights movement although they have, in fact, been preceded by a half century of activism at a modest level in the United States.

The Erickson Educational Foundation sponsors the first International Symposium on Gender Identity, held in London on July 25–27.

In *Bowe v. Colgate-Palmolive Company*, the Seventh Circuit Court of Appeals rules that women must be offered employment in jobs for which they can meet the physical requirements of the work.

California adopts the nation's first "no fault" divorce law, which permits divorce by mutual consent of the parties involved.

1970   Marsha Johnson and Sylvia Rivera form STAR (Street Transgender Action Revolutionaries), the first transgender activist organization in the United States.

1971   In the case of *Reed v. Reed*, the U.S. Supreme Court strikes down an Idaho law that automatically establishes preference to males as administrators of wills. The case is significant because it is the first instance in which the court specifically invokes the Equal Protection Clause of the Fourteenth Amendment to invalidate discrimination based on sex.

1972   The Equal Rights Amendment (ERA) finally passes both houses of Congress and is sent to the states of ratification. In spite of expectations that the amendment would be approved fairly easily, it fails to pass in the required number of states, largely through the efforts of attorney and activist Phyllis

Schlafly, who created the STOP ("Stop Taking Our Privileges") ERA campaign against the amendment.

Sweden becomes the first nation in the world to allow a person to legally change his or her sex.

President Richard M. Nixon signs the Education Amendments of 1972, Title IX of which prohibits discrimination on the basis of sex in any federally funded program or activity. The act greatly expands the opportunities for women to participate in school and college sports.

East Lansing, Michigan, becomes the first city in the United States to ban discrimination against gays and lesbians in hiring.

1973 A book by German-born American psychoanalyst Hilde Bruch, *Eating Disorders: Obesity, Anorexia Nervosa, and the Person Within*, is widely credited with bringing issues of eating disorders to the attention of the medical profession. (See also **1978**.)

1974 Congress passes amendments to the Fair Housing Act (Title VIII of the Civil Rights Act of 1968), making it illegal to discriminate on the basis of sex in the sale or renting of a house or other form of residence.

Representatives Ed Koch (D-NY) and Bella Abzug (D-NY) introduce the Equality Act, banning discrimination against gay men and lesbians in employment, housing, and public accommodation. The bill is reintroduced into every session of Congress until 1994, when it is replaced by the Employment Nondiscrimination Act. (See also **1994**.)

1975 The city of Minneapolis becomes the first city in the United States to pass a law prohibiting discrimination against transgender people.

The IOC adds anabolic steroids to its list of prohibited substances.

1976 In *General Electric v. Gilbert*, the U.S. Supreme Court upholds a woman's right to receive unemployment benefits during the last three months of pregnancy.

1977 Former Miss Oklahoma pageant winner, spokesperson for the Florida Citrus Commission, and Christian activist Anita Bryant organizes Save Our Children, a group working in opposition to a proposed Miami gay and lesbian antidiscrimination ordinance. The group is successful in defeating the proposed ordinance and inspires three additional cities—Eugene, Oregon; St. Paul, Minnesota; and Wichita, Kansas—to repeal antidiscrimination ordinance that had previously been put into place.

1978 Hilde Bruch (see **1973**) publishes *The Golden Cage: The Enigma of Anorexia Nervosa*, a book often credited with bringing the problem of anorexia nervosa to the attention of the general public.

The Pregnancy Discrimination Act is passed, amending Title VII of the Civil Rights Act of 1965, to prohibit discrimination "on the basis of pregnancy, childbirth, or related medical condition."

1979 The Sixth International Gender Dysphoria Symposium approves the formation of the Harry Benjamin International Gender Dysphoria Association, later (2007) to become the World Professional Association for Transgender Health.

British psychiatrist Gerald Francis Russell publishes the first description of an eating disorder that he calls *bulimia nervosa*. Russell called the condition a variation of anorexia nervosa.

1980 New Jersey becomes the first state to mandate sex education in all public schools at all grade levels.

The American Psychiatric Association first lists bulimia in its *Diagnostic and Statistical Manual of Mental Disorders*, Third Edition (*DSM-III*).

1981 The U.S. Congress passes the Adolescent Family Life Act, providing funding for so-called abstinence-only sex education that is based on the principle that abstinence is the only concept that should be taught in American schools. (See also **2016**.)

Venezuelan sportswoman and journalist Flor Isava-Fonseca and Finnish sprinter Pirjo Häggman are chosen to be the first female members on the IOC.

Wisconsin becomes the first state to adopt antidiscrimination legislation for gay men and lesbians.

1982   Based on a study by a committee of the American Society of Plastic Surgeons of a technology then in use in France, the procedure known as *liposuction* is introduced to the United States, where it quickly becomes one of the most popular of all forms of cosmetic surgery.

1983   Karen Carpenter, a popular American singer, dies of complications of anorexia nervosa. The death of this young (32 years of age), highly popular, attractive performer provides a striking introduction for many people to the very real medical problems posed by the disorder.

1986   In *Meritor Savings Bank v. Vinson*, the U.S. Supreme Court rules that sexual harassment is a form of job discrimination. The Court lays down the conditions under which such acts are unlawful and when an employer can be liable for such discrimination.

In *Bowers v. Hardwick*, the U.S. Supreme Court rules that Georgia's sodomy law prohibiting oral and/or anal sex between two consenting adults is constitutional.

1988   The U.S. Congress passes and President Ronald Reagan signs the Anti-Drug Abuse Act of 1988, prohibiting the sale of anabolic steroids for nonmedical purposes.

1989   The FDA approves the use of botulinum toxin (Botox®) for the treatment of strabismus, blepharospasm, and hemifacial spasm in patients aged younger than 12 years. The treatment eventually becomes very popular for a variety of (primarily) facial cosmetic procedures. (See, for example, **2002**.)

1991   Major League Baseball bans the use of anabolic steroids by players.

1992   Voters in Colorado approve Initiative 2 (also known as the Colorado No Protected Status for Sexual Orientation Initiative), which prohibits any municipality in the state from granting gay men and lesbians protection against discrimination. The new law is later overturned in *Romer v. Evans* (1996).

1993 A group of family and friends of intersex individuals found the Intersex Society of North America (ISNA), designed to advocate for patients and families dealing with the condition. (See also **2008.**)

The state of Minnesota becomes the first state in the United States to pass nondiscrimination legislation against transgender individuals.

1994 The Violence against Women Act establishes a national policy for dealing with all forms of violence against women, including holding rapists responsible for acts against their victims and establishing fair standards for criminal prosecution in such cases.

Representative Gary Studds (D-MA) introduces the Employment Nondiscrimination Act (ENDA) into the U.S. Congress. The act is offered in place of the Equality Act, on which no action has been taken for 20 years. ENDA has the more limited objective of prohibiting discrimination against gay men and lesbians in employment practices.

1996 The U.S. Supreme Court, in *Romer v. Evans*, rules that Colorado's Initiative 2 (see **1992**) is unconstitutional because it does not serve any rational legitimate government interest (the so-called rational basis standard used in such cases).

1999 The first Transgender Day of Remembrance is held in honor and memory of all those individuals killed as a result of transphobia. The day is celebrated annually on November 20.

2002 The Transgender Law Center opens its first office in San Francisco.

The FDA announces approval of Botox® for the treatment of moderate-to-severe frown lines between the eyebrows, so-called glabellar lines.

2003 In *Lawrence v. Texas*, the U.S. Supreme Court reverses its stance on sodomy (see **1986**), ruling that a Texas law prohibiting the practice is unconstitutional.

2004 A federal report on the effectiveness of abstinence-only education programs finds that 80 percent of such programs contain "false, misleading, or distorted information about reproductive health." Congress continues to fund such programs at record-high amounts.

The Unilever company launches its Dove Campaign for Real Beauty to encourage appreciation of a variety of body types, primarily among women. The campaign was inspired to some extent by an international poll from the early 2000s, showing that only 2 percent of women worldwide thought of themselves as "beautiful."

President George W. Bush signs the Anabolic Steroid Control Act of 2004, adding several hundred steroid-based drugs and their precursors to Schedule III of the Controlled Substances Act.

2005 In *Jackson v. Birmingham Board of Education*, the U.S. Supreme Court rules that Title IX prohibits not only discrimination based on sex, but also any and all actions taken against someone for complaining about sex-based discrimination, even if that person is not part of the discriminatory action.

2006 The Lawson Wilkins Pediatric Endocrine Society and the European Society for Paediatric Endocrinology recommend new terminology for the classification of people born with ambiguous genitalia, suggesting that "[t]erms such as 'intersex,' 'pseudohermaphroditism,' 'hermaphroditism,' 'sex reversal,' and gender-based diagnostic labels are particularly controversial."

2007 The House of Representatives passes ENDA by a vote of 235 to 184, but the bill is rejected by the Senate.

2008 Stu Rasmussen is elected mayor of Silverton, Oregon, the first transgender person to have been elected to such an office in the United States.

The Tides Center, a philanthropic organization, provides funds for the creation of the Action Alliance, established to work toward the new standard of care for individuals with DSD and a successor to ISNA (See also **1993**.)

2009 The IAAF conducts the first hormone testing (of South African runner Caster Semenya) as a way of verifying a competitor's sex.

President Barack Obama nominates Dylan Orr as an attorney at the U.S. Department of Labor, the first transgender person for a federal office.

President Obama signs the Lilly Ledbetter Fair Pay Restoration Act, extending and expanding the conditions under which a person can bring suit for unfair pay actions in the workplace.

2010   Phyllis Frye is sworn in as the first transgender judge in the United States in Houston, Texas.

2011   The U.S. Office of Personnel Management issues a memorandum providing guidance on the hiring of transgender persons for federal positions.

2012   The Equal Employment Opportunity Commission rules that Title VII (dealing with employment) of the 1964 Civil Rights Law applies to transgender individuals.

2013   The American Psychiatric Association officially replaces the term *gender identity disorder* with the term *gender dysphoria* in its *DSM*.

ENDA passes the U.S. Senate by a vote of 64 to 32, but dies in the House of Representatives.

2014   The U.S. Department of Health and Human Welfare rules that Medicare is required to pay for sex reassignment surgeries.

2015   The IOC announces a new policy for the admission of transgender individuals to Olympic events. Transwomen may compete if their blood testosterone levels do not exceed 10 nanomoles of testosterone per liter of blood at least a year in advance of a competition. Transmen may compete without having to meet any qualifying standard.

2016   President Barack Obama removes funding for abstinence-only sex education in American schools, ending a program that has been in operation for 25 years, that has been funded with nearly $2 billion in federal funds, and that has never been found to have any effect on student sexual behaviors.

New Department of Defense regulations permit women to serve in any position in the armed services, provided they are able to meet the physical standards required for such a position.

The U.S. Department of Education (DOE) sends a letter to all schools and colleges in the United States that receive federal funding, advising them that they are required to provide restroom and changing room facilities for transgender students.

Judge Reed O'Connor, of the U.S. District Court for the Northern District of Texas, issues an injunction against the DOE advisory letter on restrooms for transgender students cited above.

Former WASP (Women Airforce Service Pilot) Elaine D. Harmon is laid to rest in Arlington National Ceremony, on the basis of special action by the U.S. Army. It is the first time the army acknowledges that women pilots performed the same duty during World War II as did male pilots.

2017   Phil Berger, President Pro Tempore of the North Carolina Senate, announces that no new efforts to repeal House Bill 2 are likely to occur in the new legislative year.

One day after the inauguration of Donald Trump as president of the United States, an estimated 500,000 women and men march in Washington, D.C., to send a message that "women's rights are human rights." Organizers announce that 673 similar marches take place on the same day in a number of countries worldwide on all seven continents, including Antarctica. Somewhat misunderstanding the action, Trump Tweets "Why didn't these people vote?"

On February 22, President Donald Trump issues a letter revoking President Obama's policy regarding bathrooms for transgender individuals. He suggests that decisions on such matters are best left to the states.

Discussions of sex and gender often involve terminology that is unfamiliar to the average person. In some cases, the terms used are scientific or medical expressions used most commonly by professionals in the field. In other cases, the terms may be part of the everyday vernacular that some people may *think* they understand, but that actually have more precise meanings. This glossary defines some of those terms that have been used in this book, along with some terms that one may encounter in additional research on the topic.

abstinence-only sex education A sex education curriculum based on the principle that abstinence from sexual activity before marriage is the only moral and practical method of dealing with issues of sex and gender with which young people in the United States are confronted.

affectional orientation The tendency of a person to be attracted to someone of the same or opposite sex, or both in varying degrees.

allosome A sex chromosome.

anorexia nervosa A medical condition in which one stops eating in order to lose weight, often to improve one's body image.

binary sexuality The concept that only two forms of biological sex, male and female, can exist.

bulimia A medical condition characterized by repeated episodes of eating and purging (vomiting), generally with the purpose of achieving a body structure with which one is happier.

cisgender A condition in which a person's gender identity is congruent with his or her biological sex. (*Also see* **transgender**.)

cross-dressing The act of dressing in the clothing of someone of the opposite biological sex.

discrimination The act of behaving differently against an individual only because of that individual's membership in some category of individuals, such as sex (male or female), race (black or white), country of origin (Italy or Syria), or affectional orientation (homosexual, heterosexual, or other).

disorder of sex development (DSD) A condition in which an individual's genitalia do not develop normally, generally resulting in the appearance of ambiguous genitalia. DSD was once referred to as **intersex**.

drag queen A man (often a gay man) who enjoys dressing in women's clothing for his own enjoyment or for the purpose of entertaining others.

DSD. *See* **disorder of sex development.**

dysgenesis Defective development of the genital system.

dysphoria An unease or general dissatisfaction with some aspect of one's life. The term is used in psychology and psychiatry to distinguish between the *existence* of a condition (such as one's gender) and the ways in which one feels about that condition (as in feeling that one should be of the gender opposite one's biological sex).

feminism A term used to describe the movement to achieve for women legal and other rights equivalent to those available to men in a society.

gender The behavioral, cultural, and social attitudes that are associated with a biological sex in a given culture.

gender identity The sense that one has with regard to his or her own biological identity.

gender inequality The condition in which males and females are treated differently in employment, housing, voting rights, and other areas for reasons based on one's biological sex.

gender role A set of behaviors that correspond with a society's standard definition of a male and a female in that culture. Also known as **stereotypical gender roles**.

heterosexual An adjective that describes feelings or behaviors toward someone of the opposite sex.

homosexual An adjective that describes feelings or behaviors toward someone of the same sex.

intersex *See* **disorder of sex development (DSD).**

Klinefelter syndrome A DSD (q.v.) in which an individual is born with a Y chromosome in addition to at least two X chromosomes.

LGBT An acronym used to represent lesbians, gay men, bisexuals, and transgender individuals. The acronym is often extended to include other groups of somewhat like-minded and behaving individuals, as in (at the extreme level) LGBTQQ-IAAP, which stands for lesbian, gay, bisexual, transgender, queer, questioning, intersex, asexual, allies, and pansexual.

matriarchal Referring to a society, culture, or other setting in which females have the dominant role.

natural Referring to any situation or event that can or does occur in nature.

nonstereotypical gender roles Behaviors that do not correspond to the gender roles in a society established for a person of a given sex.

normal Adhering to some social or cultural standard that is generally accepted.

patriarchal Referring to a society, culture, or other setting in which males have the dominant role.

puberty   The period in an individual's life in which one reaches sexual maturity.

queer   A word that once was used as a pejorative term for gay men and lesbians, which has since been adopted by gay men and lesbians to refer to anyone who is not heterosexual. The term is often used with a sense of pride and defiance and has come to represent an academic and political approach to the study of sexual issues.

questioning   A term often used to describe individuals, especially young adults, who are still unclear about their gender identity and/or their affectional orientation.

sex   Either of the two major forms of individuals that occur in many species and that are distinguished as female or male primarily on the basis of their reproductive organs and structures.

sexology   The scientific study of human sexuality.

stereotypical gender role *See* **gender role.**

therapeutic intervention   A form of "talk therapy" in which practitioners in a field attempt to help a person who is dealing with a mental, emotional, or other problem by discussing that problem on a one-on-one basis, in groups, or in other settings.

transgender   A condition in which one's gender identity is incongruent with his or her biological sex. (*See also* **cisgender.**)

transsexual   An individual who has a strong desire to assume the physical characteristics of a gender role opposite to that of his or her biological sex.

transvestite   An individual who enjoys dressing in the clothing and assuming the social behaviors of the opposite sex, almost always without having the desire to actually change one's biological sex.

Turner syndrome   A medical condition in which an individual has only a single X chromosome.

two spirit   A term used in particular by Native American and Canadian First Nation peoples to refer to individuals who do not fit neatly into strictly a male or female role.

Index

About the Author

David E. Newton holds an associate's degree in science from Grand Rapids (Michigan) Junior College, a BA in chemistry (with high distinction), an MA in education from the University of Michigan, and an EdD in science education from Harvard University. He is the author of more than 400 textbooks, encyclopedias, resource books, research manuals, laboratory manuals, trade books, and other educational materials. He taught mathematics, chemistry, and physical science in Grand Rapids, Michigan, for 13 years; was professor of chemistry and physics at Salem State College in Massachusetts for 15 years; and was adjunct professor in the College of Professional Studies at the University of San Francisco for 10 years.

The author's previous books for ABC-CLIO include *Global Warming* (1993), *Gay and Lesbian Rights—A Resource Handbook* (1994, 2009), *The Ozone Dilemma* (1995), *Violence and the Mass Media* (1996), *Environmental Justice* (1996, 2009), *Encyclopedia of Cryptology* (1997), *Social Issues in Science and Technology: An Encyclopedia* (1999), *DNA Technology* (2009), *Sexual Health* (2010), *The Animal Experimentation Debate* (2013), *Marijuana* (2013), *World Energy Crisis* (2013), *Steroids and Doping in Sports* (2014), *GMO Food* (2014), *Science and Political Controversy* (2014), *Wind Energy* (2015), *Fracking* (2015), *Solar Energy* (2015), *Youth Substance Abuse* (2016), and *Global Water Crisis* (2016). His other recent books include *Physics: Oryx Frontiers of Science Series* (2000), *Sick!* (4 volumes; 2000), *Science, Technology, and Society: The Impact of Science in the 19th Century* (2 volumes; 2001), *Encyclopedia of Fire* (2002), *Molecular Nanotechnology: Oryx Frontiers of Science Series* (2002), *Encyclopedia of Water* (2003), *Encyclopedia of Air* (2004), *The New Chemistry* (6 volumes; 2007), *Nuclear Power* (2005), *Stem Cell Research* (2006), *Latinos in the Sciences, Math, and Professions* (2007), and *DNA Evidence and Forensic Science* (2008). He has also been an updating and consulting editor on a number of books and reference works, including *Chemical Compounds* (2005), *Chemical Elements* (2006), *Encyclopedia of Endangered Species* (2006), *World of Mathematics* (2006), *World of Chemistry* (2006), *World of Health* (2006), *UXL Encyclopedia of Science* (2007), *Alternative Medicine* (2008), *Grzimek's Animal Life Encyclopedia* (2009), *Community Health* (2009), *Genetic Medicine* (2009), *The Gale Encyclopedia of Medicine* (2010–2011), *The Gale Encyclopedia of Alternative Medicine* (2013), *Discoveries in Modern Science: Exploration, Invention, and Technology* (2013–2014), and *Science in Context* (2013–2014).